FOR COLORED BOYS

WHO HAVE CONSIDERED SUICIDE WHEN THE RAINBOW IS STILL NOT ENOUGH

EDITED BY KEITH BOYKIN

FOR COLORED BOYS

WHO HAVE CONSIDERED SUICIDE WHEN THE RAINBOW IS STILL NOT ENOUGH

Coming of Age, Coming Out, and Coming Home

MAGNUS
BOOKS

Submission Review Editors

La Marr Jurelle Bruce
Clay Cane
Mark Corece
Frank Roberts

Table of Contents

Introduction

In the fall of 2010, eighteen-year-old Rutgers University student Tyler Clementi was secretly videotaped by his roommate during an intimate encounter with another man. On September 22, Clementi drove to the George Washington Bridge, got out of his car, and leapt to his death.

On the same day, in a different part of the country, lawyers for a young black man named Jamal Parris walked into the DeKalb County Courthouse in Georgia and filed a lawsuit against Bishop Eddie Long of the New Birth Missionary Baptist Church, accusing the pastor of using his influence to coerce Parris into a sexual relationship.

These two unrelated incidents revealed dramatic differences in the way our society responds to race and sexuality. The killing of unarmed teenager Trayvon Martin in February 2012 and the death of a Florida A&M drama major in November 2011 confirm this trend.

Meanwhile, the abuse charges by Jamal Parris and several other young black men were met with attacks and criticism by members of Long's church and other religious supporters who questioned the credibility of the accusers. Despite the media attention to the story in Atlanta, there was no real organized effort to protect young black men from harm or sexual abuse, no YouTube video campaign, and no support mechanisms put in place to provide counseling and assistance for others.

It should come as no surprise to anyone who has followed the news that our society has a tendency to dismiss the grievous experiences of young men of color. A tragic shooting on a suburban campus, for example, provokes a sense of shock and outrage while similar tragedies at inner city schools often go ignored. Perhaps the best example may be the way in which society and the media dealt with several other youth suicides in the same time period as Clementi's death.

In April 2009, Carl Joseph Walker-Hoover, an eleven-year-old black student in Massachusetts, hanged himself in his bedroom. Carl was a young football player and Boy Scout who had endured months of harassment and anti-gay bullying. He was just one week shy of his twelfth birthday when he committed suicide.

In the same month, another eleven-year-old, Jaheem Herrera of Atlanta, took his own life after suffering constant anti-gay bullying at his DeKalb County school. He too was African American.

Then, in September 2010, the same month in which Tyler Clementi killed himself, nineteen-year-old Raymond Chase, a black openly gay college student studying culinary arts at Johnson & Wales University in Providence, Rhode Island, committed suicide by hanging himself in his dorm room.

In the following month, a twenty-six-year-old black gay youth activist named Joseph Jefferson took his own life. Joseph had worked with HIV/AIDS charities and helped to promote black LGBT events. "I could not bear the burden of living as a gay man of color in a world grown cold and hateful towards those of us who live and love differently than the so-called 'social mainstream,'" he wrote on his Facebook page the day he killed himself.

Sadly, these suicides did not generate much attention in the mainstream media or action in the larger community.

I was covering the 2010-midterm elections for CNBC when I first heard about Tyler Clementi and Raymond Chase and the other suicides. As I drove across the George Washington Bridge one night from Manhattan to the CNBC World Headquarters in New Jersey, I looked down over the bridge and imagined what it must have felt like to jump 212 feet into the raging Hudson River below. I've known friends who have committed or considered suicide, but I had never contemplated it for myself.

That's when I decided to put together this book. Despite the well-intentioned messaging in response to Clementi's death, life doesn't always "get better" anytime soon, especially for people of color who are disproportionately affected by many challenging socioeconomic conditions.

When it came time to start this project, the title would prove obvious. In 1974, playwright Ntozake Shange published her famous choreopoem, *For Colored Girls Who Have Considered Suicide When The Rainbow Is Enuf*, which later became the subject of a popular film in 2010. As young boys of color were literally committing suicide in the same year when the movie was released, it underscored that the LGBT community's promise of the rainbow was clearly not enough for many to sustain themselves.

To put together this book, I wondered what it would take for a young man to get to the point where he felt he had nothing left to live for. I didn't have to wonder very long. A few days after we put out the call for submissions, I planned to ask a young friend to serve as an editor of the book. David, an Ivy League-educated black gay man, had worked with me on several projects in the past and had once served as my personal assistant as well. But before I could contact him with my request, I received a disturbing phone call from a mutual friend. I discovered that David had taken his own life.

The police found a suicide note written on an envelope in

David's car. It simply said that he wanted to be cremated and buried next to his mother. He never explained what drove him to kill himself, but for some reason I always knew that he, like so many others, didn't completely fit in with the rest of the crowd.

That experience reminded me that men of color—especially gay men of color—must speak out and share our stories of how we have faced obstacles in our own lives. Many of us have endured and sometimes overcome experiences with racism, homophobia, abuse, molestation, violence, and disease. We've struggled with religion, self-acceptance, gender identity, love, relationships, and intimacy, and we've sometimes internalized the prejudices and biases directed against us.

Our stories are rarely told, except in sensationalistic tones that demonize us as predators and villains. And, so, we must tell our own stories in a way that represents us as full human beings.

I was fortunate to come out into a world where those stories were just starting to be told. While I was a student at Harvard in 1991, I came across a book called *Brother To Brother: New Writings by Black Gay Men*, edited by Essex Hemphill. I went to see Hemphill at a book reading event at nearby MIT, and his book quickly became a bible for me. But Hemphill, like many of the young black authors in his anthology, died of AIDS-related complications within a few years. That's why so much of our history has disappeared. Back then there was no real treatment for AIDS.

There were also no openly gay TV anchors like Don Lemon or comedians like Wanda Sykes, and E. Lynn Harris was just getting started as a novelist. And the idea of gay marriage was unthinkable even to gay people. There was no Internet, no hookup websites and no cell phone apps to connect you to the closest date. No one even had a cell phone back then.

In the decades since *Brother to Brother* was published, we've elected our first black president, appointed the first Latina to the Supreme Court, repealed the ban on gays in the military, and developed life-saving treatments for people living with HIV/

AIDS. At the same time, however, independent community bookstores have vanished, magazines and publications have gone out of business, and neighborhoods that once serviced the needs of minority communities have slowly disappeared.

The world is changing rapidly, and so too is our literature. The diversity of this book reflects some of those changes. We received hundreds of submissions for this anthology, and many outstanding pieces could not be included. But this collection includes writers who are African American, Latino, Asian American, British, and Jamaican. Their ages range from their early twenties to their sixties, and they represent all parts of the country and a wide cross-section of occupations, including college students, writers, performers, veterans, doctors, and lawyers.

It is not always easy to be who we are, but as we grow and mature and develop coping mechanisms that enable us to survive and thrive in a complicated world, we have a responsibility to reach back and help others still struggling along the way. In so doing, we also help ourselves. Above all, we cannot allow each generation to grow up in a world where they feel they are alone while we carry so much knowledge, history, and foundation that we can, and must, pass onto them.

Keith Boykin
May 2012

GROWING PAINS

Back to School
Craig Washington

My earliest conception of Saturday night as the unquestioned reason to have a good time is grounded in my Aunt Dee's house. Delores Dorsey was one of my favorite aunts because, unlike most of the other grownups, she liked to dance with us kids and make us laugh as much as she did with her peers. Her laughter was like a hearty musical riff that bounced and rippled through the air, from her chest to yours.

When I think of Aunt Dee's place, Tavares is performing on the wood-framed color TV. They are decked in creamy white polyester that clings to all that draws my thirteen-year-old eyes. The Frigidaire stores delicious red elixir, as impossibly sweet as it is tart, with sugar soaked lemon rafts floating on top. My lips pucker from memory. Kenny and I are in our cousins Arlette and Doreen's bedroom, just off the kitchen toward the back of the apartment. This was where the kids stayed and played games, rehearsed skits, and reported what the grownups were talking about. I hear my mother and father, Aunt Dee, Uncle Karly, and his wife, Aunt Marie, and Aunt Clara in the living room. They are all much younger than I am now, sitting at the bid whist table, drinking Johnnie Walker Black and debating whether Sammy Davis Jr. is an "Uncle Tom." Their voices are the banter of gods. Laughter, cuss words, and arguments tinkle and thunder like changing weather above our heads. When mirth or anger floods over, we stop to listen.

Everybody was having such a good time that Saturday night. It was one of the best times of the year for all of us. It was the beginning of the school year, so nobody had gotten into trouble yet. The one good thing about going back was that we all got a new chance, a fresh start. Aunt Dee was not yet fussing about Arlette spending too much time with boys and not enough on books. Dad wasn't fussing with me about spending too much time with books and not enough time "being a boy." That night everything was just fine. All the grownups were in the kitchen and the kids were in Arlette and Doreen's room. All was as it should be. From there, I could hear that Mommy was in a good mood. She loved bid whist. She kept talking about being "trump tight." I loved the thump as the side of her hand hit the tabletop, delivering the deathblow cut to her opponent. I didn't hear much from Dad. I imagined his mouth stuck out until Uncle Karly said something low toward his ear, probably something ladies were not supposed to hear. Next thing, Uncle Karly and Dad were both laughing and hitting at the edge of the table like they both lost their mind. But they were still losing.

"Mommy took us shopping at May's. Y'all wanna see what we got?" Doreen demanded. "Don't you mean Macy's?" I snapped back. Doreen scurried off to the closet, pretending to ignore me. I liked putting her in her place by showing her she did not know every damn thing. Another cousin, Brandt, was there and I didn't want to be shown up in front of him. Next to his easygoing confidence, I felt like the opposite of cool, though he never treated me as such. Doreen and I were the youngest, and each of us thought of ourselves as the smartest, so we got on each other's nerves. We fought, wielding sarcasm and subterfuge with the expert precision of children who have everything to gain from besting one another.

Perhaps sensing the impending battle, Arlette, whom I adored, stepped in. "No, Craig, she's talking about May's. The one on Jamaica Avenue."

"Oh, okay," I admitted. I didn't mind being corrected by Arlette since she often stuck up for me. Like most children, we were as fickle as cats and our loyalties might switch depending on what favors they might gain. We were obsessed with each other and generally paid little attention to the adults unless they threatened to scold or whip one of us.

"Seeeee," Doreen announced in one long suspended note as she laid out the bounty of back-to-school clothes. A chorus of oohs and ahhs followed. There were knit sweaters and mini skirts with bright red and purple buttons. Bright orange dresses with pleats and bell-bottom windowpane jeans tumbled out of glossy shopping bags. A smaller plastic bag issued a pile of Betty Rubble-sized bangles and matching bracelets. My heart began to race as the scent of new clothes billowed from the mound of garments colored like Baisley Park in October. The rest of us began to chirp about the clothes we had already gotten or had set our sights on.

"I'm gonna get, like, five leather vests, you know, like the one Michael Jackson had on last week," I told Brandt. I had a crush on Brandt and I loved to make him laugh. He slapped me five. Kenny said he wanted to get black patent leather shoes and a vest to match. Our cackling whipped into a froth of put downs and comebacks as my eyes darted to and from the heap of rainbow on the bed. Boasts, lies, and tall tales were spit out, fed upon, regurgitated, and scavenged. We were happy little sparrows dizzying ourselves. One or two of us would plop on the bed, doubled over, holding laughter-cramped bellies, panting for breath. It was a high time. And it was at that moment, when I felt so giddy, so without worry that I said it.

"Sometimes I wish I was a girl. Girls get to wear everything.

Nice things." My own words ricocheted back like darts splintering through my skin. "Oh God," I prayed, hoping they were all buzzing too loudly to notice. We all went on like this for a long while, guzzling Kool-Aid and swapping grown folks' gossip. I didn't notice that Doreen had even left until she came back into the room. Her smirk revealed she was up to something. She walked right up to me, flashing that twisted smile. "Uncle Wash wants to see you in the living room." At first everyone got quiet. Then one single "ooooh" swelled into a chorus.

A kid summoned into the living room might signal one of two things: high praise or a stern reprimand, followed by a whooping at home, if you were lucky. Either was usually meted in the high court of the grownups, Aunt Dee's living room, then later and more sternly, at home. Such beatings served as much for retribution as for correction, payback for embarrassing your parents in front of their peers.

I felt like James Cagney in a dead-man-walking scene, eyes firm, footsteps steady, crossing my last mile. Stevie Wonder was reminiscing about a "childhood sweetheart" in Little Rock as I passed through the narrow hall stretching from the kitchen toward that awaiting living room. It was the longest walk I had ever taken. When I reached the other side, I noticed the adults were still at the card table. They were in the middle of a game, so I thought this must be serious. The air was so dry and my skin felt tight, on the verge of cracking and peeling as if it needed to be shed but stubbornly resisted. Dad called me over to his side. He rested a hand that could palm my entire head squarely on my shoulder. "Did you say you wanted to be a girl?" Dad placed each word before me one at a time, as if laying out a path for me to follow.

My fear shifted into confusion. Not about how Dad found out. Everyone knew Doreen was the biggest snitch. Not about whether or not I would be punished. I was certain of this and the reason why. What confounded me was my own stupidity. I was used to handling things so well, at not saying aloud those ideas, those desires, those things that boys were not allowed to say, or to want. I knew better. At ten years of age, I already realized I was different from other boys. I knew pretty much what to say and not to say, to hide this difference, to get by. But somehow, for some reason, that night, I had slipped up. Then for a moment, I thought that maybe my father would laugh it off once I explained. I knew I really didn't want to be a girl, all I needed to do was tell him what I meant. In that instant, the air cooled and my skin soothened.

"Yeah, I did," I said at the brink of smiling at my own misstep, anticipating that he, too, would find it amusing. Perhaps I thought he might remember how he had said something out loud like this when he was a little boy. I heard one of the grownups sigh aloud, but they, too, would soon be relieved once I told the whole story. "See everybody was talking about all the clothes they got and I just said that girls get to wear neat things. That's all." I heard Aunt Dee or maybe Mommy say "umh-umh-umh" for my shameful condition, but I kept looking straight into my father's eyes, wide open and trained on me. I knew it would be alright, that Dad was ready to understand what I had to say. I felt a peacefulness rush over me.

Dad cocked his head and looked down at the floor between my feet. "Now he understands," I thought as Dad shook his head.

It was a sudden burst of light and heat that raised me. Only after my elbows hit the hardwood hallway floor did the left side of my face feel like it was missing. I thought it was a bomb. I heard a loud clap as one of my aunts shrieked. My left eye was shut and stinging and I looked back into Dad's eyes out of my good eye. Dad drew a long breath. "Get out of my sight," he said. I obeyed.

Stretched before me lay that same hallway leading back to more shame. This time it was Freda Payne's "Band of Gold" that escorted me down the aisle—"And the memory of what love could be, if you were still here with me." I wondered if Brandt heard all the commotion and what he would think of me. What jokes would Doreen make for the rest of the night? The kitchen was empty, so the kids were still in Arlette and Doreen's room, talking about me no doubt. I poured myself a tall glass of Kool-Aid and put it to my face to cool the throbbing sting. "Craig?" Mommy said as she came up to me. She was alone. I wondered if she, too, was mad. She bent down to my height and pulled me toward her. Her Unforgettable perfume reminded me of the hours I spent walking in her cranberry-spiked heels when she was at work and Kenny was outside playing with the rest of the normal boys. I wondered if she would hug me if she knew. "You alright?" she asked. "Yeah," I submitted, my face buried in the side of her Angela Davis-sized Afro.

"Your father shouldn't have hit you. Dad loves you. He was just very upset." She stopped and knelt down in front of me and there was no one around, no one but me and her. "You just have to watch what you say. Okay?" I mumbled a response. "Okay?" she repeated as if it were an oath I needed to seal. "Okay."

She took me by the hand and led me toward Aunt Dee's bathroom. As we walked I wondered just what to make of my mother. Could she be trusted? Her words made me feel special. It was not the part about Dad's love. I knew what to make of that. She said he was wrong. But she offered something else. Something I could use. Some advice, like a friend, not a parent, would give. Did she know how different I was? Could she love me if she knew? Could she be trusted and married to him at the same time. Not likely, I thought. But I wanted to give her something back anyway. She seemed to need something, too. I could tell because her always-steady hand was now trembling in mine. I thought of it as some sort of secret handshake. I was afraid but I tried as hard as I could to keep my hand sturdy for her.

I thought we would need each other to be a little stronger now.

This story is dedicated to the memories of my mother, Anna Ruth Washington, and my Aunt Delores Dorsey for all the love, laughter, and music they gave me.

Guys and Dolls
Jarrett Neal

Coach Walker was the first man I ever saw completely naked. I was in eighth grade at the time, and I was miserable. My mother was about to marry a man I didn't particularly like, and after the wedding, she and my future stepfather planned to move to Omaha, Nebraska, leaving me behind in Kansas City with my grandparents.

At school my classes were either so easy that I found them insulting or so difficult that the low grades I made convinced me I was an idiot. I didn't have cool clothes. I didn't have a girlfriend. My complete lack of athletic ability excluded me from the popular group of boys, the ones who hooted and hollered in the back of the school bus; the ones, who, at fourteen, already possessed the brawny, robust physiques of full grown men; whose laughter pealed from the mischief they caused and the misery they inflicted. This, I later assumed, was one of the reasons our school didn't force students to shower after gym class. Packs of rowdy pubescent boys given running water, towels, and permission to remove their clothes—boys fascinated with all things sexual and imbued with the rampant homophobia that codifies their behavior well into manhood—augured nothing less than disaster, and our principal wanted to avoid it.

Our junior high school employed three gym teachers: Coach Smith, a tiny African American woman who taught girls' PE; my gym teacher, Coach Manning, a man so overweight that he could be heard wheezing from several feet away; and Coach Walker, a brash and brawny young African American man with sandy hair, honey skin, and a goatee. He roughhoused with the boys and was every girl's fantasy. In college he had excelled at virtually every sport, and the proof of his athleticism, a physique stacked head to foot and front to back with bulging hard muscles, was unquestionable. Coach Walker was the only teacher who got away with cussing at us and telling us dirty jokes. He zoomed through the school's parking lot in a black Corvette while NWA quaked from his speakers. To my classmates and me, Coach Walker put the "kool" in Kool-Aid, and we were as mortified as he was when we filed into the locker room after spending gym period outside playing football and happened upon him naked in the communal showers. The sight of him stark naked inspired a rowdy response from most of the boys, yet stunned silence from me and a couple of my peers. Seeing Coach Walker standing under the steamy shower that autumn afternoon, his golden brown body glistening, his tumescent penis bouncing from one tree trunk thigh to the other, ended my boyhood. I never knew anyone could be so beautiful, certainly not a man, a naked man. It was like watching one of my action figures come to life.

Two years earlier, when I was a small boy in elementary school, *He-Man and the Masters of the Universe* was the most popular cartoon among boys. I raced home every day after school to watch timid yet Herculean Prince Adam extend his long, heavy Sword of Power, shout, "By the power of Grayskull!" and magically transform into He-Man, the half-naked blond, bronzed barbarian who defended the planet

Eternia from Skeletor and other half-naked barbarians (with such blatant homoerotic imagery, Mattel can probably take more than a little credit for captivating an entire generation of gay men). My mother bought me a new Masters of the Universe action figure each payday, and when I played with them my imagination soared. Eventually I amassed a collection of action figures so large that there wasn't one character on the cartoon I didn't have a figure for. Castle Grayskull itself, a three-foot high plastic structure colored green and made to look as ghoulish and ferocious as the castle on the cartoon, was the bulwark of my collection. My mother gave it to me for Christmas. Three months later I turned twelve and decided I was too old to play with toys, so I packed up all of my action figures and dumped them into the trash along with Castle Grayskull. Mama went berserk.

We call them action figures: miniature plastic replicas of superheroes marketed to little boys. And boys love them. I recall spending countless hours of my boyhood running, jumping, and stomping all over my grandparents' house with my action figures, lowering my voice when I spoke for them and imaging storylines that were much more complex than the ones I saw on the cartoon each afternoon. In this regard action figure seems to be the most appropriate term for these toys. Yet the language our culture uses to describe these figures reveals our own anxiety regarding masculinity. They're dolls. We know this. Yet the cultural fear that boys who play with dolls become sissies demands that we rename them. I wasn't the only boy who enjoyed playing with action figures, and I doubt I was the only boy whose sexuality quite literally sprung to life when we packed into the locker room too early and surprised Coach Walker in all his naked beauty. Many of my classmates cackled and pointed; some even whistled. Embarrassed, Coach Walker snatched his towel from the hook just outside the communal showers and barked, "Get dressed!" He boomed the same words over and over, as if the thunder of his voice and the repetition of the words themselves, like Prince Adam's magical invocation, would be enough to enrobe him, to eradicate the image of his body, and the diversity of feelings he inspired, from our crude adolescent minds. How could we be comfortable with nudity when we were forbidden to disrobe and bathe in front of each other? Our only model for manhood, in mortifying incident, had been made human and all too fallible.

Men were scarce in the environment I grew up in. There's an old joke about Father's Day in the ghetto. The punch line: What's Father's Day? As tasteless as the joke is, it underscores the reality of boyhood for untold numbers of African American boys who, like me, had no male role models. Our mothers, almost in desperation, relied on He-Man among other superheroes and action film stars, toys, and games, sports and social interactions, to fill the void left by our absent fathers. They were poor substitutes, yet a starving child can transform cracker crumbs into a banquet. I took great pleasure in the hours I spent playing with my action figures. Indeed, I, like so many of my creative peers, credit playtime with cultivating my imagination and providing the genesis of my desire to write. Happy in my world of make believe, He-Man and his ilk allowed me to become anyone and do anything I wished, whether it was battling Skeletor or riding Battle Cat through the untamed wilderness of Eternia. Yet at no time during these play sessions or my pubescent years did it ever occur to me that He-Man was an undeniable stud. Mattel, the company that created not only the Masters of the Universe line of toys and games but also the thirty-minute animated series, states in his biography that He-Man stands six feet two inches tall and weighs around two hundred and twenty-five pounds. But anyone with keen eyesight knows that these measurements, like the character himself, are utter fiction. Wimpy boys like me could only dream of attaining the physicality and confidence He-Man, a veritable muscle god, possessed. The daily taunts from my peers and the ache of fatherlessness, an absence I feel even as an adult, crippled my sense of self-worth. Like He-Man's alter ego, Prince Adam, I scarcely knew what to do with myself. I needed to become He-Man just as much as he did.

A man with the body of a gladiator walks through a fantastical world populated by anthropomorphic creatures, robots, warriors, and sorceresses wearing only jackboots, a furry brown Speedo, and a metal harness that bears a flaming Iron Cross. His muscles are swollen to outrageous proportions, striated and pumped, resembling an archetype of masculinity found, in the real world, only on the covers of bodybuilding magazines. This is He-Man—perhaps the single most striking and iconic image of my boyhood. Introduced to boys in the mid-1980s, He-Man represented the nation's "bigger is better" zeitgeist: a decade when Americans were trouncing competitors in the Olympics, in the nuclear arms race, and on the silver screen. Arnold Schwarzenegger, Jean-Claude Van Damme, and Sylvester Stallone were knocking down doors and kicking in dicks in a string of action flicks that capitalized on their steroid-pumped bodies and athletic prowess. Coach Walker, with his hunky sculpted physique, hairy chest, and husky drill sergeant's voice, could easily have taken a place beside these box office behemoths. In the fleeting moments I watched him step out of the shower, grab his white towel, and bound into his office twenty feet away, my own Sword of Power jousted the air. Though my classmates and I had come upon Coach Walker by surprise, catching him in the most exposed and vulnerable situation a person can find himself in, at no time after the incident did any of us think less of him. He scared and fascinated us before we saw him naked and wet, and he continued to exude charisma and strength in the months and weeks that followed. This, I think, makes muscle men so appealing—their ability to simultaneously arouse and terrify, to meld brutality and fear with beauty and sensuality, inhabiting the roles of father, hero, lover, and disciplinarian.

I didn't acknowledge my sexual attraction to men until my freshman year of college. Four more years passed before I gained the courage to admit to myself that I am gay. These years were marked by anger, frustration, fear, despair, and, most of all, loneliness. Yet with maturity comes perspective and wisdom, the ability to sort out the past and find solace in truth. I would have given anything to be as powerful as He-Man or as attractive as Coach Walker but one was a cartoon, the other was a man, and I mythologized both of them. They gave me comfort and amusement and taught me many lessons in their own ways. The most valuable lesson of all was to save myself, be my own hero, and gather strength from within. Still, I wish I had kept those action figures. They might be worth a lot of money today.

Pop Quiz

Kevin E. Taylor

I grew up a black, fat, gay, pug-nosed, asthmatic, dictionary-reading nerd in the projects of Southwest Washington, D.C. I was terrorized by a gang of boys who chased me home from school throwing bottles. Confusingly, each of them later tried to seduce me, offering to be my "first," but the words they screamed told me they'd never want anything to do with me. They said they knew why boys like me had fat butts. Odd, I didn't. I thought it was just fat because the rest of me was, too.

I was pushed down the street by a girl who thought she was more boy than me. She thought I was a sissy. She knew I couldn't return the punches because my mother had raised me not to hit a girl. I didn't, until she tried to push me into oncoming traffic and I had to break the code.

I was tortured by a boy, reaching into the window of the basement classroom where I was sitting in detention for defending myself, who pulled a plug of my Afroed hair out at the root, laughing until I grabbed his arm and pulled him into the room, onto the ground, and almost lost my mind while being restrained from pummeling him.

I have been terrorized and ostracized and criticized, and I have had to fight for my life a few times. I have been harassed because of the words I chose to use in sentences, out loud, in front of people who said little, fat, gay brown boys couldn't speak like that in the projects. As a boy who liked to read books and watch television and whose asthma forced him to stay inside when kids were playing and summer was calling, I was a prisoner to my sickness, to my smartness, to my surroundings.

But I remember the day it all changed.

It was in eighth grade Social Studies class, when our teacher divided the room in half and gave a verbal pop quiz on social and cultural news events. I did well in school, and despite the other challenges I faced, I was always expected to shine in the classroom.

Most of the questions that day were related to local politics and major news events. Late in the quiz, each side was tied and my teacher pulled out a tiebreaker question.

"Who is the newly re-elected president of Mexico?"

None of the students had any idea. One by one, student after student failed to provide the correct answer. I thought the teacher would change the question and allow us to move on to see who would win. But that's not how things played out. He stood in front of the classroom, alternately pointing to students on either side of the room, first left, then right, clear that he was going to exhaust each of us until he proved we hadn't actually read the newspaper or done our assignments. He glared at us with the familiar look of disappointment that parents give children when they don't complete their chores. The story was on the front page of the *Washington Post* and we should have read it, seen it, or noticed it; I did. But chair-by-chair, each student seemed to have skipped that particular story.

With four students left on my team before me, the

alternating count left seven chances for someone else to answer. I never imagined the question would get to me because Taylor was in the back of the alphabetized seating chart, and I almost never got called upon.

I loved that class and I loved reading the newspaper every night when my mother brought it back from one of the homes she cleaned for a living. I would fold it, just like I had seen gentlemen do on TV, and cross my right leg over until the ankle rested on my left thigh. I felt grown up while reading, but more importantly, the newspaper allowed me to escape my surroundings and explore a world outside the abusive one in which I lived. I needed Rome and London, New York and California and the news of the day. I needed anything outside of my own little world. So I loved to take in information. I never knew it would make me a hero.

As the teacher got to a girl on the other side of the classroom who sat in the same row as I did, she, too, could not offer an answer. The pressure fell on me, and I realized this could be my moment.

"Mr. Taylor," the teacher said. "Who is the newly re-elected President of Mexico?" I could see people staring at me, finally hopeful that Mr. Brainiac would fail. Even members of my own "team" seemed to hope I wouldn't get it right.

Alas, I lifted my head. I had read the article.

"The newly re-elected president of Mexico is José López Portillo!"

I had to resist the temptation to cheer for myself, but I had read the article and I knew I was right. And from then on, something changed. My side of the class got an A and the other side got a C. But I received so much more than a letter grade that day. My teammates hugged me, because for some the A made the difference between passing and failing. A boy I liked also hugged me, which I think was his way to reveal his feelings for me. And from that day on, things were different. I got smiles and hellos in the hallways. Things even changed with the fat boy who always wanted to fight me. When we fought in the seventh grade, we were just the two fat boys fighting it out. The next time we fought, however, people called out my name in support during the skirmish. Two guys even pulled us apart, saying to me "Kev, man, that's beneath you. Stop." Somehow, I got people to realize that being smart could pay off, even for them.

Of course, in the eighth grade, I also grew about six inches and grew more proportionately into my weight, which enabled my pug nose to fit onto my face in a new and maturing way. My voice also changed, and I appeared a bit more intimidating to potential bullies as I developed.

It wasn't just that one day in the Social Studies classroom that stopped the bullies from bullying. But I remember that day more than most.

I was always uncomfortable being "Young, Gifted, and Black," a song I had heard both Donny Hathaway and Nina Simone sing during those days of cultural awareness and celebration. I wanted to be able to walk with my head up and be proud to be young, gifted, and black, but my neighborhood, my community never seemed to support that, until the day I raised my hand and raised the standard of how you treat Kevin E. Taylor. That was also the year when Kevin Taylor was called to the front office and more than one person arrived, and I demanded that the E. be placed in my record, which separated me from every other Kevin and any Taylor so I could proudly be anywhere in the world as me.

Being young, gifted, and black wasn't always "where it was at" in the concrete jungle of my neighborhood or in our Southwest tenement with its sticky floors and imposed limitations. But just a few blocks away, at Thomas Jefferson Junior High School, where I walked with children of elected officials and their maids, on a fall day in October, I didn't mind at all.

Bathtubs and Hot Water

Shaun Lockhart

Reading Comprehension, fourth period. I looked around the room at my seventh grade classmates. Everyone's head was bowed, searching for the deeper meaning behind Aldous Huxley's *Brave New World*. The only sound heard came from the light hum of the fluorescent lighting overhead. An entire five minutes would pass before a voice broke everyone's train of thought.

"Hey, Shaun!" My neck jerked. It was Natalie, the class bully, calling from across the classroom in a husky voice. "Come here for a second," she continued.

Now everyone's attention turned to me. Would I dare walk over to see what she wanted? Hesitantly I tiptoed across the floor, hoping that if I were quiet enough, maybe everyone would return to his or her reading. But no such luck. "Do you know why I called you over here, Shaun?" Her voice was even louder now. I could hear nervous laughter from a few classmates, and my chuckle echoed their anxiety.

"Um, no, I don't, actually," I replied, bracing myself for the punch line.

"You don't have to be a bulging, masculine guy. But you—you are very effeminate. I have never met such a weak man. You need to start hanging around more black males. Honey, you are a sissy white boy trapped in a black boy."

"Natalie!" a friend of mine shrieked. "Knock it off."

"Somebody needs to tell him," she said, cutting her eyes in my friend's direction. I was frozen in humiliation. Nobody else said a word. Natalie had spoken and nobody challenged her. Her eyes returned to connect with mine and then she grinned.

"Oh. You can return to your seat now." I walked away and I wanted to keep walking out the doors of Noe Middle School, never to return, but I wasn't a student who would play hooky.

My grades were good, I consistently made honor roll, and my teachers loved me. Classmates were my problem, particularly the other African American students who reminded me daily that I did not fit in. Things began to heat up when LaTosha wanted to date me, and I became nervous. Struggling with my sexuality, I was forced to make a decision between suffering the humiliation of being one of the only guys in my class without a girlfriend, or to start dating LaTosha and embarrass myself even further. I decided to concentrate on academics and find friends where I could.

That did not work out too well. LaTosha ran with a large group of other girls, including Natalie as the ringleader. It seemed Natalie's sole purpose at school was to create conflict and draw negative attention. So after turning down LaTosha's advances, Natalie began to pull my card.

"You do like girls, don't you?" She asked one day, her head tilted to one side as she placed her hand on her hip.

"Of course—why would you ask that?"

"I have my doubts," she replied.

"Well, really, that's none of your business, is it?"

Natalie stepped in closer to my face and grinned. "You are

a faggot, number one. And number two, you are an Uncle Tom. So that's two strikes against you. Crossing me would be your third and final one."

And the last thing I wanted to do was cross Natalie. She was very popular, very intelligent, and very feared. I could never understand why someone who had so much potential and was such a brilliant speaker would use her talent to channel so much evil and hatred towards others, especially me. She considered herself the Sister Souljah of Noe Middle School. Everything was pro black and everything that black males did in our school had to be done a certain way, according to her criteria, or she would publicly ridicule them.

So I became Natalie's target and I was devastated. I knew people listened to her, and she could ruin my life. My goodness, I thought. What if she found out my house didn't have a bathtub and hot water? That would certainly kick it up a notch.

I grew up on the south side of Louisville, Kentucky, with a very loving family. My mother, father, older sister, grandmother, and I lived together in a cramped, yellow shotgun house that had two bedrooms and one faucet in the kitchen that ran only cold. There were no sinks, hot water, or bathtub anywhere in the house. During the summer months, plug-in fans struggled to keep the house cool, but really just circulated dry, hot air. During the cold months, kerosene heaters and one wood-burning stove fought to keep everyone warm.

Our frail faucet sat at the end of a long pipe that ran from under the kitchen floor and poured water into a green bucket we constantly had to empty into the toilet. From this faucet we drew water for every purpose necessary, and to get hot water, we had to boil tea kettles. This took place at a time (the '80s and '90s) when most children of my age lived in homes with basic plumbing necessities. Despite our poor living circumstances, my family shielded us from the reality of our poverty. It never really dawned on me that I was poor. My grandmother headed our household with an ambitious spirit when it came to raising her family properly.

She worked as a cafeteria cook at Iroquois High and made certain that neither my sister nor I ever went to school wearing dirty, torn, or wrinkled clothing. None of our peers would have guessed we came from such modest living conditions. We did not have much, but we took pride in what we had. My mother, who worked as a supervisor for a local package delivery service, helped out with our household needs as well. My dad, who battled alcoholism, found odd jobs here and there. So there we were, making it the best way we could, but I was happy growing up. Except for the hell that was middle school.

"Hey, Mr. Shaun, how was school today," my grandmother asked every afternoon.

"Good."

But most days were bad. I came home humiliated but never told my family what was going on because doing so would open even more doors and questions. They might have asked, "Well, why would they think you were gay?" Or they may have asked, "Well, why don't you have a girlfriend?" So I did not say anything. Instead, I turned to television and absorbed Oprah Winfrey—her lessons, her life, and her modest background. I thought to myself, "If Oprah can get through it, I can get through it because I have always believed God uses people and holds certain people to the light by which others can see the way." And I knew undoubtedly that Oprah spoke to me with her lessons. Oprah's own childhood struggles validated my struggle and became a grounding force that allowed me to walk through my experiences at school. I once read an article where she explained that lessons of adversity teach us about ourselves and allow us to emerge on the other side with a greater sense of joy.

What I began to realize is that life is all about finding important lessons and realizing your particular purpose for being on earth and using your life to magnify that purpose to help others. So after I "got it," I started going to school and behaving nicely to Natalie and others who were mean to me. Once I did this and told myself that their words did not define me, my self-esteem improved drastically. The mean comments and jokes from classmates didn't bother me as much because I was none of those things. I am not a bad person because I act a certain way or hang with certain people. I am not a bad person because I am gay.

I would no longer own those negative comments that were spit at me. Their comments only painted a picture of who they were, what they believed, and how they lived their lives. I lost my fear of things that happened around me once I realized they were doing just that—happening around me. I became outspoken and stood up for myself and others. When Natalie began belittling others, I reminded her that she, too, had faults. Teachers began to admire me as one of the few students who stood up to Natalie.

My middle school experiences taught me valuable life lessons. My family lacked a bathtub and hot water so we had to improvise. And my family didn't always have money so we had to improvise. That taught me that if life doesn't give you what you want, when you want it, or how you want it, you have to improvise. And I knew that lesson well.

Strange Fruit

Antonio Brown

I see myself from above. I'm in this little room and the door opens. He enters the room, light-skinned, and comes closer. His eyes, I'd never noticed the intensity, the beauty of his eyes. Drawing nearer, he parts his lips, preparing for the kiss. My eleven-year-old self is now wide-awake.

Vince?

Vince was the neighborhood bully, back when we had neighborhoods, bullies, and fist fights instead of drive-bys. I had bought into Dr. King's nonviolent message and applied it to my life. I never liked to fight. Not terribly practical when surrounded by testosterone-rocked boys trying to grasp fleeting notions of manhood with tales of "tappin' that ho" or "bustin' Pookie and them's ass" in a street fight. And then there was Vince, who plagued me and my best friend, Kenny.

Kenny and I would ride our bikes, play board games, eat candy, and hang for hours. Then Vince, who was at least three years older, would come along to spoil our days by taunting us with our shared nickname, "Faggotry." My young mind's eye always saw a "faggot tree" dangling strange fruit.

Even as a child, I had identified with Billie Holiday's torch song "Strange Fruit," a curious dirge depicting lynched victims swinging from poplar trees in the Jim Crow South. Vince's taunts of "faggot tree" sent shudders through my adolescent body, overflowing my mind with images of cadaverous gay boys swaying like unholy ornaments in the towering oak tree that shadowed my family's backyard. My gut sank as I willed myself to shrink into invisibility.

"So, what you punks wanna do?" Vince asked.

"We're hanging out playing some games, 'bout to go to my place and do some homework," Kenny said.

"Yeah, I'll bet," Vince said. "Hmmph, faggotry."

Kenny and I bristled and puffed up our chests.

In response, Vince asked, "What choo gone do?"

We looked at each other. Should we double-team him? Could we take him down? But then what?

I never understood street fights. I mean, how do you know who won? And unless someone died, when would it end? I could never see the point. So Kenny and I walked away, demoralized and angry, but proud to take the higher road.

"Yeah, I didn't think so, punks," Vince yelled at us.

Kenny and I had lost our patience with Vince, but we convinced ourselves his accusations weren't true. We both had girlfriends and many more girls pursued us with love notes handed our way. *Check here if you like Arneta, Cythnia, or Theresa —yes, no, maybe so.* Vince didn't know what he was talking about.

That summer, Vince's cousin Denise came to visit. She was my age, a cute brown-skinned girl with long braids and a mad crush on me. And she always smelled like my grandmama's banana pudding, complete with Nilla Wafers.

I wouldn't say I was an eleven-year-old on the down low, but I was still coming to terms with my gay self. I just didn't know. I didn't know that living a loving life with another man was an option, and I wasn't clear if that was what I wanted. So I still went with girls, including Denise.

One day when we were kissing in the entry to my family's basement, we looked up and every kid from the neighborhood—Tweet, Stank, Hugie, Carmen, Tom Tom, and Estelle's *entire* crew—was in my backyard oohing, aahing, chanting, and cheering.

"Wait till Vince hears about this," someone said.

I took the walk of shame through the crowd to escort Denise home, walking right into Vince along the way. The whole neighborhood had been waiting for something like this all summer. Would "Pretty Tony" bring it or punk out?

Vince was in our faces in an instant. "Denise, what you doin' hanging with this punk?"

I tried to walk around him with Denise in tow, but the neighborhood had gathered, ready for a fight.

"Look, Faggotry, I don't want you all up on my cousin."

"Its cool, Vince, we're heading home now," Denise said. "And he definitely ain't no fag."

Vince, unconvinced, looked around. "You don't know what you talking about. Tell her," he demanded.

"Tell her what, Vince," I asked. "Look, I'm just walking her home, then going home myself."

"You ain't going nowhere till you get past me."

Folks were standing around like they'd paid money for this show. I'd already turned both cheeks, and all it had gotten me was a sore ass. Was it time to fight?

Before we could find out, my mother's voice called me from a distance to come inside. Everyone knew the "fight" was done. Vince never confronted me again. The summer passed and soon he and his family moved away.

By the time I made it to high school and college, those threats seemed far away. But college had its own challenges, including folks who were ready to shame me for being who I am. The fraternities and athletes became the new neighborhood bullies, still trying to scope out their manhood while standing on the necks of others. Although no one directly threatened me, I felt that familiar shrinking feeling when the jocks' oppressive presence drew near. And yet many of the frat boys and jocks shared an open secret we always knew as the "down low." I never played that game, but some folks in my new queer circle held all the secrets and did not mind sharing.

College did offer new opportunities and options for love. Critical analysis of Foucault and "queer theory" opened my mind. Education became a space of praxis, bringing theory to life and loving. Aside from hitting the books, I also used that time to hit the sheets. Love, exploration, and self-acceptance all walked hand-in-hand. Although I ran on my high school track team and had always been physically fit, the university gym helped fill out my body and boosted my confidence along with my biceps. The images of emaciated strange fruit dangling from the "faggot tree" faded as I found love for my body, mind, and spirit. And I experienced my first real love for a man.

It was my lifelong love of jazz that connected me with my college love affair during sophomore year. Curt was a tall, dark-skinned graduate student who loved Nina Simone. He was fine, sexy, smart, and smooth as silk as he handed me a Hershey's kiss before leaning in for a kiss of his own.

Some time later, on a long weekend home from college, I took a walk through the old neighborhood. And there was Vince. Instinctively I began to shrink in the shadow of the "faggot tree." Then, suddenly, I was no longer invisible.

We were both adults now. I was twenty and had come into my own. Bulked up and ripped from countless bench presses and bicep curls, I was fit for battle and in no mood to turn the other cheek.

Vince was wearing a black leather motorcycle jacket. I wasn't sure it was him at first. His honey-kissed skin wrapped a taut but slight physique. He had seemed so large back when I felt so small. With my now broad and solid chest puffed out, I fixed my gaze and knew I could wreck shop on Vince for all my boys dangling from the "faggot tree." Then I saw those eyes.

He stared at me, smiling, and asked, "So, you gonna hit me now?" He leaned in with those intensely beautiful eyes, now glassy with the look of hunger and regret that brands the shamed, the vexed, the blessed. And, finally, I—we—understood.

THE FAMILY THAT PREYS

Teaspoons of December Alabama

Rodney Terich Leonard

Moten Johnson was my mother's high school sweetheart. His name seemed to butter her tongue when she spoke of him. He was a married man and father of eight children. One of his daughters and I were classmates and cackling friends. Along with my mother and four sisters, I adored Moten. We admired his light-hearted ways and windy laughter while he drove us to summer softball games and hauled firewood for us every winter. In the absence of our various fathers, we found him noble and father-like.

We lived in Cottage Grove, Alabama, a tiny, jerkwater town near Alexander City, which once headquartered Russell Corporation, a textile company. When mother became ill, I began to buy the groceries and pay the bills. The only son of a divorced mother meant chopping the wood and fashioning the fire at fifteen and holding two part-time jobs at local beauty salons as a shampoo boy. I also styled hair out of our $15 per month rented house, which lacked indoor plumbing. The scent of poverty was distinct as spilled camphor. The tardiness of our

$88 monthly welfare check and $103 food stamps forced mother and me to play bingo at the Elks Club in hopes of winning extra money. My father lived in the neighborhood but was living with and raising another family.

One cold Tuesday December night my mother sent me to play bingo with Moten. On the way home from Montgomery, the rain poured for the hour-long drive. As we neared home, Moten turned off onto what was called "The Dirt Road" in Nixburg, Alabama, where my mother was born and raised. The spook of the kudzu-strewn road sparked many town ghost tales. I asked Moten why were we taking the out–of-the-way, obscure route.

"Let's ride off a piece and talk," he said, eyes on the road.

I thought to myself, "Talk about what?" We'd been laughing and talking for hours about fishing, baseball, how to make homemade coconut candy, and how times were improving for black Americans in the 1980s, on the drive to Montgomery and back.

After about ten minutes, he pulled off the dirt road onto a long, muddy familiar driveway. It led to my grandparent's old home. They'd abandoned it for the city projects because the place had become structurally unsound. I remembered the front yard, now flecked with wild weed, the place of my favorite "hide-and-go-seek" memories. My grandfather played the guitar under the sweet gum tree in this yard of my childhood. I used to eavesdrop on my grandmother's Eastern Star meetings, from underneath the tall porch. The frame of the home place still stood, powerless and watching.

Moten switched off the car's headlights and ignition. His rough-warm hands fumbled for me. "I've been watching your round, girl-butt for a long time. Bet you been reading about this in books, huh? I see you always somewhere reading. You ever had a man in you?"

I stuttered, "No."

He grabbed my left hand, placing it on a hard, rising lump

in his khakis. "Let me take it out for ya,'" he said. "'This is me, Rodney. Go on and feel it. "

Moten cupped my trembling hand around his penis. "Let's move to the back seat. Won't take long to get used to the feeling. You want it anyway," he said.

Nervousness caused my armpits to heat and itch. Raising my voice, I said, "Don't do this to me. I don't do this."

His face was streaked with sternness. I followed his order and climbed to the back seat. He followed. As he kissed me, I smelled onion on his breath. Breathing hard, he turned me on my stomach then pulled down my pants and underwear.

"Why aren't you hard?" he asked. He spat in his hand and into my rectum and roughed forty-three years of heat inside me. I dug my fingernails into the velvet seat cushion, gnawed gashes into the fabric to manage the shock of torn flesh. The floorboard scraped my knuckles. Moten pinned me down with his arms tightly wrapped around my waist. My pleas and wails went unheeded. His low moan-growl finalized the act. He switched on the dim overhead light, made me promise not to tell anyone as he wiped red clots of rape off of himself.

The rain fell softly. Later I slammed Moten Johnson's rust-colored Monte Carlo door and broke the news of no bingo luck to my mother. I didn't tell her. Instead, I brushed my teeth for a long time, the smell of Moten's breath still on mine. My bloody underwear were wet and torn, and I rolled them up in a plastic bag and threw it away.

The next day was Wednesday, which came with its expected ninth-grade ordinariness.

Years ago mother phoned with the news that Moten Johnson had died of lung cancer. She sobbed for quite some time about Moten's virtues, his upright character, and how we had lost a mighty fine family friend. Her tearful and lengthy eulogy complimented my own reverence and shame and need for reflection about Moten. In truth, I fell for his and my loneliness again and again. Through sexual abuse I was awakened, exposed to an opportunity to research versions of my being. I left that southern town, at nineteen, tied and committed to knotted secrecy and complication. Gentler and older men, throughout my twenties and thirties, in several cities, whose lives were living rooms of emotions and mirrors, refused to be branches on which my pains and issues could rest. Tears, for Moten's life-trot through rain and for my own turbulent flights for survival, found me that day. I remained silent until I spoke.

"As far as I'm concerned, the Moten Johnson you *think* you knew died in 1985, when I was fifteen, December of that year."

Then I told her.

A House is Not a Home

Rob Smith

I was well into my twenties before I remembered that my stepfather had spent two years raping me, starting when I was just seven years old. If the saying is true that God only gives you what you can handle, then that's certainly true about the mind. It closes, opens, expands, and contracts. It gives you flashes of something that may have happened long ago, the tiniest glimpses of what may have occurred. One year it's the flash of a Polaroid camera bouncing off of a glimmering gold tooth in the dark, scary and disturbing enough to wake you up in a cold sweat during a hot summer night. In another, it's the memory of the slanted door to an attic that you were desperately afraid of as a child, because something bad happened there, though you're not entirely sure what. Then one night, it all comes together with the blunt force of a sledgehammer to the forehead as the result of an ill-advised pot brownie, a techno concert, and far too much to drink.

After finally making it back home and drifting into a troubled sleep, it all comes back to you and you remember your hated stepfather. He was the man who verbally and physically abused your mother, but was for some reason always so nice to you. You remember his caramel-colored skin and the gold tooth that seemed to make his smile ominous, like that of a snake closing in on his prey. You remember the brown rims of his bifocal glasses, the loud clap of his hand against your mother's cheek, and the lick of his belt against your thin, naked body after you were sent home from school for mouthing off in the first grade.

And finally, you remember the attic itself. You remember the dust particles dancing off of the gauzy rays of sunlight breaking through the lone window that connected the attic with the rest of the world. You know that was where it happened, always on Saturday afternoons when your mother was playing softball with her friends. You remember feeling your thin arms clasped against your bare body as you struggled to control your trembling while he took the photos. You remember his gargantuan penis blocking out your field of vision for a second before you close your eyes, open your mouth, and wait for it to be over. You remember the minutes afterwards that felt like days as he held you in his big arms and forced you to lay with him as those sunrays cast odd spotlights on your nude brown bodies. You remember hearing the distant sounds of kids playing in the distance, and desperately wishing you could be one of them.

I sunk into a deep depression soon after I remembered what had happened to me. After telling my sister, I wanted to take her advice to try to forget it when she reminded me that the ex-stepfather who'd abused me was dead, buried, and probably burning in hell. Why, then, did he feel so alive in my heart, my mind, and my dreams? Nightmarish hours turned into days and weeks spent practically immobilized on my bed in the sweltering August heat. Days and weeks spent hating my stepfather and myself for what had happened. I felt used. Dirty. Stupid. Damaged.

For a month I saw little more than my legs poking out of white briefs as I watched television through eyes reddened and puffy from crying. Whenever I closed my eyes, it seemed to bring some fresh horror of the experience back to me, and I spent those weeks reliving what had happened to me in that attic over and over again, like some nightmare version of that old movie *Groundhog Day*. I saw his face grinning at me from behind the Polaroid camera. Tasted his semen in my mouth. Felt his strong arms clamp down forcefully over my shoulders when I tried to move away from him afterward.

Day by day, the darkness crept over my life like a slow moving cloud until it eventually covered all, turning the usual sounds of joy and laughter that emanated from me into sounds of pain and fear. The darkness that consumed my life was in direct contrast to the bright summer days that were passing me by, and I wondered when the all-consuming feeling of emptiness would end. I feared I would end up like the other abuse victims I read about online, the ones who were consumed by depression until they decided to end their own pain entirely. I needed help.

Shortly after, I found myself in a psychiatrist's care once a week as a part of a program offering no-cost mental health care to Iraq War veterans. For the next few weeks I bared my soul about my life, my upbringing, my worries, and my triumphs, so that when the talk inevitably made its way to my abuse, I felt comfortable enough to be frank with him. "I think I know what happened," I told him on one afternoon as I shifted uncomfortably in my seat. "But I want to find some way to let go of this because I feel like it's eating me alive." The room was deathly silent after this, filled only with the sounds of the scribbles on his writing pad. After what seemed like an eternity, he asked only a single question. "Have you ever tried hypnotherapy?" he asked.

I hadn't, and we began.

The psychiatrist tells me to think of the last place where I felt completely and totally safe, and I rack my brain trying to figure it out. It isn't the uncomfortable bed in my apartment, nor is it the home I shared with seven fraternity brothers in college. I think back to a night earlier in the summer when I shared a moonlit walk on the beach with a close friend, how we laid out on the beach together, me with my head on his burly chest, and how the last thing I felt as I drifted into a calm and dreamless sleep with the sounds of the waves crashing just a few yards in front of us was the gentle touch of his soft lips on my forehead. Yes, I felt safe there.

I think of this place as I close my eyes and hear the psychiatrist's steady voice telling me to listen as he counts backwards from ten to one, and sometime after four I find myself in some world deep in my subconscious while hearing his voice guide me from somewhere else. I see the house I grew up in, with its small yard and green shutters cupping the two small windows that face out front. I am a fully grown man now, not the boy who once lived there, but I see him, me, as he runs out of the house to play with his favorite toy in the driveway, a yellow Tonka truck that he races down the driveway over and over again. "I see me," I hear myself say. "God, I was so small." The thin, small little boy with the curly black hair bears little resemblance to the beefy adult man he will become, and as I find myself staring at this small person, the flicker of a shadow in a window above catches my eye. I look above and to my right and know what I'll be looking at before it even enters my frame of vision. That is the window of the attic. That is where it happens.

I look back over to the little boy and I see that he's looking at the window as well. His smile is gone. He looks at me, and we share a knowing glance. He silently places the truck to the side and walks into the house with his shoulders slumped and his head down. I blink and now I'm in the attic. My nose fills with the acrid smell of sawdust and mothballs. I am clothed but the boy is naked, and he sits in the corner with his thin body curled in the fetal position and his knees cupped tightly against his chest. I hear him sobbing. I look to my right, and I see my stepfather standing in the corner, completely shadowed save for the curve of his penis and a small flash of light where a sunray meets the lenses of his glasses. He is much larger than the boy, but I am larger than he. I look at him with all the hatred and fury that I can muster, but I say nothing. Instead, I turn my attention back to the boy, vaguely realizing that somewhere in the other world, my entire body is convulsing with sobs so severe that they seem strong enough to rip my chest open at any moment, and the collar of my shirt is soaked clear through with my tears.

I place my hand on the boy's shoulder, shocked again at how small and thin it is. He acknowledges my presence, but doesn't turn to me. He also doesn't tense up. He knows that I won't hurt him. "I'm gonna get you out of here," I say to him. He says nothing, but looks to the corner where our stepfather is. Stepfather is silent and motionless, and his breathing is the only sound in the room. I look back to our stepfather, and I feel my hate dissipating into something else. I think that it is pity. I look into the boy's deep and fearful brown eyes as I stand him up. "I don't think he can hurt you anymore," I say as I gently guide him out of the attic forever. I blink again and we're outside during a bright and sunny day, both fully clothed. In the other world, I hear the psychiatrist's voice asking me if I know of anywhere safe I can take the boy, and I do.

Just a few blocks away my paternal grandfather and his wife live in a small, pink house with an enormous oak tree in the front. I call his wife my grandmother because I love her as such. She is warm, maternal, and caring. I know the boy will be safe here when I see the joy radiating from her eyes as she sees the two of us walking towards her. She takes him into her fleshy arms, and he returns the hug warmly. She starts to guide him into the house, and he looks back at me when I don't move. When he looks into my eyes I can tell that he wants to know why I can't come, but I don't say why. I just tell the boy that he can trust her. I tell him that she will take care of him, that she will love him, and that she will protect him. He smiles at me now, and it is bright and warm, made somehow more endearing by a front tooth that is missing in his mouth.

The last thing I see is him walking into the house with our grandmother as I continue to walk down the street. Our backs are both turned to the old, white house with the attic.

Mother to Son
Chaz Barracks

My mother always seemed to have issues with masculinity, or
rather with my apparent lack of it. Maybe it was because she
felt guilty that I didn't have a father. Or maybe she had dreams
of me becoming a macho sports star. Whatever the reason, for
as far back as I can remember, she seemed to be obsessed with
it. When I was little, there were continual comments like, "stop
acting like a girl," "stop acting like a pussy," "stop acting like a
lady."

As I got older, "faggot" became her word of choice. She
used it in casual conversation: "Take out the garbage, faggot,"
she would say, as if faggot was simply my nickname. At other
times, she would scream it at me in a rage. Anything could set
her off. Something as simple as my asking, "Can A.J. sleep over
this week?" And she would say, "No." I would argue back that I
didn't understand why not. "Because I don't want any fucking
gayness in my house; you are not bringing your little boyfriends
here so you can play with their dicks under my roof. I will not
have any faggot stuff in my house! Do you hear me, faggot?" I

didn't even understand why she was saying that. At this time, it wasn't sexual or anything. I was just asking to have a friend sleep over like the other kids.

It made me angry, but it also confused me. I didn't understand why my mother spoke to me like this and made me cry, because I knew she loved me, and our good times together proved that. When it got really bad, I would retreat to my sister's room. Although she usually regarded me as an annoying little brother, when I was hurting she never turned me away. I would walk in and she would know, and she would let me sit on the floor and watch TV with her. When my sister wasn't there, I would go into my own room, take the phone off the hook, turn off the lights and TV, and cry in the dark until I began to think about other stuff...like my grandmother. I used to call my grandmother late at night, and hearing her voice would take the pain away. When I would cry to her, she would tell me I was not a faggot and to ignore the comments. But it was hard to ignore; it hurt so bad.

For a while, I did try to ignore it. I would focus on the good times, but Mommy's mood could change on a dime. We could be watching a movie, and she would rail at me about how gay I was, then that same night we would go get ice cream as if nothing had happened. That was the way it was—every day was up and down with her, and it could shift in an instant. During the good moments I was always aware that anything might happen to set her off, and when a painful attack was coming my way, I would hold onto the thought that it would pass, it would get better. There would be ice cream and shopping and good times to come.

Then one day the routine changed. That car ride was one of the hardest experiences of my life. It was a Saturday morning. It was pouring rain. The night before, the house was completely silent. My sister stayed in her room, I stayed in my room, and Mommy was in her room with her boyfriend. No one was watching TV. It was like someone had died in the house, and nobody knew what to say. It was still like that in the morning, completely silent, except for the sound of the rain. Mommy didn't pack anything, because, well, you don't bring anything for the type of trip we were taking. So we just brought her. No bags, just her and the clothes she had on, sweat pants and a T-shirt. Everybody was silent in the car. We stopped at a drive-thru and got breakfast, and for a brief moment, it felt like a family outing. But no one was speaking; there was just a deathly silence in the air.

Mommy's boyfriend, Tony, drove slowly in the rain and approached a really long driveway. My sister and I watched from the window in the back as we arrived at the correctional facility, which was out in the hills far away from everything. We entered a large crowded waiting room, where Mommy walked up to the window and checked in. They told her she had only a few minutes to say good-bye, which she did, one-by-one, but it didn't feel private or personal in the busy room. We gave her short hugs. She cried and apologized. Tony was first; I could see he was crying when he hugged her. My sister cried, too, when she gave Mommy a hug. Then it was my turn. Mommy was still crying uncontrollably; she told me how much she loved me and to be sure to behave for my sister. I gave her a hug, but I didn't cry. I had prepared myself for this day. I was twelve. And I was not going to cry.

The saddest part was that none of us looked back. In the movies, people always look back and wave in the good-bye scenes. We didn't do that; we just left. When she turned to go into lock-up, we turned and headed for the exit. We just walked out the door and got in the car, numb from the experience.

The car ride home was awkward. Now we were with her boyfriend. My sister in the front passenger seat wasn't crying, she was just staring straight ahead, stoic and seemingly without emotion. I sat in the back. We weren't even halfway down that long driveway, and it happened: I started to cry, and I couldn't stop. Tears were pouring down my cheeks. I tried to pretend I was asleep, so they wouldn't see. At one point, my sister turned and asked if I was sleeping, but I didn't answer. It was all I could do to hide the flood of tears and silence the impulse to sob out loud. I wasn't crying because Mommy was gone. I think I was crying because I realized this was a breaking point for the family. I didn't know what was going to happen, and that scared me. I was crying because I officially had a mother in prison, and the thought of that stigma was hard to bear. I was crying because now I was not only a "faggot," I was a faggot with no mother and an uncertain future. And there was something inside I couldn't put into words.

When we got home, I went in my room. Tony went out and brought us back dinner. We ate in our rooms and watched TV, and that was it. My sister came into my room and said, "Are you okay?"

In two more weeks, school was over, and I went to my grandmother's for the summer. When I returned at the end of summer, Mommy came home. The first three months she was back, she was "under house arrest"—I actually saw them put the ankle bracelet on her—and she was nice to us. Maybe that was because she felt like a guest in her own home; by that point, my sister had taken charge of everything, and the house was in perfect order. Mommy joined in and did our laundry. It was almost idyllic, except that there was something about her that seemed so soft and broken. But, on the whole, everything was good for about a year.

She had difficulty getting a job; then she got one, but she was fired. I could tell there were problems. Whenever my mother stressed out, she aimed her frustration at me, and the faggot stuff would increase. And it increased dramatically. With the reality of my mother's incarceration, I began to put the pieces together. Even as a young child, I had been aware of the fake names. Magazines would come to our house in different people's names. The phone bill, light bill, and cable bill were in three different names, and none of them were my mother's name.

Mommy would always get pissed if I threw out mail. I thought it belonged to someone who used to live in our house, so I threw it out, and then she would rail on me, "Don't touch my fucking stuff!" I didn't know it was hers. My sister finally clued me in and explained that my mother was using different names and aliases. And once I understood, I automatically knew how to handle calls that came into the house for these various names: "Sarah Spooner? Yes, she lives here, but she isn't home right now. Do you want to leave a message?" "Ann Marie Browne? Yes, but she's out. Can I take a message?" At that point I didn't know about the bad checks or the credit card fraud. My sister, however, had noticed that something was amiss; when we would go shopping, it would always take a little longer than normal at the register. I didn't fully understand it as a child, but now as I was going on fourteen, I began to realize the extent of my mother's criminal activities: mail fraud, identity theft, forgery, and providing false statements.

With my mother back home on probation, the warning signs were gathering: there would be trouble ahead! She continued to struggle to find a job, my sister moved out, and Tony moved out. I was alone with my mother in the house. Then I noticed the cable bill arrived with a new alias, and I knew she was back at it. I was on the receiving end of more and more of those old verbal attacks. But now I had a better sense of what was going on, and I had some ammunition to fight back and defend myself. If she was going to attack me verbally, I was not going to ignore it anymore. I would confront her rather than retreating in silence. In a way that only self-righteous teenagers can, I was going to hold her to account. If she attacked me verbally, I would counter by pointing out her moral failings. When she started to go after me with the faggot stuff, I countered with a sharp verbal retort: "I may be a faggot, but I'm not a criminal; and *I* won't be going to prison." That hit a nerve. And that's when all hell broke loose. The arguments got worse, more violent, and sometimes she would kick me out of the house for days. In a year of what seemed like ever-escalating confrontations, I did everything I could to avoid the conflict, and she did everything she could to keep me there: "You faggot! You are going to sit here and take this like a man! You better get used to it!" As if this barrage would somehow cure me or toughen me up.

When my grandmother bought me a car in the spring of 2005 that sent my mother over the edge. Now that I had wheels, I would leave whenever the arguments started. I was the one with the car and the job. But when I left for work, she would yell after me, "You're not going to work, you're going to your boyfriend's house!" Then she'd call the police and tell them I ran away from home. It was a crazy, ongoing battle, but I had stopped crying. I couldn't take it anymore. It wasn't even making me sad. I just wanted it to be over. And I don't really know which came first—that I stopped crying when I started fighting back, or that when I started fighting back, I stopped crying. But whichever it was, it was a fundamental game-changer. And although the tension escalated in the short run, in the long run the experience saved my life.

It reached the point where the arguments would occur in front of my friends. My mother, who had always been so careful about public impressions, didn't seem to care who saw our battles. She would taunt me in front of my friends: "Come on, faggot, I dare you to hit me!" She would toss my stuff out on the lawn and throw furniture at me. It was out of control. My friends who witnessed these incidents would tell their parents, and soon I had a network of friends and parents who were offering me a place to stay. It was at that point I realized two very important things: first, what was going on in my house was not acceptable; second, moving out was a viable option.

Finally I left. Three friends came to help run interference if things got ugly. And they did: Mommy came out of her room like a charging bull—yelling, slamming doors, and trying to block the way. But my friends helped to gather up my stuff, threw it all in the car, and we were off. I stayed at my friend Carrie's house for the summer. Her parents were very generous, but it became clear this could not be a permanent arrangement, so in the fall, I moved into the unfinished basement of my sister's building. I slept on a futon mattress I had to hide everyday before I left so that no one would discover someone was living in her basement. I got through my last two years of high school by keeping busy; I worked four part-time jobs and ran track. My mother lost custody of me. She returned to prison and was eventually deported to Jamaica. Months passed and I would speak to her on the phone from time to time but I felt nothing because I knew I didn't need her.

I was on my own, and it was a mixed blessing. Although I was relieved, there was also a gnawing sense of loss. My mother would not be at my high school graduation or at my graduation from college nor any of the other milestones in my life. Still, I had grown strong and relatively self-sufficient, and I had friends and mentors in high school that defended me and loved me regardless of what I was or would become. Occasionally I was called gay or faggot throughout high school, but it never hurt. Once I overcame my issues with my mother, I didn't care what anyone else said. The rules were also different in school; once a boy even got suspended for calling me a faggot. Coming from a home where my mother called me a faggot every day and never got in trouble for it, I thought suspension was pretty harsh. But it reminded me not to tolerate verbal abuse.

I made it through high school and landed a scholarship for college. It was a fresh start, out of Connecticut and away from all the pain of my life. I didn't think bullying happened in college. I was wrong. In West Virginia it started immediately, and it was unexpectedly harsh.

I was assigned to a dorm occupied largely by athletes. The thought crossed my mind that it might present a problem, but I dismissed it. After all, I had a great roommate and a couple of good friends on campus. But one guy took the lead: Larken. He was not much taller than I was, but he was bigger, he played baseball, and he always had a mean look on his face when he saw me.

Larken would walk past me in the hall and stare in my face and whisper "faggot," as he walked past, his friends laughing from a distance. The guys on our floor always had their doors open, and they were always loud, running from room to room, throwing balls and playing video games. But whenever I appeared, they suddenly got quiet and would just stop and look at me. Then when I went into my room, I would hear an explosion of laughter in the hall. As time progressed it fell into an ugly routine: I would swipe into the residence hall, walk to the third floor and pull out a paper towel from my bag in order to wipe off the whiteboard outside my dorm room. Everyday, the board would have messages from Larken: "faggot," "dick lover," "gay person lives here." Larken would see me in the hallway and purposely bump my shoulder, then stare into my eyes as if he was daring me to react. I never did. Every night when I went to the showers, guys would follow me into the bathroom and stare, push in the curtain, and make gross advances, then they'd leave in a pack, their laughter echoing through the hall. I started showering later and later, just so I would have some peace and quiet.

I was surprised how much this all hurt. First, because I wasn't expecting it, and more importantly, because it wasn't just name calling, it was full out harassment. It was the daily remarks on the door, the constant intimidation in the hallway, routinely getting kicked out of parties, and the sexual taunts in the showers. It was the wedge that was driven between me and my roommate, who was afraid to stand up to them, and between me and my friends, who kept advising me to "just ignore it." But I wasn't going to ignore it. Ignoring it was not an option. I knew very well where ignoring it would lead: nowhere. I was going to confront the problem right away.

I told Larken's friends and teammates that my patience was running out, that enough was enough, and I set up a meeting with the Dean. While I hoped Larken would heed the warning and stop, I was fully prepared to go through with the formal complaint. He did not stop, so I met with the Dean of the College and relayed everything that was happening. Surprisingly, she was very impressed with my "strength" and my "ability to come forward without fear." (Was it possible that I was the first student to come forward and challenge the homophobic culture on campus?)

The Dean had no idea what I had already been through, that I had a mother who called me the same names and thought the same things about me. The harassment at college was nothing compared to that, and my tears were all used up long ago. Furthermore, I wasn't doing this solely for me. I was also doing it for other students who might be pushed to the edge but were afraid to speak out. Larken's friends begged me not to press the matter, and others threatened me not to take it further, but I did. I demanded that Larken be removed from the residence hall, no matter how many people threatened me.

The day he moved out, I made sure I was home. I sat in the hall outside my dorm room and watched him carry his things out of the building. Although I was tempted to walk past him and bump into his shoulder, look into his eyes, and dare *him* to react, I didn't. After he was gone, not one boy in that hall ever called me a faggot or wrote on my white board again.

I told my sister about the incident, and without my knowledge, she told my mother. A week or so later, my mother called me from prison and asked what happened. I couldn't believe my sister had told my main bully that I was being bullied again. My mother wanted me to give her the school's address so she could write to the Dean and complain. I actually started to confide in her, because I felt so alone—especially since everyone on my floor hated me by then. But something suddenly snapped inside me, and I realized I couldn't sit there and tell her what he had done to me and listen to her tell me how proud she was of me for standing up to him, when she had done *exactly* the same thing to me my whole life. Yes, I could empathize with her, and I could rationalize why she might have behaved that way to me all my life, but I was not going to deny my experience, and I was not going to tolerate lies anymore. It was over. So I thanked her for calling and I chose to move on.

I finished my freshman year free of Larken, thanks to a campus restraining order that kept him away from me. Then I transferred to a different university in Virginia, where I found a more welcoming environment.

Since that time, my mother and I have spoken occasionally. She's always excited about my endeavors, but we both refrain from discussing the past. I often think I forgive her and that I can love her as my "mother," but because of everything that's happened I really don't know what that means. In fact, I really don't look at her as "my mother" because she is not in so many ways. A lot of what she did I can forgive, but I fool myself in thinking I will ever forgot. You grow from being hurt but you don't grow away. The pain is always there; it just gets lighter because you become careful to never let someone else hurt you the same way.

I'M COMING OUT!

Pride

James Earl Hardy

DIFFERENT
is what his Mama called him
"He's special
He's sensitive
He's sweet
He's my Baby
No child of mine can be that way
It's a phase
He'll grow out of it"
But even she knew that wasn't true

FAGGOT
is what his father called him
A fruit
A fairy
"Boy, take your hands off your hips!"
"Boy, don't you roll them eyes at me!"

"Boy, don't be suckin' your teeth!"
"Boy, don't..."
Soon his father stopped saying don't
His father stopped saying boy
He just stopped

SISSY
is what his older brother called him
Cause he threw and ran like a girl
Played with Barbie
Jumped rope
But they must've been the right things to do
Cause he became an A student
and his brother wound up in jail

FUNNY
is what his Nana called him
Too neat, too nice
Too much sugar, too much spice
In his bowl
"Get him in church, he need Jesus!
Jesus gonna save him!" she testified
And Jesus did
At least that's what the minister said
Every Wednesday night after choir practice
When he had him fall on his knees
But not to pray

PUNK
is what the block boy called him
He always had a 40 in one hand
a blunt in the other
Gyratin that pelvis like Elvis
Kissin the air as he walked by
Announcin to the 'hood

"Ain't no nigga s'pose to switch!"
"Ain't no nigga's ass s'pose to twitch!"
But he always knew that was the cue
to meet on that roof top
that night at midnight
and once again be his bitch

QUEEN
is what his good girlfriend called him
He taught her how to wear that wardrobe
beat that face
walk that runway
and give the Chil'ren grace!
Ah, and don't forget the hair!
Wash and wear weaves
Pass the hot comb, would you please!
But she was jealous
You would be, too
If your best friend
looked better in your drag
than you

STRAIGHT
is what City Hall called him
Marriage and a baby carriage
One child, a boy
No home in the 'burbs
Just three small rooms in a tenement
A car that needs a new battery
Too many bills to pay
And no money in the bank
But it was still the American dream
And he knew it would please everyone
except himself

BI
is what she called him…out on
When she came home from work early that night
and found them naked on the living room floor
The next door neighbor's teenage son
on top of and inside of her husband
as their son lay asleep in their bedroom
What could he say?
There was no fighting, no high drama
Her harshest words: "You're a freak!"
And she took off like Tina
but she had the car keys
and she didn't leave the baby behind
and he hasn't seen them since

QUEER
is what the white folks called him
Act-Up Come Out of the closet
Do Ask and Do Tell
Silence Doesn't Have To Equal Death
Wear a Pink Triangle
Wave a Rainbow Flag
But he soon sensed that this fight
was to protect the divine right of white
And the European he called his lover
just couldn't
or wouldn't
understand

GAY
is what the world called him
It's a short-cut, shorthand
A convenience
A fantasy
A lie

He doesn't feel…gay?
Could someone explain how he's supposed to?
But nobody can cause nobody knows
And the anxiety, the angst, the anger grows

But today he knows something else
he knows someone new
It ain't about a name
that's all a game
What somebody else thinks
What somebody else wants
What somebody else is
He always looked in the eyes of others
to define who he is
But now he looks in a mirror
and the beauty of his own dark brown eyes
he loves in another's
He's no longer a figment of his own imagination
or someone else's nightmare
He's not on the outside looking in
He looked inside—himself—and found it

And PRIDE
is what he called it

Age of Consent

Alphonso Morgan

By the second grade I was obsessed with getting molested. Where I got the idea? Phil Donahue: kindergarten. If you are too young for *Donahue*, as you will more and more invariably be, picture Harry Potter fifty years from now. As Mama Marabelle dozed on the couch, her long hair parted down the middle like the Mona Lisa and her Old Gold corkscrewing up its smoke, the fifty years from now Harry Potter looked at the thirty-five years ago me through his glasses and the concave television screen and told me to beware. I coughed a little in the smoke and felt the tingle down in my corduroys.

That same year I had molested Cindy Sweedle in the coatroom of Ms. McKinstry's class. Ms. McKinstry prudently separated the boys and girls for nap time onto two sets of little mats on either side of the room. But the coatroom had two doors, and Ms. McKinstry underestimated our motivation. As she scribbled at her desk, Cindy and I signaled past her ankles, laying on our stomachs and alternately humping our mats. I do not know how we knew this signal, or which of us invented it, but we understood it as instinct, and wound our ways by imperceptible degrees, patient and slow and relentless, in the light dimmed to encourage rest, past chalk boards and building blocks and under tables, humping, like two little inchworms, until we entered through the coatroom's opposite doors. In the coatroom I molested Cindy ruthlessly through her clothes, although it occurred to me that possibly she had molested me because she humped harder than I did and because she was on top.

The liaison was unsatisfactory, in any case, and I tried again with the Nichols boys, ages four, six, and seven, when their mother Carla dropped them off to spend the night. I lined them up on the floor with their pajama bottoms next to them, and layed on top of each of them one at a time. All our little penises erected and the tingle in my own felt so good, better than scratching a mosquito bite, better than the way it felt when Mama Marabelle cleaned my ears out with a bobby pin. Somehow I liked the middle boy, Bobby, more than his brothers. Bobby was the black sheep, the bad boy of the family, the first and the last one always to get in trouble. If any of them was capable of molesting me for real, it was Bobby, but he never showed any interest because he was past tolerating our little game. Somehow, anyway, I realized that a molester would need to have some power, be bigger and stronger than I was, and so I changed my tactics.

Going forward, I focused on the older boys in the neighborhood and tried to position myself for future tortures. There was Peter, down the alley, whose house was missing most of its siding, and whose parents kept a falling-down camper from the 1950s in the backyard. Right off the alley. So convenient for sexual abuse. Peter took me in there once with the neighbor girl Chrissy. I was seven or so by now, Chrissy perhaps four, and Peter told us we both better suck his dick if we knew what was good for us. He took it out of his pants and though he was eleven or twelve at least, I noticed he had no hair down there like some of the older boys I had seen in the shower at Holiday

Lake. He told Chrissy to do it first, and threatened us both that if we didn't he would make us walk around the block naked. An unnecessary threat for my part because I was going to do it anyway, though the absence of hair was dismaying, and in spite of the fact that this was not exactly the way I had envisioned my molestation. I don't know what I imagined it to be exactly, in the most logistical sense, but generally speaking it involved someone getting on top of me.

Well, Chrissy did it first, mechanically, the way you might drop a nickel in your pocket. Then I did it, with similar enthusiasm, and Peter peed a little in my mouth. Furious and double-crossed, I spit on the camper floor and went for the handle of the door, but Peter reached it first and held it a second. He told us not to tell, but he was mainly looking at me, and said if we did he would beat us up and make us walk to 7-Eleven naked. Chrissy said okay and I just nodded a little, but as soon as he let go of the door, I jumped down and ran through the alley. A few steps in I turned and yelled back at the leaning camper: "I'm tellllliiiiing!" I left Chrissy in the dust and ran down the alley and into our little house and told my mother everything, except that he had had no hair.

A half hour later, having re-parted her Mona Lisa hair and smoked two Old Golds back to back, she took my hand and tramped down to Peter's house with me at the end of her arm, not the short cut through the alley but the longer, official route around the block. When Peter's mother opened the door, there was no time for pleasantries or small talk. Mama Marabelle said straight at her face: "Peter made Phonso fellate him." "Fu-what?" the woman said stupidly through her peroxide bangs. She turned red as a Corvette as my mother refreshed her vocabulary.

The next year there was P.J., whose yard backed into ours and who terrorized the neighborhood on a white bike doing an impression of a police siren. So good an impression that cars would pull over in the street when he rode by and all of the housewives on Lane Street would look and pull back their curtains to see what the emergency was. My adult self might have thought of P.J. as a high-functioning mentally challenged person. My eight-year-old self just thought he was a dumb "retard" and a bully. When summer break came P.J. stayed home by himself during the day while his mother went to work. When he wasn't endlessly circling the block doing his police siren, he played demolition in his back yard with model cars. I would be just across the fence, largely unsupervised, making streams and dams and entire river towns sometimes with the green garden hose on full blast. He had never paid much attention to me generally, except once when he karate chopped a caterpillar I had caught that had become a chrysalis.

But one day he needed help with his demolition, or so he said, and he invited me through the hole in the fence. He said his mother didn't allow anyone in the house when I said I wanted a drink of water, disingenuously, now that I think of it, since the water hose was still blasting just across the fence. But he got around this little rule by letting me wait in the basement for him, which could be reached through a cellar door around the side of the house. When he showed up, he had a plastic machete in his hand instead of the water and held it to my throat and ordered me onto a piece of foam rubber on the floor. He did get on top of me, and I remember being very excited by this. He said the word "cunt" three or four times, but it was wasted on me. I thought "cunt" was what a cow chewed. I was very scientific. The whole thing was over in a less than a couple minutes, and I never did get to see him without his clothes on.

The Thomases lived across the alley. They were Catholic and had ten boys. I had never noticed their family because of the way they were built. They were all big and husky and played football in the fall. Somehow I knew my molester would have better proportions. But at some point before we left Lane Street, the Thomases started taking in foster kids, and one of the first was a troubled seventeen-year-old named Jake, who was mixed. He was the first man of color I had considered in my saga. It was Waterloo, Iowa, in the seventies. There wasn't much color to choose from. But Jake and I never panned. I was close to ten by now, and I started to hang out in front of the Thomas's house trying to act cool. To that end, I once hawked a loogie right onto the sidewalk, and Jake picked me up by my feet and cleaned the spit with my sandy Afro.

Around the same time, I spent the night at my Aunt Tam's, and one of her boyfriends came in the middle of the night drunk. I was asleep on the couch, roughly the same size as my aunt, beneath a thin sheet, while he fumbled around in the dark. I believe he mistook me for her, and put his head under the sheet, and kissed up my legs until he found something that definitely did not belong to my Aunt. But in those few seconds before he found his folly, I reeled with pleasure and fear, thinking it was really about to happen after all that time. To manifest my disappointment with the drunken interloper, I stared ruthlessly at him the next morning from my cousin Josh's Sit-n-Spin. He never looked at me once. I was invisible again. But at least I knew what a man's stubble felt like between my legs.

Around eleven or so, driving back one night from Grandma's house on Holiday Lake, I lay in the back seat, pretending to be asleep under my jacket. My mother and her boyfriend sat in the front listening to something on Public Radio about a man who had been raped (somehow) by another man. The program said how such a thing was an act of aggression and power rather than sex. This was good enough explanation for me, but I rubbed myself furiously and silently through my parachute pants.

By this time we had moved from Lane Street to a bigger house on the West Side, which Mama Marabelle and I shared with Tam and Josh. The house was nice but pretty smoky between Mama Marabelle's Old Golds and Tam's Kools. There was a grapevine in the back and a little black boy named Montreese who lived around the corner. I had given up (kind of) being molested. I was in middle school and I figured I was too old. But I had more sexual energy now than ever before. So I started messing around with Montreese. He was several years younger than I. And there were many times he didn't want to, but I talked him into it. My main course of action was to make him lay on his stomach and I would pull his pants down and grind around on his butt. But once, right in the middle of it, I felt an overpowering sensation down there with all that grinding, and I jumped up and ran to the bathroom, thinking I was peeing on myself. Montreese ran in after me and looked down at my penis and said, "Ugh! What's that, Fonzo? Snot?"

The next year we moved back to the East Side on Smith Street, the blackest neighborhood we had ever lived in, and my mother worked nights at the halfway house downtown, so I ran the neighborhood. Two brothers lived at the end of the block: Jermaine and Antoine Brown—identical to each other almost except that one was bigger than the other. They were both very dark with very defined bodies and walked around a lot without shirts; each had his hair cut in what we used to call back then a shag. The little one, Antoine, would come over sometimes after school and tell me about all the girls he had fucked in the pussy. We wrestled a lot, and it got pretty heated—once he even pulled my pants down over my butt and moved around a lot on top of me until he told me he came. That was the first I had heard of the term, and he showed me his dick, as proof I suppose, but I didn't see anything there except a small green booger. I wasn't as disappointed at this as I was at the fact of it not being his brother. Antoine was smaller than I was and his brother was bigger. I was sure Jermaine could have produced a more exciting result.

That year we moved to Minneapolis, and I had talked my mother into my first Jheri curl in the frenzy of celebration. I was pretty sure I looked like Michael Jackson when I reached the South Side of Minneapolis, sleek and mature and ready as could be for the eighties. There was a porn shop a few blocks from our house at the corner of Lake Street and Fourth Avenue, and I would pull a baseball cap low over my curl and sneak in. Past the fat, dozing proprietor sitting at a desk high above the racks of magazines and into the quarter booths in the back of the place. Once the man was awake, and asked me if he could see an ID and I tried to give him my Social Security card but he told me to get out. So I took to waiting behind the store, in temperatures well below freezing, in the middle of my first Minnesota winter, until someone came out the back door. I would catch the door and slip in the back to where the quarter booths were without having to walk by the man at the counter. It was inside those booths, with my hands quivering from nerves, dropping quarter after quarter into the slot, that I first discovered what gay sex actually was. I really don't know what I had believed up to that point, but I honestly didn't think that men fucked each other like that. Once or twice a man approached me or tried to enter with me into a booth, but I resisted. I guess the right one simply never came along.

When I was fifteen, I worked at Wendy's a few blocks further down Lake Street from the porn shop. I had braces by this time and contact lenses and my curl had gone a little red in front as per the times. I had a lot of regular customers so I was not alarmed at the cash register when I started seeing the same little man over and over. He never ordered much, maybe a small fry or a side salad, but he looked past my auburn curl, deep into my contact lenses. One night after closing, as I was walking home in the dark I heard a voice suddenly beside me there on the sidewalk. He asked me if I knew where to get some weed, which I certainly did by this stage, but there was something in his voice that I knew wanted more than marijuana. I didn't recognize him at first as my customer from the restaurant, but he did seem familiar for some reason as I led him home. I was shaking in my shelltop Adidas, pretending I might have a stash at home, and when we reached the duplex on Fourth Avenue I looked in the window and saw Mama Marabelle sitting there on the couch. Without now the part down the middle, her hair was home-permed and voluminous. Think: Stevie Nicks only long mousy brown instead of blond. I was surprised and a little angry to see her; she worked nights at the prison in Shakopee and chose, of all nights, the one of my final deflowering to be at home. But, of course, I wouldn't let a little thing like the presence of my mother deter me from a path at least ten years now in the making. So I led my guest around to the back, broke in through the basement window, came up the basement stairs, let the man in through the back door, and led him down to the basement. The actual event was as anticlimactic then as my recounting of it may be to you now: a hurried affair on the cold, cracked basement floor, with none of the paraphernalia or know-how that might really get the pleasure receptors going. It felt physically good when it wasn't complete agonizing pain, but somehow the power relationship was off; I was fifteen, he was twenty-four. In most states, I suppose, the law would have protected me as the victim. But I felt myself then in control. And I believe that even today, all these decades later. I would make him beg for my affection, just to see if he would do it, and deny him it outright because all I really wanted was to submit.

Years later when I was in Cuba, I would see girls in their Quinceanera dresses, floating by in the beautiful old Chevys, addressing to the world the news that they were women. At fifteen they announced their alertness, their full capacity for sexual knowledge, their full citizenship in adulthood and all that follows. Their eyes would blink in the sun and their trains would rise in the wind, and I would watch them in silence and whisper to myself simply: "Yes!"

The Luckiest Gay Son in the World
David Bridgeforth

My toddler memories of my father were filled with wonder.
When I heard my mother say, "Your father's home," I would
look up to see this man walking into our house wearing what I
now know to be a suit with a skinny tie. He was kind, charming,
and humble, and he loved my mom. My parents' happiness
inspired me, and I felt love in the soft palms of their hands.
Then my mother was diagnosed with AIDS and all that ended. I
did not know what those four letters meant, but I watched from
the hallway shadows of our home as their tender love slipped
harshly away.

I now know my father cheated on my mother, and my
mother out of spite cheated on him. She did not use protection,
and the man she slept with gave her HIV. All the love ended
after that. There was no more light laughter, no more smiles, no
more bright Sunday mornings filled with warm hugs. My family
arrived on a cold, frightening nightmare, introduced by divorce
and lingering words of hate.

I was shocked by the quick change in my tiny world. My

mother, younger brother, and I soon arrived in a modest and not-so-friendly ghetto with not enough money or food. Because my father did not have HIV, I felt it was his responsibility to care for our mother in sickness and in health. Instead, he left and I became the "man of the household" at eight years old. Drugged up and drowsy under the influence of HIV medication, my mother slept most days, leaving me with the responsibility to cook, pay the bills, and keep the house running.

Eventually she became too skinny and frail to get out of bed, and I could see her sunken cheeks and the furrowed circles around her brown eyes. One morning, I brought her favorite green tea with honey and lemon. I woke her up and kissed her softly on the forehead and set her French teacup and saucer on the antique table next to the bed. Her bony fingers extended to grab my wrist, which felt like I was caught in the grasp of several dry twigs. She looked at me with a deep stare, as if she was being dragged away, never to return again. "If anything happens to me, make sure you take care of ya' brotha," she said.

"Of course, Mom, I will." I was afraid but tried to play down the drama. I gave her some tea, kissed her again, and went downstairs to feed my brother.

I could not understand why this thing called AIDS would cause my father to leave his family, and I grew to hate him for jumping ship. I was a spitting image of my father—he stood 5'8," with brown eyes, a full head of dark brown, wavy hair, and a perfect white smile—but I spent the next several years wanting to be nothing like him.

I started by dying my hair. "What the hell is this?" Dad asked. "What are you doing? Who's gonna hire ya with a damn blond streak up in ya damn head?" At the time, blond was the color I felt represented freedom in my conservative Indianapolis community. I had moved back to my dad's house downtown and I needed to liberate myself, to do something outrageous. So dying my hair was my statement of defiance. My father was not pleased with my choice of coiffure or with my push from conformity to liberty. My coming out statement scared him.

Dad did not like gay people, even though he would never say that. He said he didn't like being around them because they hit on him. Here was a man open to different religions, opinions, and ways of thought, a worldly man who knew the rich and poor, but he just couldn't be around homosexuals. I assumed if he didn't like gays, then something must be wrong with them. And I could also tell from his smart-ass comments when I was a teenager that he could see the femininity in me and was disappointed. He often referred to my tight skinny jeans as "nut huggers," and even though I laughed along with the guests and friends he would entertain in his house, I knew he disliked my style. He told me to "diversify" myself, which most likely meant beef it up. And he discouraged me from watching and following too many women on television—especially Oprah, Beyoncé, and Juanita Bynum. Nevertheless, I wanted out of the controlled life and into a world of bold, bright colors. I knew my dad could see that, and I knew he did not like bold bright colors.

After I had moved out, at nineteen years old, it was time for me to introduce my father and others to the person I was becoming. For that to happen, I needed to fully accept my sexuality, not to bleach with shame the beauty of my rainbow. But instead of "coming out" face-to-face to my family and friends, in the summer of 2007, I wrote, stamped, and mailed twenty-five personal letters. In each letter, I explained what attracted me to guys and answered every question I could think of, from having children with a woman to gay marriage.

By this point, my mother had survived her near-death experience with AIDS, and when she was strong and the virus was undetectable she remarried and moved on with her life. I sent her a letter to her new address on the other side of town. My father was still living at his same place in downtown Indianapolis. It would not take long for the letters to arrive across town.

A few days later, my father sent me a text message in response to my letter. It arrived literally moments after I received a supportive letter from my mom. "To my beloved first born son, I love you and I am always on your team," she wrote. That was a relief, but I knew all along that my mother would accept me. It was my father who concerned me. I thought of almost every possible response he might communicate, but the one he gave I never expected. Until I read his text message: "Live ya damn life son, I am proud of you, and I love you."

I cried and in that moment my heart beat in an unknown rhythm. My father had celebrated my life, the femininity, the gayness, the rainbow in me.

I responded to his message: "Thank you Pops, I will and I love you too." I was free, and all the hate I felt for him began to melt away. By the end of the evening, I had received twenty-three additional responses, each one loving and accepting me for who I am.

Most importantly, I saw how lucky I was to have a father who had the courage to overcome his own hang-ups on my behalf. And I knew if my father could open his heart to his gay son, then I could open my life to him.

Coming Out in the Locker Room

Rod McCullom, DeMarco Majors, Wade Davis, and Will Sheridan

Pop quiz: What class did you absolutely dread in high school?

Ask most gay men that question and the answer probably won't be physics or calculus. Many—if not most—gay men would probably say their worst memories were of gym or physical education.

Not because many of us couldn't pass a ball or play a simple game of one-on-one. It was because high school was where many of us discovered our sexuality—and often were teased, bullied, or mocked by the more athletic or "masculine" boys. Sports and the locker room represented fear...as well as masculinity and an overwhelming sexual intrigue.

Flashback to my own experience growing up in the 1980s. I was an advanced student and fairly popular at middle school in an integrated Los Angeles neighborhood. By the time I hit high school? Not so much. My parents had divorced, my mother had less money, and we relocated to Chicago's South Side. It was light years from the multicultural, aspirational, and feel good vibe of Baldwin Hills. This was the 'hood, where boys were expected to be men—hyper-masculine, thugged out, and a terror on the basketball court.

Being the captain of my swim team didn't count as playing sports in the 'hood, because there were no swimming pools. And talking "like I was white"—or so many of the kids sneered—didn't help either. Of course, I was also discovering at that time that I was gay. Not the best of times.

Running track and making the football team in high school became the perfect opportunity to reinvent myself. That continued in college and even afterwards when I started working out and hitting the weights seriously—to build not only muscle but psychological "armor" to protect against feelings of inadequacy.

For many other young men who were discovering their sexuality in high school and/or college, playing sports and the locker room offered a similar refuge from the outside world. With that in mind, I gathered three athletes to discuss coming out in sports, homophobia, and expectations of masculinity among black men.

Former Villanova University basketball player Will Sheridan came out publicly on ESPN in May 2011. DeMarco Majors played for the American Basketball Association and was seen on Logo's *Shirts & Skins*. NFL player Wade Davis played with the Tennessee Titans, Seattle Seahawks, and Washington Redskins. This interview marks the very first time he has publicly discussed being gay and his experience in the NFL.
— *Rod McCullom*

ROD MCCULLOM: Let's hear your coming out stories. Let's start with you, Will.

WILL SHERIDAN: There is my first coming out story and my first public coming out story. My first coming out was on ESPN's *Outside the Lines*. I basically said that I liked dudes and everyone should get over it.

But my first coming out was to my parents the summer after my first year of college. I was nineteen years old. I was watching a game on television and I said, "I have something to tell you." It was hard…but I felt I had to tell them. My father said, "Son, tell us whatever is on your mind." I told him and he was shocked. He told my mother and there was drama the next day. But I feel that it was the best thing I have ever done. My father respected it and it improved our relationship as men. My father respected my courage.

WADE DAVIS: My coming out story is a different. I came to New York City when I was twenty-six or twenty-seven. I was dating a guy for a long while and he was out to his family. I was very jealous because he had this open relationship with his family and I didn't. So I went home to Colorado to tell my mother and sister. I told my sister first because I knew my mother would be difficult, because I was so close to her. I asked my sister for advice on how I could tell Mom, and she said that I couldn't. "You're her favorite, the perfect son coming home, she can't handle that," she said. She was adamant about me not telling her. But I was going to tell Mom anyway. I drove over to my mom's house, and we went out for a walk. I told my mother that I had something to tell her. I said, "I like boys." I couldn't mouth the words gay. And she said, "What?" I repeated it and said, "Okay. I'm gay." She paused and looked out into space. "That's an abomination," she quietly said. She told me these other things—and stressed that I couldn't tell anyone. Then we headed back home. She didn't look at me or make eye contact with me. It was hard because I felt like I was watching this person decay and become this person I had never seen before. To this day, our relationship is not the same. We don't talk very much, and we have a very strained relationship.

ROD: So she knew during the years that you were playing in the NFL?

WADE: Yes. There were a lot of factors that went into this.

We were raised in the South, very religious. Plus, I was the so-called "star" of the family and taking care of a lot of people. For me to tell her that I was gay, maybe she thought that was a reflection of her and that she couldn't brag on her son anymore. My mother and I were extremely close, especially when I was in college. We talked once or twice a day. Possibly she had an inkling but never wanted to go there.

DEMARCO MAJORS: I was about to turn twenty-five years old. I was playing professional basketball in Argentina and Brazil. My father was about to pass away, I returned home. I didn't know what was going on with me but I understood that I had this attraction to men. I stopped going to church and stopped praying because I believed that my father died because I was gay. And I thought I lost my father because of what I was going through.

Then I went to the Gay Games in Sydney, Australia and was recruited to play professional basketball in Australia. I was trying out for NBA teams. Contracts that were previously being offered were pulled away from me. Without any explanation. And I was getting very angry.

Then I was asked to become part of the "Out 100." I had to fly home and tell my mom. We had this relationship where we could tell each other everything. I pulled out the magazine and said, "Mom, well, you know I'm gay. But this is how involved in the community I am. They choose 100 of the most influential members in the community." I was prepared for her to shoot me or go off on me. But she smiled and said for the first time in my life she was proud of me. "I'm so proud of you because you are using the gifts that God gave you."

ROD: Did you start to have feelings about other boys in high school? And did you see any anti-gay taunting in school and the locker rooms? Will?

WILL: Of course. Growing up I definitely had feelings when

I was young. Long before high school but I mostly denied it. Growing up, I was awkward—I was tall, walked funny. So I was teased and people were calling me gay, and I didn't understand why. It hurt my feelings. And I didn't understand how kids knew these things about me. I just wanted to be normal and wanted to fit in.

As far as bullying is concerned, I was never beat up. But I became a very aggressive player. I would always elbow another teammate or player. Having a wild, no limits personality probably helped me on the courts. And off the courts, too. I didn't want people to focus on how I walked or who I hung out with.

WADE: My story is a little different than everyone else's. I was actually the bully as opposed to being bullied.

ROD: Was that to over compensate or coming to grips with your sexuality?

WADE: Yes, that was primarily the reason. I don't think that I realized I was gay until [I was] a junior in high school. I was so focused on playing sports, it never crossed my mind. I grew up playing Little League or running track. I was also a class clown.

When I finally realized that I was gay, I turned up the comedy routine…I would just make fun of everyone, be they gay, straight, or whatever. And teasing and taunting kids, too. It was a way to keep the focus off me and on others. As I look back now, it was because I was so afraid that people would see through me.

ROD: Just to go a little further. You were in the NFL for many years. Did your teammates know or do you think they suspected?

WADE: I don't think my teammates ever suspected. Many of my teammates who I later came out to, don't believe me to this day (laughing). Several have asked for proof or pictures of me with a guy. That's because I did such a great job of hiding who I was. In the NFL, I was always the guy in the strip club throwing out lots of money or going home with all these girls. I didn't have sex with the women, but gave the impression that I was a womanizer.

But twice there were incidents. When scouts visited me in college, one of the coaches made a comment that "Wade is not as much a ladies' man as some of the other guys on the team." That was the first time that I thought someone had seen through my shield. It freaked me out. The other time was when I was playing for the Titans, there was another player that many teammates knew was either gay or bisexual. That was my first year and I was signed as a free agent. One of the other players advised me against hanging out with that particular player. I don't think he said it because he thought I was gay. He just thought it would give me unwanted attention.

DEMARCO: I also had feelings about boys in high school but [didn't act] on them.

Growing up in the Midwest, in the country, growing up poor, you heard lots of gay slurs. People were always saying, "Oh, that faggot" to get into their head. I was always the nerd stuck in the jock's body and saw that.

Skin color and complexion was a problem for me. Being light skinned was sometimes a problem. [Some black students] fought me or pulled guns on me because of my skin complexion. Then when I went to school, I had [white students] who wanted to fight because I was too dark. And some parents told their children not to play with me.

ROD: Okay, let me ask the question that many guys want to hear about: Can you talk about being in the locker room. How did you deal with that? Was there fear of being discovered?

WILL: The most common comment when people read my story is—how did you deal with those hot guys in the locker room? The locker room wasn't a problem for me. I wanted my teammates to respect my position on the team as a player/leader so I rarely if ever played the jock grab-ass games. Just so no one would ever think—once I came out—"Oh, Will violated me."

So in a way, I was hyper aware of it. I wasn't afraid of them knowing—I just didn't want it to change our family dynamic as it did with my blood family. I guess in the end, my actions, dress, and sociability gave me away, but I never wanted (my actions in the) locker room to confirm anything.

WADE: I'm often asked this question. The answer is different at each level of football.

In high school, it wasn't a worry of mine because I realized I was gay late in my junior year and didn't have an overwhelming attraction to men yet. It was such an awkward time in my life. I look back at all the sexual exploration that went on in the locker room between my teammates, that even if I did something inappropriate, it probably would have went unnoticed because there was so much other "questionable" stuff going on.

I quietly began to understand my own sexuality once I began playing college football. I had to be careful about letting my mind wonder about men in general because sometimes those innocent thoughts would manifest itself at inopportune times. There's a lot of innocent male-on-male play in the locker room, and sometimes you think those playful actions are not as innocent as they really are.

During my senior year, I mentored one of the younger guys on the team. We spent so much time together, my attraction to him was inevitable. I eventually removed myself from our friendship in order to protect my own identity and not cross that line. But I can remember being in the shower with him and having to leave immediately before I finished because I felt myself becoming aroused. I know that if I were "out," I would have been more comfortable with myself and not spent so much time trying to determine who else was or wasn't gay. But at that time in my life, anytime a man showed me the least bit of attention,

I'd panic because I thought they could see through me.

When I entered the NFL, my only focus was on making the team. I didn't have time to worry about being discovered. The minute I stepped into that sanctuary, most of my worries about being discovered were removed and replaced with an intense focus on football. Also being in the NFL was such a huge honor for me, it was initially easy for me to function in the locker room without the fear of being discovered. But I also had been in or was in a relationship with a man, so those urges weren't lying as close to the surface and ready to come out like in college, and my "control" was much greater. Ironically, later in my career, the need to be gay and free made it harder to focus on playing the game on the field.

ROD: Church is very important in the black community. How important was church growing up? And did this impact your sexuality?

DEMARCO: When I was thirteen I started going with my grandmother to the Church of Christ. I became a minister at thirteen years old. God was always my imaginary friend, because I was uncomfortable with myself, what was going on in my life, and talking to other people.

WILL: I went to a Christian, non-denominational church. I enjoyed the music a lot. To me, church was about invoking a fellowship, and similar to DeMarco, I didn't want to get to know everybody. At church we had a great youth group but I didn't become very invested in it. I believe in God, I believe there is a higher power, but for me religion has always been more divisive. I have seen too many Christians say that you can't do this or that if you are a Christian.

And speaking as a black man...our community is deeply rooted in the church—and that has held us back from embracing our gay community. Thankfully, the youth are changing. So many are accepting black gays, they really don't care. I see even black gay youth attending church, having their own churches, being comfortable and openly gay in church.

WADE: I grew up in Louisiana so I was in church almost every day. Monday was Prayer Meeting, Tuesday was Bible Study, Wednesday was Youth Group, and Thursday was another meeting. Sunday was Sunday school, early morning service and then regular service. Sometimes an evening service, too (laughter).

Church is also where I grew up idolizing my mother. When she wasn't singing in the church choir, she would sit in the pews and wear those big floppy hats that you couldn't see around.

When I realized that I was gay, I began to question the Bible. If the Bible says "Thou shalt not lie with men," but on the other hand it says, "God is love," it became very confusing. I went from becoming a very religious person to more spiritual. But that is the reason why my mother and I are so far apart. She's very religious, takes the Bible very literally. She believes the gay thing is black and white. Can I say one more thing?

ROD: Of course.

WADE: One thing that I found interesting about the black church: Where I grew up my choir director was obviously gay. And I have been in so many other black churches and the choir directors and pianists are also very obviously gay. Their partners are seated in the back pews. The church is fine with that and loves them because they don't make it known, they don't announce it.

It's very similar to playing sports. There are so many athletes that players suspect are gay or know that they are. But as long as they don't announce it to the world they are fine. That's why I think so many players don't come out. There is this parallel between sports and the black church that I find almost comical. There are so many players that I know are gay. There are so many choir directors that I know are gay. I know the preacher knows. My mother knows and loves this man. But yet when her son announces that he is gay she says, "Nope, I'm done, gotta go."

ROD: I was just about to ask about that. It's like "Don't Ask, Don't Tell" in the black church. We know, you know that we know, everyone knows, but we just don't talk about it. And if we don't talk about, it's accepted. Did you see that in sports?

WADE: The parallels are almost identical, it's scary! It's like "Don't Ask, Don't Tell." When you see what happened with Pastor Eddie Long, there was a rush to forgive him and it was swept under the rug. There have been other gay athletes who were outed but they weren't on ESPN or the news. It's like [NFL Commissioner] Roger Goodell made a phone call and it was [silenced].

Will, DeMarco, and I believe that it's our job to spark a conversation or dialogue. We won't change everyone's mind or heart, but as long as the conversations are being had.

DEMARCO: Wow. I agree with both of you! I can agree with what I've seen in church and in professional sports. It's not about whether there is a conversation or not. You just want people to acknowledge what is going on with the person. And not acknowledging another person as a human being is not acknowledging yourself. It's the same as in church or sports.

WILL: It's important to open up the conversation to all churches. My church was not a black church, it was predominately white, a mixed crowd, and white pastor. But you could say this about almost all churches. It's very applicable to the Catholic Church as well. And there are so many former or gay men in the priesthood in that church.

The most important thing about my coming out story is for the next generation. I was approached to do ESPN three years ago, right after I [graduated] from college. But my parents were like, "Don't do it." My dad loves me unconditionally, but, of course, he is still concerned about walking down the street, or what the brothas may say to him in the barbershop.

I was able to do ESPN this year because I feel like I want to be a stronger person for the community.

ROD: Will touched upon perceptions of masculinity in the black community. All of you were jocks and many people don't consider gay men as masculine. How do you feel about that, Will?

WILL: Masculinity in the black community? Generally the more alpha male you are, the better. That's generally been our history. I had a conversation with my father, and he said that I was being more of a man by coming out as opposed to hiding or lying.

There are many parallels in the sports world with the music community, because I'm involved in music now. I'll do shows and the audience is mostly straight men. Offstage I might be less masculine, but onstage my delivery is very masculine, so they are drawn to that masculinity. Rappers are considered ultra-masculine and are among the most successful in the music game.

WADE: I'm at a point in my life where I hate that people refer to me as "straight acting." It took me a while to get to this point. Years ago I would act ultra-masculine to over compensate and act as if I wasn't gay. I thought people wanted this from me as a black man. The black community also reinforces this as well.

As I become older, I realize that men who aren't trying to hide their femininity and are less masculine are so much stronger. They are never able to hide who they are. I might be able to walk down the street and no one knows about my sexuality but that has nothing to do with strength. It has taken me so long to understand that. I used to wear thirty-eight size pants when I was a thirty-two, or triple X tees, all of this uber-masculine gear, because that's what I thought people expected. When I got my first check, I bought a truck and twenty-two inch rims because that's what I thought people expected. That was my idea of what it meant to be a masculine or a black man.

Now I have no problems with that. I'll wear jeans that fit me. I might not be able to wear skinny jeans (laughter). There is a maturity level that our community reinforces with masculinity. I work now at a school with LGBT youth. I am so amazed and think they are so much stronger than I was at that age. Unfortunately, black culture does a horrible job in projecting what it means to be a black man. And it's not just gay men. Straight men have to overcompensate, too.

DEMARCO: I've always been a watcher. The one thing I've learned about the black gay community is that most of the femme men were fighters. They've had to fight their whole lives. They were feminine since they were young and always had to fight. And they kicked some ass, too. On the other hand, I see a ton of masculine men hide behind "I'm straight acting." And that's all it is—an act.

I play sports. But am I perceived as masculine or feminine? I don't know. To be honest, I came from a single parent household, so if you tell me to "act strong," I would look to my mother. My mother was real tough, a very strong woman, to help her family.

ROD: Finally, since most of you have come out, you have become somewhat public figures. DeMarco, you've been on a reality show. Will, you were on ESPN. Are athletes and players coming up to you and asking for advice? DeMarco?

DEMARCO: Rod, you've seen my journey since the beginning. The one thing that I always tell people is to come out on your time. The time that it took you to accept yourself, allow other people that same time. Just be patient in your giving, be patient in your loving, and be compassionate. If they truly love you, it's about you and your process. If you're ready, you'll tell people. If you're not, you're not.

WADE: To be honest, I don't get many sports guys asking

questions about coming out. But if I were, I would say to come out when you're ready.

Many people want to see a gay person being out and playing sports. An out player would do much for society, but coming out is a very personal decision. I would just tell that person if they were going to come out, make sure that they have a very strong support system. I was not ready to come out until I had a partner who I felt could support me emotionally and mentally. I would tell youth to make sure they were doing it for the right reason. Not to be famous, but for the right reasons. That's my advice.

WILL: A lot of people have reached out to me via Facebook, Twitter, email, and other forms of communication. It's overwhelming and humbling that people think I am a source to help make their life better. I agree with these two gentlemen that you should not come out until you're ready. I also agree with DeMarco's point that you have to give people time, as much as you gave yourself.

I speak to a lot of black gay youth and tell them not to let coming out fundamentally change them. Don't try to become a "diva." Try to be amazing and try to change the world. Do some good in the community. Because as black gay men, we have to do things ten times harder than the next person.

When I Dare to Be Powerful
Keith Boykin

It began with a white-haired white woman in a white windbreaker. While the four of us plotted our conspiracy, the grandma in slacks approached us awkwardly in the hotel lobby. It's not every day that an older white woman feels comfortable enough to engage a group of young black men, so I turned to greet her. "Can I help you with something?" I asked.

"Are you folks gay rights?" she said.

I looked at her with a transparent expression of bewilderment, as though my brain would not allow me to process the illogical syntactic construction that reduced a group of humans to a cause in which they believed. I responded tentatively to correct her.

"We support the *idea* of *equal* rights for gays and lesbians, if that's what you mean."

"Well, I just want you to know it's wrong," she blurted out.

Again my face must have given away a sense of ire because she moved a few steps back as though I had threatened her. But she had been the one to initiate the conversation, and the look on my face was more of confusion than confrontation. What she was doing was almost inconceivable to me. Did this old white woman really just come up to a group of black men who were minding their own business just to tell us we were "wrong"? This isn't happening, I thought to myself.

"What do you mean it's wrong?" I asked, knowing full well what she meant but wanting her to say it aloud.

"Homosexuality," she shot back. "God says it's wrong."

"Oh, really, when did he say that?"

"It's in the Bible."

"Really, and what did Jesus say about homosexuality?" I asked.

"It's wrong," she repeated.

"Actually, Jesus never mentioned homosexuality anywhere in the Bible," I responded. And then as I began a furious litany of biblical quotations and citations to challenge everything she thought she knew, she quickly retreated down the hallway toward the reception desk.

I jumped from my seat and followed her, demanding that she respond. "How dare you come over and challenge us and not have the courage, the knowledge, or the moral integrity to defend your viewpoint," I said.

She kept walking, promised to pray for me and turned away. I've heard that "I'll pray for you" line many times before from religious critics and I know exactly what it means, so I refused to let her go without an opportunity for dialogue. I positioned myself in front of her again, dropped to my knees and clasped my hands in prayer, just as I noticed a seal on her jacket for a conservative group called Concerned Women For America. I asked her to join me in a prayer for God's love. She rolled her eyes and walked away while I continued my theatrical stunt on my knees in front of the concierge.

I don't imagine I changed her mind about "gay rights" by creating a scene in the hotel lobby, but at least she knows she can't go around interjecting herself into other people's business and expecting them not to respond. Maybe the next time she planned to open her mouth and criticize someone she didn't know, she might think twice about it. And besides, our conversation had nothing to do with what she thought we were discussing. We were not focused on the mainstream gay rights struggle that day; we were simply trying to get our own community of African Americans to acknowledge our existence. But sometimes you have to fight on several fronts at once.

It was a few weeks before the Million Man March in 1995, and we had been plotting details to assemble an openly gay contingent in the historic but controversial all-male event. The march was being organized by Minister Louis Farrakhan of the Nation of Islam, and five of us were meeting to draw up plans to get hundreds of black same-gender-loving men to join our ranks.

We decided at that hotel meeting to hold our own rally before the official march, and I called upon some old friends to help lend some credibility to our gathering. On the morning of the march, I thought of that old woman in the hotel lobby as my trembling hands scribbled nine words on a poster board in the brisk air at our pre-march rally: *Black by Birth/Gay by God/Proud by Choice.*

Despite our best efforts to get an accurate headcount for the event in advance, we were never really sure if anyone would attend our rally. It was a lot easier to get people to say they would attend than to get them to show up. As the leader of the group, I arrived early, secretly hoping for a huge crowd to surprise me, but only a handful of early birds, reporters, and photographers milled about. A couple of my fellow organizers expressed concern about the turnout, so I reassured them that the crowd would come once we got started. In reality, I had no idea if anyone would show up. A lot of people had personally promised me they would attend, but I had learned from life experience that it's easier for some people to lie than to disappoint you.

One of the organizers set up a podium with a microphone, while another unfurled a huge black banner he had designed himself to announce our presence at the event as black gay men. There would be no way to hide our identities behind that banner. We were out for good and everyone would know it. Meanwhile, a third organizer began distributing stickers with a rainbow-colored image of the continent of Africa. I knew the sticker would be controversial, but I affixed one to a trench coat I wore over my favorite suit.

A few minutes after our scheduled start time, the crowd had swelled to several dozen and the speakers began to fire up the participants. Derrick Bell, a longtime civil rights activist who was my former law school professor, spoke to express his support as a straight ally. Kenneth Reeves, the black openly gay mayor of Cambridge, Massachusetts, delivered a speech that only a gifted politician could deliver. Phill Wilson, the founder of the National Black Lesbian and Gay Leadership Forum, spoke out. The entire rally had been his idea from the beginning. But the responsibility to finish the event was left to me, as the new executive director of Phill's organization. I was supposed to rally the troops and then lead the crowd on a march to the Mall. By the time I took the podium, our numbers had grown to several hundred, and we were feeling much more confident about our mission. Still, we wondered if most of the participants had only come for the rally or if they would follow us on the march to the Mall. We would only find out once we started marching.

We had no clear vision how the day would unfold after we left the rally and no idea how we would be received. Uncertain of what might lie ahead, I summoned a few words I hoped would inspire the crowd and ended the event with a call to join me on the fifteen-minute procession to the larger assembly on the Capitol Mall. I was acting on faith, remembering a lesson I had learned a few years before, but others were now learning it as well. It came from my favorite quotation from Audre Lorde. "When I dare to be powerful—to use my strength in the service of my vision—then it becomes less and less important whether I am afraid."

Without a legal parade permit or a police escort, we flooded out from the sidewalks and took over the street. A few passersby hurriedly moved out of the way, a couple of people driving their cars along the adjoining streets honked their horns in support, and a number of pedestrians stopped and stared. A few even snapped photos of the unexpected demonstration.

Sensing no negative reaction, our group grew increasingly ambitious and empowered. We began to chant:

"We're black!

We're gay!

We wouldn't have it any other way!"

Still, almost no one along the street reacted critically.

They say there is safety in numbers, but on this day we had not convened in search of shelter. Our numbers were our strength, not just our sanctuary. And what exactly did we have to fear in the first place? That someone would call us out? We were doing that ourselves. That someone would attack us? Not on this day of peace and atonement. And not unless they were prepared to confront hundreds of fellow tribesmen. Rather it was the fear of the unknown, of doing something you've always been led to believe you should not do. It was one thing to be out and proud in the comfortable gay bars and nightclubs of Dupont Circle. It was quite another to do the same outdoors with a million black men surrounding you.

We pushed down Ninth Street toward the Mall, where hundreds of thousands of black men had already begun to gather. No one in our group had any idea if anyone down there knew we were coming, but many of us were prepared for whatever might happen. We were tired of being left out of the conversation, or quietly discouraged from acknowledging our participation, in our own community, and on this day we decided to assert our rightful place as black men.

Two blocks away, the huge crowd gathered on the Mall could surely hear us coming well before our shoes would touch the grass. Inching closer to the inevitable, the rush of adrenaline drowned out the churning in my stomach. My balmy palms still held a firm grip on the hand-made sign I held in the front of the crowd. I was the ringleader. I had to show confidence. So I straightened my tie, raised my fist, and turned up the volume.

"We're black!
We're gay!
We wouldn't have it any other way!"

I have my own quirky way of dealing with fear. Ever since my first high school track meet, I've always psyched myself up at the starting line by imagining the worst thing that could happen to me. Yes, my father, the former track star, would be watching closely in the stands and expecting me to carry on the family tradition, but what if I did not win? What is the worst thing that could happen to me? I'm not going to die just because I lose a race. All I can do is try my best. And only with the acceptance of the possibility of failure and humiliation was I able to realize that my fear was not as powerful as the goal itself. Once you realize that the thing you fear is not the end of the world, you begin to understand that your defiance of fear gives you power to change the world.

I had little time for deep reflection on fear once our march down the street had begun, but my instincts told me to keep moving forward no matter what. Focusing on the logistics of moving our procession safely to its goal left me little opportunity to ponder a worst-case scenario.

One block away and I could see the heads turning on the Mall as a steadily moving stream of black gay men prepared to connect with a larger sea of African American men flowing across the lawn. Fists punching against the air, voices rising to break the morning solitude, step-by-step we marched.

Less than fifty yards from the Mall, my eyes started scanning the crowd ahead to find a path big enough to accommodate us, as we would try to move into the larger group and find a position of maximum visibility. If I had been walking by myself, I might have been able to negotiate a route to the front of the stage, but it looked virtually impossible to find enough room to fit nearly 300 people in the thickly saturated assembly. Sometimes when you don't have an answer, you have to keep moving forward and act on faith. So we kept marching and chanting as though we knew where we were going.

I felt the stares of thousands of gazing men as the first footsteps of our group soared above the street curb and landed on the Mall. Where do we go from here? Still no answers. Twenty feet away and marching. Ten feet away and chanting. Five feet away and still no way forward. I thought about an old riddle I had heard years before. *What happens when an irresistible force meets an immovable object?*

And then it happened.

Like a scene from the Hollywood version of Exodus, the sea of men literally parted in front of us, creating a clear path of dry ground for us to follow. Some in the crowd moved to the left while others stepped back on the right, and into the empty chasm we marched.

"We're black!
We're gay!
We wouldn't have it any other way!"

We plunged into the crowd, marching and chanting for several city blocks, pushing our way almost effortlessly eastward toward the Capitol building where the main stage had been assembled for the rally. More stares, more cameras, more looks of shock and surprise, even a few claps and smiles greeted us. But there was no homophobia, no insults, no violence or conflict. For many march participants, that day was probably the first time they had ever seen a group of black gay men openly, visibly, and unabashedly acknowledging themselves as a part of the larger African American community.

We moved as far as we could, finally coming to rest much closer to the stage than we expected, and when we stopped, the parted sea of black men quickly reshaped around and embraced us.

FOR COLORED BOYS

To Colored Boys Who Have Considered Suicide

Hassan Beyah

To colored boys who have considered suicide
on dark and cold winter days
in closets and rooms confined and strangled by their own
insecurity
searching for peace and acceptance
in a place far beyond their imposed social invisibility
where dark skin turns red then white then blue
fragile young men who have never climbed mountaintops
or marched on Washington
but have had a dream
and feel neglected and abandoned by communities and
environments
that practice and preach hypocrisy
from pulpits and podiums
justifying hate with biblical text and Quranic verse

To colored boys who have spent too many late nights
in darkened clubs
masquerading as uber-masculine contemporaries
in fitted caps, wife-beaters and spankin' new Timbs
seducing their senses and egos
with colored alcoholic beverages and promises of sexual
encounters
and maybe the occasional fantasy of commitment
and relationship
but knowing all too well that the closet has only room for
one
and it is easier at times to love the many than to love the few
or even to love one's self

To colored boys who have never been asked,
never tell
and spend lifetimes defining manhood and masculinity
in terms of sexual roles and positions
hiding preferences in shadows
and becoming pop culture references
sexualized, marginalized, objectified, crucified
and then forgotten

To colored boys who spend countless hours
In testosterone-scented gyms
developing biceps but never finding salvation
in the development of the soul.

To colored boys who die
a thousand painful deaths of rejection
long before the cold black barrel
ever reaches the temple of self-doubt
or the colored pills of racism are ingested
Or the toxic, poisoned liquids of homophobia reach and
destroy the liver

but die slow and lonely deaths
filled with fear and insecurity,
chasing dreams of acceptance
slicing socially chained wrist with the flesh-ripping
blades of self-hate
and hang from the ropes of silence and shame
suffocated by their false sense of invincibility

To colored boys trapped in the windowless isolated boxes
of limited opportunity
with restless souls and deferred dreams
seeking love in unromantic late-night cyber encounters
and journey unprotected through the wilderness of
instant gratification
finding peace in death but never in life

To colored boys who have never
been offered a hand to hold
or a shoulder to cry on
who tell narratives that go unheard
who have fears that go unspoken
who have dreams that go unrealized
and
who give and rarely get anything in return
for the poet
the writer
the part-time escort now turned "model"
the photographer
the dancer
the dreamer
for Jamal, Henry, Taylor and Byron
and
all the colored boys who have considered suicide
This poem is for you.

Mariconcito

Emanuel Xavier

I was on a field trip in kindergarten the first time I saw a pair of tits on the big screen. I had no interest in them. I was more enthralled by the film's leading man. While the rest of the preschool kids were watching *The Swiss Family Robinson*, I wandered off on my own into another theater to watch *Saturday Night Fever*. The topless stripper shown in one scene in the film was no match for a half-naked John Travolta taunting his grandmother in his undies. I was in love.

For some time afterwards, my wildest dreams involved John Travolta as a vampire coming in through an open window and standing over my bed, hungering for a taste of my blood. It was far from a nightmare. I looked forward to going to sleep so I could dream of this hot adult man watching over me. I would eventually develop awkward crushes on other male celebrities and on other boys long before reaching puberty.

As an effeminate little boy, I was constantly picked on by the boys at school and by my stepfather at home. The boys taunted me for speaking too softly, for befriending girls, and never fighting back. My stepfather had his own special word for me: *mariconcito*.

He came from a culture tainted with machismo, where women were meant to be subservient to men and men were allowed to beat their women if they got out of line or dinner was not ready when they got home from work. My mother, also a product of this culture, was ashamed of me and seemed to think she could beat the gay out of me anytime I did anything that was not manly for a little boy. There was no tolerance for a queer child in that world.

As a teenager, I fell in and out of love with a Puerto Rican named Richie, who would often call the house to talk to me. Growing up in the living room of a one-bedroom apartment made it easy for my mother to eavesdrop on our conversations. Then one day she quietly picked up the phone line in the bedroom and listened to a call that confirmed her worst fears. She confronted me and slapped me until I cried. When I told her I was gay, she told me she was disgusted with me. I ran into the bathroom and locked the door to kill myself before she or my stepfather would hurt me first.

The bottles in the medicine cabinet provided an easy option. I started swallowing pills and stayed there until I passed out. When I finally woke up, I was vomiting charcoal given to me by hospital staff as a nearby nurse watched in horror. Assigned a social worker, I told her what happened and she then tried to comfort my mother. But I could see in my mother's eyes that I was going to get beaten for exposing our family's shameful secret once I got released.

Sure enough, my return home was a physical and emotional nightmare, and I was asked to leave the house. I could not live a lie, and my mother could not live with a gay son. We would both come to regret it, but any chance for reconciliation was destroyed by my stepfather who felt that kicking me out of the house would teach me a lesson.

I was sixteen, homeless, picking through garbage for

leftover food, and sleeping underneath parked cars to avoid the rain. Ashamed to ask my friends for shelter, I remembered rumors of a place in Manhattan where homosexual men openly congregated. A few train stops away from Brooklyn and I found my way to Christopher Street.

The hustlers and drug dealers who "owned" the West Side Highway piers at the time welcomed me, and I became a hustler myself to get food, money, and shelter. Angry, young, and curious about sex, I felt valued by hustling at a time when I had no other support from family and friends. Soon I started experimenting with drugs and later I began selling them myself. Both hustling and drug dealing were ways to survive and taught me, in the most difficult way, to become a man.

Before I had left home, I had heard whispered rumors that my mother had a gay cousin. He had served in the Army and had a daughter, and I would only see him at Christmas during family gatherings in the Bronx. We hardly ever spoke more than a few cordial words to one another, but if he ever came to Christopher Street or the Village, we were bound to cross paths.

One night while I was hustling, I positioned myself around the corner from the Monster Bar off Christopher Street, hoping to pick up an older drunk and horny man. Instead I ran into my cousin. The Monster was apparently his favorite after work hangout spot.

A stroll to the West Side Highway piers that night led to an open conversation about our lives that made us feel like family for the first time ever. He had already heard that I had "run away from home" and invited me to stay with him in his small but comfortable apartment in Riverdale. I accepted the offer to crash in his living room until I found a decent job or a permanent home. He never judged or criticized me, even though he was well aware that I was still hustling. He had his own demons but gave me advice he hoped would pave a better path for me.

My cousin repeatedly suggested I call my mother and let her know I was alright. I resisted at first but eventually gave in and called. She allowed me to return home so I could finish high school and instituted an unofficial "Don't Ask! Don't Tell!" policy about my sexuality. Back at home, I repressed my feelings and focused on school and as many after-school activities as possible. None of my high school friends or teachers had a clue what I had experienced during the summer, and I was fine pretending I had a home life as great as theirs.

My repressed desires were bound to surface eventually, and it wasn't long before I started doing drugs again. I probably tried everything except crack and heroin. Ketamine, or K, was a very popular drug at the time along with cocaine and ecstasy. I preferred snorting horse tranquilizers and going into "K-holes" instead of the jittery effects of cocaine or crystal meth. My return to drug dealing began by packaging crack for a neighborhood dealer. As things worsened at home, I left again to live with my gay cousin, who had moved in with his boyfriend. We would all live together as a sort of makeshift family, and I became unofficially adopted as a gay son.

Despite all the turmoil in my life, I somehow managed to get a grant to attend St. John's University and attempted to go to college for a few years. But I eventually dropped out and was introduced by a group of club kids to a popular club dealer who made the drug scene seem glamorous and fun. He revealed secrets of the trade and took me under his wings. But he also took advantage of my situation and sold it to me as friendship as I became addicted to K and immersed myself in the gay club scene.

My main "competition" in the business was a young, gay Colombian-born drug dealer named Angel Melendez, who ran around in angel wings and platform boots. When the police discovered his dismembered body floating in a trunk in the Hudson River, it forced me to take a good hard look at myself in the mirror. I realized my life was headed in the same direction if I didn't pull out. At the same time, as I had become more popular in the gay club scene, my visibility was becoming a liability to the drug dealer I worked for. Several times I was nearly arrested and soon it seemed I had only two options—either leave or end up in jail.

I left the club scene, started working at a bookstore, and discovered my passion for poetry, which provided a creative outlet for unleashing my heartaches. Writing about the horrors I was forced to deal with and subjected myself to helped heal the wounds but not the scars. I eventually found some success as a "controversial writer," even though my parents were never too impressed. The relationship with my mother and father improved a bit, but the "Don't Ask! Don't Tell!" policy was only slightly modified. At least my parents were willing to meet someone I loved if I had a serious relationship, but until then they'd rather not know.

Just as things started to get better, I suffered another setback in 2005. On my way to visit my mother in Bushwick, on an October Tuesday night, I saw a group of rowdy teens heading in my direction while I was walking alone on an empty street. As a former badass pier queen, I walked right through the crowd to get to my destination. Just as I passed the group, one of them punched me in the back of the head and tried to knock me to the ground. He went on to punch me in the face, and soon enough they were all taking turns pummeling me with their fists. The girls in the group watched proudly as their "men" ganged up on one individual, blow after blow after blow. A gypsy cab driving on the next avenue slowed down long enough for me to run toward it, jump in, and be whisked away to safety. Bloodied and bruised, missing my keys, I had been a victim of a probable gang initiation, according to the police.

The attack on an openly gay public figure in the community aroused suspicion from queer Internet bloggers, who speculated on everything from rumors of my death to questions of what I was doing out on a weeknight in Brooklyn to what I might have been wearing and how I might have sashayed down the street. Just as rape victims are often blamed for their rapes, I was blamed for what some perceived as a gay bashing. I read comments on the Internet like "He deserved it!" and silly stuff like "This is probably because he co-starred in *The Ski Trip*, which aired on Logo and one of those kids recognized him from that movie." Even if I had been wearing daisies in my hair or red patent leather high heel pumps (or both), or one of these kids happened to watch a gay cable network and sit through an independent film, the comments from my own gay community made me feel worse. This drove me to silence until I finally accepted an interview with a fellow gay Latino activist, Andres Duque, for *Gay City News*.

The attack left me completely deaf in my right ear and forced me to get hearing tests and an MRI, which showed that I had an "acoustic neuroma," a tumor of the nerve that connects the ear to the brain. If there was a silver lining to the attack, it's that it alerted me to the growing golf ball-sized tumor in my ear canal. I had to choose between radiation therapy or invasive surgery to have it removed or, I was warned, it would grow to the point where it would block the fluid surrounding my brain and I would unexpectedly die one day from what would probably be rumored to be a drug overdose. Despite the possibility that my face would be partially paralyzed from the procedure, I opted for the surgery. The tumor was successfully removed, and I was fortunate that I only experienced partial paralysis for several weeks after the surgery.

After years of broken communication, my family was there for me throughout the entire ordeal from the attack to the recovery from the surgery. My mother was recovering from her own battle with cancer—the reason I was on my way to visit her the night of the incident—and we shared a bittersweet time when we both sported shaved heads; hers from radiation treatments and mine as a requirement for invasive head surgery. We were surprised this had happened at a time in my life when I had overcome so much adversity instead of when I was indulging in decadence. Looking back, the experience provided an opportunity for healing, both physically and emotionally, and helped to bring us closer as a family. Holding grudges and harboring hatred is useless when the great cliché of life is that it really is so short and you never really know what will happen tomorrow.

The scar that surrounds my ear serves as a constant reminder of that brutal night. I still believe it was a random gang-related incident and it didn't matter whether I happened to be gay or not. But those teenagers themselves were victims of a society that distorts masculinity. According to this thinking, my stepfather and those boys from my childhood had a right to make fun of me and hurt me because I needed to be a man. My mother had a right to throw me out of the house because I was evil and needed to learn a lesson. Years later, those teens had a right to attack me because they needed to establish their manhood.

All of this begs the question, "Does it really get better?" On the one hand, I made it to adulthood, became a successful writer, and I've done a great deal of work for the community. On the other hand, I've still been a victim of physical violence, just like so many other young gay men. I suppose my answer would have to be "It needs to get better." Whether there is a God or not and whether he or she made us this way for a reason, we should have the same opportunities as everyone else to pursue freedom and love.

Chicago
Phill Branch

I saw his personal ad in the back of *Frontiers* magazine. *Frontiers* was my gateway to a world I didn't quite have a grip. It was one of those magazines you see in the gay ghettos piled up in front of small boutiques and adult novelty shops; an unholy invitation. Shirtless white boys with perfect abs and perfect teeth mocked you from the cover pages. Still carrying the burden of being black and being "that way," it took me a while to actually pick one up.

No one knew about me.

I don't count the men I met at adult theaters or the football player from Grambling State University I met one random night in college or my adviser who seduced me with the assistance of an International Male catalogue. They didn't count because no one else knew. I could always walk away.

The night I finally picked up a *Frontiers* magazine I was bored, unhappy, and horny—a cocktail for disaster. He lived in Norwalk. I didn't even know where in the hell that was. I'd only been in Los Angeles a couple of months. I hadn't been any further west than the Beverly Center, south of Venice, or east of La Brea.

I'd moved out here to be the next Spike Lee, but somehow I ended up answering phones at Levine/Schneider Public Relations instead.

I was alone and didn't want to be. I was poor and didn't want to be that either. I was gay...and didn't know how to be. On top of all of that, I was going to miss Christmas back home in New Jersey. I think missing Christmas bothered me most of all.

I love Christmas. My family wasn't especially religious. For us, Christmas was all about the gifts and spending time with family. As kids, my brother and I got everything we wanted. We'd open gifts, then hop into a cab over to my grandmother's house where we'd open more gifts. It was always a magical time. Well, except for the one Christmas my dad left to get a tree and didn't come back until after Christmas.

My first Christmas in L.A. was magical, too—in a black magic sort of way. I thought I wanted to kill myself, but I took a passive aggressive approach to ending it all. I didn't have insurance, so there were no prescription pills. I was late with rent and considered jumping from my tenth floor Park La Brea apartment window, but that was too dramatic, even for me. At some point during my downward spiral I realized that I didn't want to kill myself. I really just wanted to punish myself for not having the life I was supposed to have.

I'd imagined I'd be engaged to my high school sweetheart, Dana. We had it all planned out. We were going to have three kids, two girls and a boy—Ebony, Essence, and Elijah. I don't know why we went with names that began with "E." I'm sure there was some reason that seemed profound in our teenage minds. Instead of engagements and kids, however, I found myself trying to face a life that was completely unrecognizable.

That first Christmas in L.A. was unlike anything I'd experienced—no snow, no Yule log, no presents. People were wearing shorts for God's sake. What kind of Christmas is that?

Since I decided against suicide, I went to the movies instead. I remember wearing a turtleneck and brown corduroy pants. I thought maybe it would make me feel like I was home if I dressed in winter clothes, despite the warm temperatures outside.

I ended up seeing *Dumb and Dumber*. That choice didn't make things much better. On the way home, feeling completely lost, I picked up *Frontiers*.

When I got back to my apartment, I locked myself in the bedroom. I didn't want one of my roommates to see what I was reading. I sat on the floor of my bare room and flipped to the back of the magazine. I've always gone to the back of the magazine first. It's a habit I developed reading *Jet* magazine. *Jet* printed a list of the top twenty songs and albums in the back of the magazine. I've always liked lists. I would read the "Top Twenty" lists first and then work my way back to the beginning.

Frontiers had ads for everything under the sun. I'd seen personal ads in mainstream newspapers before: "man seeks woman for walks on the beach and romantic dinners." *Frontiers* was no walk on the beach.

"Hot guy in WeHo, with hot mouth looking to take big meat all day and night…anonymous only."

I was disgusted by the vulgar ads and seemingly classless nature of the people who posted them, but I kept reading and then I found "him."

He was tall, swimmers build, and liked *The Simpsons*. He was a "blk," "btm," into "ff," "ws," and "k." I didn't know what any of that meant, but I figured it couldn't be so bad.

I called him.

"Come over," he said. He lived in Norwalk.

"It's ten o'clock," I said.

"I'll pay for a cab and I won't try anything; don't want to be all alone on Christmas."

I didn't either.

I showered, got dressed, and left a note with his address and phone number on my bed, under my pillow. Even in my reckless abandon of meeting my faceless, nameless Norwalk date, I tried to be responsible. "If I am missing, I am in Norwalk at this address."

I sprayed on some cologne and went downstairs into the waiting cab. Fearing getting murdered by an anonymous man in a town I was unfamiliar with is how I began my dating life. I knew it was dangerous, but part of me felt like I deserved whatever might happen. This was my lot, for being "this way."

I may have well been driving across the country. I'd never been on any of these freeways—the 5, the 110. It wasn't until I realized that I'd been riding for about a half hour that I begin to think the driver may have gone too far.

I began making a list in my head. People who will miss me if something happens: Mom, Qadir, Nana, Dina, Shekira, Brian, Rudy, Larryce.

The list went on. It went from a being a list of people who love me to being the list of people who'd come to my funeral. I wondered who would take the trip to New Jersey for the services. I wondered if people would be disappointed by how I had died and if they'd not show up. I started to wonder if my roommates would find the note. What if no one found my body?

I wanted to tell the cab driver to turn around, but the meter was already up to fifty dollars and I didn't have fifty cents. I had to go the distance if not for anything but the cab fare. I was already in too deep.

After about forty minutes I arrived in this foreign land of Norwalk, and a tall, cute, lanky black man met me at the curb. The cab driver asked for $85.

The stranger paid the cab driver, looked at me, and said, "You better be worth it." Without any other prompt, he turned around and started walking toward his open apartment door.

It had to have been only seconds, but it felt like an hour as I watched him walk across the street. My legs were cement. I didn't move from the side of the cab. A piece of me, the piece that still kinda liked me, mustered up enough strength to lean into the cab driver's window and say, "Please come back at six."

The cab driver, an older Russian man, stared at me for a beat and gave me a slight nod before he drove off. As his car pulled away, I felt shipwrecked. All I had was a pager. No one would think to even look for me in Norwalk. They certainly wouldn't be looking for me at some man's house. For the first time in my life, I felt completely isolated.

"C'mon now," Chicago yells. I call him Chicago because that's where he said he was from. I don't remember his real name. I'm sure he told me. Actually, maybe he didn't. I'm not even sure if I used my real name.

I walked into his townhouse, and he locked the door behind us. I can still remember the sound of the deadbolt closing. I saw him, from the corner of me eye, take the key out of the deadbolt. I pretended not to notice. I didn't want to be impolite.

We sat on the couch at opposite ends. His stare was piercing. This was a game and he'd already won. I could feel myself shaking, so I know he could see it. He was older, probably not by much, but enough to have been down this road before.

What's Love Got to Do with It? played in the background. It felt appropriate. As I pretended to watch TV, he watched me. In the moment, I suddenly realized that I'd skipped a few steps. I had never been on a real date with a man before, but there I was sitting in Norwalk with Chicago, in a dead-bolted apartment.

"Do you like videos?" he asked.

"Of course I do."

I thought he was going to turn to BET. I was so naïve, that's what "video" meant to me. I expected to see SWV. Chicago turned on some porn and pulled out his dick. It was all moving too fast.

"Do you have any eggnog?" slipped out of my mouth. It's Christmas. I wanted eggnog. I wanted my family. I wanted presents. Really, what I wanted the most was the key to the front door.

He laughed at me. "Eggnog?"

As he laughed, I noticed a long scar on his head. He noticed I noticed. "I have a plate in my head," he grunted matter-of-factly. I wasn't sure what having a plate in one's head meant, but it sounded like a bad deal.

Time ticked. I just sat there, pretending that his penis wasn't hanging out of his black jeans while he talked to me. On his wall I focused on an ugly, mass-produced, black street fair type of painting.

"You want a Zima?"

"No."

Chicago jumped up. "You said you liked Zima, I bought some."

I forgot that I'd said that. It wasn't true. I didn't really drink. When he asked me what I'd like to drink, Zima is the only thing that came to mind. That's what my crew was drinking at the time, so that's all I knew to say.

He hands me a Zima. "You need to drink all these."

I take a sip. It's not bad, but I don't want it. I didn't see him open it. I didn't know what was in it. I didn't want to make him angry, though, so I continued sipping. He smiled. The smile was like someone looking at a child trying to do something grown up.

"How old are you?"

"Twenty-one," I whispered.

He rubbed my chest. "You look like you're in high school."

I just kept drinking and staring at the painting.

"You nervous baby?"

I was, but I thought that drinking the Zima made me look more comfortable. He took it from my hand. "You playin' with this." He downed it.

"You a freak, ain't you?" he growled.

I wasn't, then.

His hand moved from my chest to my throat and he was not quite choking me, but it still didn't feel good. I tried to adjust; he squeezed tighter.

"I can do anything I want to you and nobody knows where the fuck you are," he said while smiling and still holding my neck. All of a sudden, my receptionist job and my miserable lonely life in Los Angeles didn't seem so bad at all.

He let me go and laughed, "I'm just fucking around." Chicago grabbed me by the shirt and pulled me off of the couch. "Let's go."

I couldn't stop looking at the front door. I wanted to run. There were bars on the window. I looked for the phone, but I didn't see one. Besides, who would I call? The police? What would I say? "Hello, 911...I am at a stranger's house and he promised me sugar cookies, but instead, he pulled out his dick."

"You ain't going no fucking where," he snarled, noticing my eyes locked on the door.

All I could think about was my mother and my little brother. At once, I began to feel afraid and sad that I might not see them again. I thought about all the years of getting straight A's and being student council president.

How did I end up here?

Chicago's place was a two-story townhouse-style apartment with ugly beige carpeted floors. I resisted a little bit as he pulled me up the stairs. He shook me and glared at me like he'd learned some things from watching Fishburne's interpretation of Ike Turner. "Don't fuck with me."

After what felt like two hundred steps, I was in his bedroom. It was normal. In a way, the normalcy was frightening. It would have made more sense to see a messy room with walls covered in pages ripped from porn magazines. Instead there was a flowered bedspread.

He pushed me down to the bed, then seemed to remember something. "Come here."

He pulled me back to the staircase. I stood at the top of the staircase, he kneeled at the steps. "I've always wanted to do this," he whispered. He began to unzip my pants.

"I could kick him down the steps," I thought. That always

works in the movies. The person stumbles down the steps and then collapses, unconscious on the landing. Then I realized that between there only being about sixteen steps and the fact that they were carpeted, I'd probably only piss him off. While my Lifetime movie scene ran through my head, his lips pressed against my dick.

Men are special creatures. My body, despite the fact that I was more scared than I'd ever been, responded to his touch. I felt myself grow inside of Chicago. Maybe I wanted this.

Bored with the staircase set-up, he dragged me back into the bedroom. We laid facing each other, like lovers. He caressed my face and kissed me gently. I preferred the head. I could detach from the head. But the kissing, his breath on my face, and his eyes facing mine made everything too real.

"You're shaking," he taunted. "What would you do if I didn't let you leave?"

I laughed.

"I think I'm going to keep you," Chicago said like it was the easiest decision he'd ever made. He took me by my hand into the hallway and opened the door to another room. It was dark and all I remember is that a birdcage sat on the dresser. "This is your room now," he said proudly.

My room?

He told me that if he decided to let me leave tomorrow, that I can go home and pack all my things. I didn't think it was funny, but I laughed again.

"Stop fucking laughing at me," he snapped. He slammed the bedroom door and pushed me back into his room. He tore my shirt off and threw me down on the bed. He kissed me hard, and then bit me. He bit my lips. He bit my chest. It hurt, but he was bigger and I couldn't move.

"You're gonna be sorry you came here if you keep pissing me off."

I'd imagined that being gay would come with some obstacles, but I'd never imagined being trapped in a townhouse, in Norwalk, by a man with a plate in his head would be one of them.

I found out very quickly that all of those initials that I didn't understand in his personal ad were very critical. "Blk": black. "Btm": bottom, "FF": fisting, "WS": water sports, "K": kink. He liked pain. He enjoyed hurting me. It's a blur, but at some point I was stripped down to my underwear, writhing in pain as he twisted and contorted my body while he kissed, licked, and sucked voraciously.

He gave me a thick strap and told me to beat him. Again, I laughed. I didn't mean to, but I was frightened.

"Don't fucking laugh at me, I will fucking kill you!"

I hit him across the face with the strap.

I stood paralyzed as a tear rolled down his face, "Yeah, just like that."

Once I ruled out the idea of jumping out of the second floor window, I decided to do what Chicago wanted me to do. For the next couple hours I experienced something that was a cross between sex, wrestling, street fighting, domestic abuse, and a horror film.

After one of the longer sessions, consisting of me being on the receiving end of a well-worn wooden paddle, he held me in his arms again and asked me to move in with him. I'd learned my lesson about not agreeing. "Of course," I said.

He told me that he'd get a truck and help me pack my things the next day.

"Thank you," I said as if I were truly appreciative. The whole time, my eyes were on the clock, it was 2:30 A.M. I knew the cab driver wasn't coming back like I'd asked, but I still looked forward to 6:00 A.M. I needed to feel like this could end. He wrapped his arms around me and told me he loved me.

Being chopped up in Chicago's freezer wasn't how I wanted my story to end. Wanting to survive this, I rolled over and gave Chicago a big kiss. I told him that I loved him and that I couldn't wait to move in. He held me close. I told him I was going to go home and pack and would be back in time for dinner. He was thrilled. I was sick. Within moments, he was sleeping. I sat listening to the clock tick for hours. Six o'clock comes and nothing.

Chicago woke up smiling, "Good morning, honey." He hugged me. It hurt. My body was sore. My skin was raw.

"Good morning," I said.

"You ain't going nowhere," Chicago moaned. Just then I decided I was going to have to do whatever it took to get out of that house. There was some card tournament trophy sitting on the nightstand. I didn't want to hit him with it, but hell, he liked pain.

"I need to go home," I said as assertively as I could.

"I said you aren't going any fucking where."

I rolled over, he spooned me, burying his face into my neck. "Don't make me mad this early in the morning, okay, baby?"

"Okay."

I closed my eyes, fighting back tears; nervous and unsure if I wanted to physically fight my way out of this house. It didn't occur to me to call the police; besides, what was the crime? I realized I might have never actually said "no." I realized that through every horrible thing that happened to me, I'd possibly given reluctant and frightened consent. Why in the fuck did I pick up that *Frontiers* magazine?

We lay there for several minutes in silence, his chest against my back.

The doorbell rang.

I didn't react. I was afraid of Chicago's response.

The doorbell rang again.

"Hello!" a voice yelled from outside.

Chicago jumped up. "Who the fuck is that?"

"I don't know."

He rolled out of bed, grabbed his pants and headed downstairs. I jumped into my pants and barely put on my shoes and shirt. I bolted downstairs and pushed past Chicago and the cab driver as they stood at the open door.

I ran out of the house and into the waiting cab. I could barely catch my breath.

A few moments later, the cab driver got into the car, looked at me in the rearview, but didn't say a word. I cried the entire way back to civilization. L.A. has never looked as good to me as it did that morning on December 26, 1994.

We pulled up in front of my building, and I remembered that I don't have any money. I started to speak but he said, "It's okay."

It would be years before I could truly recognize the gift the cab driver gave me. I have so many questions that will never be answered about why he came back.

I limped into my apartment. My entire body was sore. Seeing myself, naked, in my full-length mirror felt like a punch to the gut. Bruises covered my body. I was still in the closet, so I couldn't tell anyone what had happened. How could I explain the bruises? My roommates were right there, sleeping in their rooms, clueless about what I'd endured. I knew that I'd have to go through my regular day with them as if nothing had happened.

After lying on my floor for about an hour, I called the one friend I felt I could cry on the phone with and not be questioned. I was too embarrassed to really tell her what I'd done.

I was supposed to go to work the next day but couldn't. When I returned to work and faced my over-eager office manager, Deb, I had to explain why I missed work. She stood there, berating me about responsibility as I tried to think of a lie that would excuse my absence. But I was broken and just needed someone to hear me, even if it was this woman I found annoying.

"I was raped."

I don't think I'd ever experienced such a silence. Office

managers go through all sorts of training, but I'm sure Deb wasn't ready for me to say that. Those three words slipping out of my mouth changed everything.

Deb took me to her office and explained that I'd have to talk to a counselor on the phone. She said it was state law. I agreed. I then did what many others in my situation do; I blamed myself. No convincing from the counselor was going to get me to give her Chicago's address.

Deb wasn't my favorite person, but on that day she was my hero. Having her and the counselor treat me like a human being and not like someone who'd shared a dirty secret helped me stop clinging on to the life I'd once imagined for myself and start dealing with the cards I'd been dealt.

I am now far removed from being that twenty-one-year-old who was afraid of living his "real" life. But after fifteen years, I can't drive through Norwalk without my heart palpitating—and I still hate Christmas in L.A.

Better Days
Jamal Brown

One morning during recess I decided to skip a snack with friends and play on the jungle gym. A crowd of kids took turns sliding down the slide and eager to join the fun, I jumped in line and waited my turn. In front of me a group of girls huddled around a fellow male classmate, giggling and glancing in my direction. Not thinking anything of it, I focused my attention back on the slide.

The sun blazed high above and, wearing shorts, I worried about the hot plastic of the slide burning my legs. But before I could second-guess sliding down, I felt a pair of soft lips pressing against mine, and a small hand clenching my left arm. My fellow male classmate had rushed up and kissed me in plain view.

What just happened? Why didn't I viscerally react by pushing him away and reinforce my boyhood by shouting "Ewww!" so the whole playground would know my distaste? It may have been a dare or insignificant to him, but his lips rocked my universe. At the time I didn't understand why, but I secretly enjoyed that kiss.

I told no one of that day and surprisingly no one on the playground mentioned it again. I was coming to learn that boys weren't supposed to like other boys, and those who did were "sick" and "perverted."

My single-parent mother carried the sole burden of raising me in our predominantly lower-middle class neighborhood in Sacramento County. Within my family and the black community, gay was synonymous with white and I grappled with understanding how I could like other boys and be black. What did that mean in terms of my blackness? What is a boy supposed to do when the very feelings he holds are completely shunned by his loved ones and the environment around him?

While my attraction for other boys continued to grow and I wasn't at all attracted to women, I learned the consequences of revealing my attraction could be serious. Those considered gay were socially ostracized, harassed, and sometimes physically harmed, and I feared becoming a victim. So I did what I thought I needed to do to survive: I pretended to be straight.

I dated girls and became actively involved in sports to prove my masculinity. When women complimented or hit on me, their advances meant I was passing. But as I got older, it became more difficult to force my attraction towards women, and sports provided easy excuses with evening practices and weekend games.

At the same time, I found myself exuding more effeminate mannerisms. The more pronounced and flamboyant my gender expression became, the more I threatened my male peers' sense of masculinity, which, in turn, ignited their teasing and harassment. My only recourse, or so I felt, was to retreat deeper.

I pushed myself farther into the closet and developed serious thoughts about suicide. There seemed to be no alternative. I knew of no other black gay men, and because the only image I knew of what a gay man looked like was white, I developed a heightened sense of isolation and self-disgust. The catalyst for my action finally came on a winter night in 2004.

A rowdy and spirited crowd packed the school gym for a men's varsity basketball game between my school, Center High, and our rival, Highlands High. Some dubbed the contest as "the ghetto school versus the white school," but I had ties to both. I had grown up with the kids from Highlands, situated in a lower-middle class black and Latino neighborhood with gang problems and a high crime rate. But I had switched to the mostly white Center School District after junior high.

As the Center High School mascot, I was a visible figure at the game that night and our team narrowly beat Highlands in overtime. A big crowd lingered in the school parking lot after we won. I posed for a few photographs in my cougar costume and then hurried to store it away in hopes of seeing old friends, but by the time I made it outside much of the crowd had disappeared.

The full moon lit up the cloudless sky as I waited for my aunt to pick me up at the corner of the parking lot. After some time, most of the cars had departed and I didn't want to be left alone waiting in the dark. I buttoned my decorated varsity letter jacket to keep me warm and called my aunt to gauge her arrival. "I just had to drop your cousin off so I'll be there in five minutes," she promised.

A group of teens from Highlands approached the corner where I waited, and I recognized one from junior high and motioned to say hello. But he beat me to the punch.

"What's up, faggot? I'm trying to get faded tonight." Much like I reacted as a kid on the playground after that first kiss, I froze in confusion. His desire to get faded was code for marijuana and I didn't smoke, but it was the F-word that confused me. Did he figure me out? What signal did I give off?

"You hear me, faggot?" Before I could respond, I felt the weight of his fist slam into my head. The gang surrounded me as he went for a second swing. I lost my footing and stumbled to the street.

"Leave him alone, Jermaine, he's not worth it, man!" One of

my attacker's friends didn't see the need to waste time on me, so as quickly as I fell to the ground, I saw an opening and stumbled away towards the campus. I lost partial feeling in my face and was barely able to speak through the pool of blood that filled my mouth. Within minutes, both my mother and aunt arrived and drove me to the emergency room.

When the doctor questioned me about the night's event, I left out the "faggot" part. Even as I sat there, a battered victim of an anti-gay assault, I dared not reveal any clues of my sexuality.

I spent the next few days numb on Vicodin to soothe the physical pain, but I badly needed something to cope with the mental and emotional trauma. That Friday night my mother stepped out for the evening, and I found a remedy.

I can still remember the feeling of the knife slowly piercing my stomach. The room was pitch-black, save a slither of streetlight, and my panting seemed to be the only breath of sound giving life to the space. I braced my legs, shoulder-length apart, balanced my left arm on the wall, and clenched the blade inward.

"I hate it. I hate it." The streams became heavier and my cries ached louder.

"God, please get it out." I crouched on my knees and began desperately pleading for the pain of guilt to leave my body. I was tired of living, and living with the shame of what society considered an abomination. The walls I built to protect me finally cracked, and I could no longer bear another day wrestling with my sexuality. Suicide would be the cure to free myself from the shame and stigma that enveloped my life since childhood.

The knife dented my stomach further inward. A warm stream dripped down my inner thigh. But what I thought was blood were actually tears. I could not go through with it and crouched in a fetal position and cried for what seemed all night.

"Jamal? Jamal, wake up!" The next morning my mother's voice rang throughout the house to wake me for breakfast. Somehow during the night I made the transition from the floor to my bed. I quickly leaped into a pair of suitable mesh shorts and a tank top and followed the smell of buttered grits and burned bacon to the kitchen.

"Morning, fathead." Much to my utter annoyance, and for reasons unknown to me, my mother loved calling me a fathead rascal. It was her adoring mother-son name for me so I went with it.

"How was last night?" Bingo was her hobby.

"Eh, it was okay. Didn't win nothin,' but hey, that's life." It seemed her night was as unsuccessful as mine. "What did you do last night, ol' man?" She loved those pet names.

"Went for a run and then watched some television. What are you doing today?" The crispy bacon strips shattered against my teeth in my frantic attempt to avoid conversation. I had developed the ability to mask my emotions and appear happy without a care in the world, but this morning was different.

As we shared conversation over a seemingly normal meal, the world oddly felt at ease. For once I wasn't overbearingly conscious of every word from my mouth or each bend in my limbs.

"I just want you to know something," my mom said. "I love you so much, Jamal. You are the light of my life, and everyday I am proud of you. You are my son."

"What an odd thing for her to say without any revelation about my actions the night before," I thought.

It's difficult to name a specific moment that led to self-acceptance, but the night I failed at suicide was also the night I realized something important; that is, that pain is also my guide, and I could not live a life dictated by the prejudices and expectations of others. I had sunk to a low point, but it also marked the beginning of a journey towards loving me for me.

One Day a DJ Saved My Life

Jonathan Kidd

I made up my mind to kill myself when I was twenty years old. I like to think of it as an "era" of suicidal thought. There wasn't just one time, one instance, and then everything was perfect. It was a constant thought because my problems, well, they were constant. Just like learning to love yourself is a process, moving away from negative thoughts of self-harm is also a process. But two moments from that era helped me to believe in the power to proceed.

I started to acknowledge my same-sex attraction in college. It was probably clearer to many of the friends I had constantly debated with about gays in the military and whether homosexuality was a sin. My friend Jeff joked recently that during our freshman year all I ever wanted to do was "argue about politics and eventually homosexuality." By the time I was a sophomore, I was wound so tight that if friends came over to watch football with their shirts off, because that's what you do when you're in a dorm bro-ing down, I'd run to the bathroom and splash cold water on my face. I know. Real dramatic.

Somehow, during the course of the year I got involved in a relationship with the resident advisor, who I had sought to counsel me about my feelings. It was a whirlwind. I gave in to a crush for the first time in my life and it was a secret—a thrilling, amazing secret. But as relationships go, he wanted more—in this case for us to be public and open about our relationship—and I got scared. I thought about all of the things that would change, how my family would react, my church, and the girl with whom I was madly in love. Up until this point, I had done a good job of compartmentalizing my affections. Because gay activity was a "sin," somehow it wasn't "real" and thus had no bearing on the rest of my life. My goal to get married and have three kids would not change.

Change did occur, however, when I informed my counselor boyfriend that I didn't want to see him anymore, and he lashed out. All of the fears, insecurities, and dread that I had shared with him were suddenly thrown back in my face with twisted flare. In retrospect, I get that he was hurt by my rejection of him and reacted as many people would have in that situation, but at the time, it felt like my entire world had collapsed. I started having panic attacks while sitting in class, grabbing hold of my desk to prevent myself from running out. I envisioned my parents getting a letter in the mail like a kid the year before whose parents received a *Michigan Daily* photo of him kissing a guy at the Queer Kiss-In. I wondered how hot Hell would actually be. Finally, the tears and fears culminated one blustery night in February.

I grew up Pentecostal; don't go to the movies, listen to non-gospel music, or wear sneakers to church because that's a sin. I believe I was called to be a minister when I was a teenager. But I didn't follow through because of anxiety about my sexuality. From as long as I can remember, I knew I was gay, but I also knew homosexuality was not sanctioned by the church. AIDS had arrived on the scene as "God's punishment for them nasty mens" when I was six, and I wondered if I would get AIDS by holding hands with boys as I desired. I witnessed many an altar call to "pray away the gay" from members of my church and the community. It was mad stressful to say the least.

Fourteen years of pent-up Pentecostal frustration led to a chilly winter night when I was about to jump off a building on the University of Michigan campus. My theory went like this: If I am destined to end up in Hell and undeserving of God's love, why not just kill myself and get it over with?

I didn't wear a jacket but it was cold. For some reason, I thought about Dante's *Inferno* and the depiction of a frozen Satan encased in ice. The rapid removal of heat from your body burns like dry ice. It was a brilliant idea, but also an extremely scary one I felt doomed to experience firsthand. I did not think about my family who adored me or what affect my death would have on them. I just wanted my pain to end. I wanted God to love me "just as I am." I got to the edge and looked down. Then something happened.

When I was growing up attending evangelical tent revivals, the elder saints used the phrase "call Jesus." If your brakes go out on your car, call Jesus. If you don't think you have enough money in your bank account to cover the mortgage this month, call Jesus. Whenever trouble comes your way, call Jesus, and he will fix it, by and by. So as I was looking at the ground, preparing myself for the unknown, I asked God for help with my heart. I called out the name "Jesus." What transpired is why for the rest of my life, whether I attend church or not, regardless of what preacher so-and-so says on TV, I know that I am a child of God.

My knees buckled and landed on the roof of the building. At the same time, I felt a wave of love wash over me and I started praising God for that wave, for that love, for that blessed understanding and assurance. I tried to stand but I couldn't. I kept praising and praying in the cold on that chilly roof for what seemed like forever. And when I was finally able to rise to my feet, I turned around as I stood up and headed back inside, crying my eyes out. God had literally picked me up, turned me around, and placed my feet on solid ground.

I still get chills just thinking about it. And I am crying a little bit as I write this because it was my faith that brought me back from the edge and sustained me ever since that day. So my response to all of the spiritual haters in the world is that God, Yahweh, Adoshem, Lily of the Valley, Bright and Morning Star, Sweet Jesus showed me the light on a dark winter night, and no matter what you say or how loudly you say it, my relationship with *my* God is personal and you can never take that love away from me. No matter what.

I could end right there. But my sadness, despite knowing I was a child of God, did not end that winter. I was on a path, but I did not know where I was headed. I took baby steps for the next several months, falling into and out of exploratory relationships with guys, trying to fix things with my girlfriend and even dating new women, meeting more LGBT folk on campus, telling more of my close friends that I was open to dating guys…then changing my mind. Who knew what was in store for the future?

When summer came, I made plans. I lived up the street from an independent video store that carried awesome gay-themed movies and around the corner from a club, The Nectarine, that had "gay night" twice a week, and I was there every Tuesday and Friday night shaking my groove thing. I was "out." Sort of…but at one point I went back "in" after what I found in the club—people obsessed with casual sex, drug use, and gossip so vicious you'd think you'd need a rabies shot after talking with them. In retrospect, most of my friends, regardless of their sexual orientation, enjoy sex, have dabbled in drugs, and try to get rid of gossip as fast as they can by telling others. But I had imagined a homo-utopia where everyone was supposed to get along before they paired up and got married. Homo-Utopia?

One night I felt particularly vulnerable, and I don't know what the trigger was. It could have been any number of things, really, but I felt like crap and I went to the Nectarine because it was gay night. Yet, I didn't dance. I just sat in a daze, looking out at the people and judging them all. Maybe what I was seeing was their pain acted out upon themselves and each other. I couldn't take it and wondered what kind of life I was trying to live. I wanted to be a ho with one partner, not half the town. I wanted kids, even though the debates over gay marriage were more than a decade away. I wanted to be who I was before I acknowledged I was attracted to men, not some wild bizarro version of that guy who numbed himself with unprotected sex. Life as I knew it felt meaningless.

I went home determined to kill myself. I decided I would take my life by asphyxiation this time, and I wrote some letters to loved ones. According to my plan, it was all going to go down the next day. I just had to get some supplies from the store in the morning. I set my alarm for early. I hated the "wa-wa" sound my clock made and had it on radio alert. So on that day, which I believed to be my last, I woke up to music. It would have been a miracle if the three songs I am about to list played back to back, but they did play in the same set and they are the only ones I remember. They were Biggie Smalls's "One More Chance," Mary J Blige's "My Life," and Chantay Savage's "I Will Survive." It felt like the disc jockey on the Detroit radio station was spinning just for me that morning.

The series of those popular songs on the radio may not seem like a big deal to some, but it was for me. I grew up playing music; piano since as long as I can remember and trumpet beginning when I was ten. Classical and jazz gave way to funk, rock, and doo-bop as I got older, but what stayed consistent was the role of music as a transcendent energy with the power to make me feel alive. When I heard tree frogs in Mississippi, car horns in New York City, and drummers chanting in Ghana, I felt the power of music. And when I finished graduate school, I spoke during one of the commencement ceremonies and offered praise "to the most high who is the melody of my whistle." I'm the person who turns up his car radio because I've noticed the person in the crosswalk is walking in rhythm to the song I'm bumping. So on that fateful morning, what started off as an alarm telling me I'd come to the end of the road, ended up being a signpost letting me know that everything was going to be alright.

"One More Chance" made me begin to weigh my options because the words from the hook reminded me to "give life one more chance," but still I didn't budge much. "My Life" made me weep and sob because it always did; and usually I found it to be depressing because it made me think of all the things I'd "seen," but on this morning I heard empowerment in the lyrics, "cause he'll give you peace of mind/and you will see the sun shine/and you'll get to free your mind/and things will turn out fine." By the time Chante came with her take on Gloria Gaynor's classic, I felt born to sing, "I *will* survive...so long...bye-bye-bye-bye-bye...so long...bye-bye-bye-bye." I came to realize that God could love me, but if I didn't love myself, it wouldn't matter.

Good-bye, suicide; hello, life.

WHEN THE RAINBOW IS NOT ENOUGH

No Asians, Blacks, Fats, or Femmes

Indie Harper

It was seven o'clock and I was already more tipsy than appropriate for daytime. The sun was starting to set, the Hudson River burning yellow, orange, and red, melting into cooler blues and purples, the outline of stars just starting to crackle across the sky. The scent of water drifted across the pier onto the rooftop bar, where I sat with my friends drinking half-priced margaritas from aquarium-sized glasses. I turned from their smiling faces, breathing in the cooling air, feeling the blush of heat rising off my drunken face, it was one of those moments, one of many, where New York seemed full of magic.

"Fuck!" I heard as I quickly turned back to discover one of my boys had spilled his drink over his boyfriend. There was the quick, sharp staccato of heels and biker boots as everyone rushed to find him a napkin, a towel, the edge of a tablecloth, anything to dry him off. The unfortunate boyfriend excused himself to the bathroom as the rest of us cackled.

"Well, you could just take it off," I suggested when he came back, a dark uneven spot sat across his crisp, blue button-up like a sinister bib around his neck. "I'll even stuff a dollar down your pants if it makes you feel better."

"Ha ha," he answered, "I'd like it better if you could wash it for me, it's dry clean only." I was thrown. *Huh?* But then it dawned on me, dry clean + me = "Herow, Meesta Jo-son, two dolla, me lova you a-long time."

"Oh, ha ha, ha ha," I found myself pretending. Ever found yourself laughing awkwardly at a joke you've heard a million times before? No, just me? That's cool. I know it's new and edgy for some, but for me it's old. It's like running into that friend who will beat a joke to death, bury it, dig it back up, run to a hardware store, pay ten bucks for a saw, run back, saw off a new branch, and then beat it some more. The first time is hilarious, *Oh the memories!* the second, an utter joy, *I remember that!* but the third, fourth, and fifth times start getting tedious, *yup, that happened.* You may be able to walk away, never have to think about it until we meet again, but I'm Asian all the time. I heard it this morning, I'm hearing it now, I'll probably hear it thirty minutes from now. But to spare his feelings, I laughed along. "Five percent off if you get the pretty unicorn nail package, happy ending required."

When I was a young gaysian boy, back when I was the only gay I knew, I used to dream of the gay community like a warm blanket. I had read stories of all the outcasts and runaways, the freaks, the geeks, the nobodies, and how they came to the big city, lost in its endless corners, and found a place where they belonged. I dreamed, mercilessly, sitting behind my desk in high school, of the gay community I knew one day I'd be a part of. I'd have gay friends and go to gay bars and restaurants and one day, hopefully, fall in love, at sixty-three, with a young eighteen-year-old gay boy sex slave who'd fallen in love, with my money. You know, just like Cinderella. I'd always imagined gay people were different. That somehow they'd understand. But when I opened that black and white door and entered the Land of Oz, dazzled at first in the richness of blues and reds and yellow brick, I found my magical land had a wicked witch.

My first gay experience was like most other gay boys'. A friend, already out and more established, took my hand and casually asked if I wanted to go a gay bar. I nodded and smiled, trying desperately to pretend that my heart wasn't exploding. She took me to the Gay 90's in Minneapolis, a large building with every activity possible crammed into its two stories. Three dance floors, several lounge areas, a drag stage, a pool table, and a "secret" room accessible only through the first floor men's room. The first people I talked to were thin, lanky gay boys who wore tight pastel colored T-shirts with skinny jeans and white belts. I said hello and smiled. They just stared at me. One grunted and rolled his eyes before they turned and walked away. My small balloon of hope, my shaking hands, my legs that couldn't seem to get there fast enough, the smile I couldn't take off my face, fell from me like sand spilling from a broken jar.

Ten years later, my experience in the gay community hasn't gotten better. As a young man, I didn't know there were other options. I just wanted to be where other gay people were. I wanted others like me. Others who could tell me who I was, what I would become, what all of this could mean for me. But no one told me. No one seemed to care beyond what I could do for them or to them or on them. And really, no one should. That journey was mine to take. On the surface the gay community may seem different—Leather Daddies! Twinks! Jocks! Rice Queens!—but where it mattered, where it really counted, gay people are just like everyone else. And I was heartbroken for a long time. But as I've grown, I've become less and less angry at the community and more disillusioned with myself. After all, it wasn't the community that had built up my hopes. It was me, imagining what I'd hoped the community to be, only to be disappointed that gay people didn't live up to those expectations. Gay people are just like everyone else. There are people who are brave and kind and funny and beautiful, but mostly there are *a lot* of assholes.

My friend Thomas and I were sitting in the straight metal chairs of a popular Chelsea eatery, playfully arguing about who had it worse in the gay community: black people or Asians. We laughed over the wavering light of a dozen tiny candles, our raucous chuckles floating over the heavy beats of house music and Top 40 radio.

"No one will fuck you if they're scared of you," Thomas said.

"You mean scared of your giant dicks?" I answered. "'Cause I've never met anyone who turned that shit down."

"Motherfuckers smile and talk to your ass, but at the end of the night, they slip out, some white boy bullshit on their dicks."

"I wouldn't take you home either." I shook my head. "Never know what goes missing in the morning." We laughed, the same melancholy recognition in our voices.

"I'd snatch that shit, too. Lock. It. Up. Motherfucker."

"Hey, at least, black guys will fuck each other. Sometimes its easier to pull a white boy than an Asian."

"Fuck off, black motherfuckers do the same shit." We shook our heads. I stared at my plate of food, feeling the color of my skin seep into my bones. I looked up at Thomas and smiled.

"Fuck 'em."

I don't like most Asian people who *only* date white people. They're always so smug about their boyfriends, parading their whiteness around like a trophy. But the stain of his skin won't save you. His skin won't bleed onto yours, covering your feelings of doubt. Your skin will always be gold, your hair as dark as the other side of the world.

I know it's hard to feel beautiful. I get it. Most days I wake up and feel hideous. Every blemish a chasm on my skin, I sigh at every raised pimple, every minor imperfection, somehow, illogically blaming myself like I've failed, disappointed myself somehow. And when you're a minority in America, there can be layers of doubt. Your insecurities tinged with color. For me, there is the lingering, nagging question every time I meet a boy

I might kinda, maybe sorta like of whether my race matters, if he's already discounted my worth as a boyfriend because of the slant in my eyes, the yellow of my skin. In fact, when I met my first boyfriend, he uttered the line I've grown to hate more than anything else in the world. His name was Steve. A man named Steve, I've always imagined, would be an accountant or a banker who wore sneakers with his power suits and carried around a briefcase to feel official. But my Steve was a writer. He was tall-ish with dark ginger-brown hair, green-specked eyes, and a grin so mischievous it seemed to crawl out of the highlands of a Scottish romance novel and take my virginity against the rough hard bark of an evergreen forest.

We met at the Abbey in Los Angeles. He had been chatting with my moppy-headed friend Mark for a week, and they were meeting for drinks. Steve walked in, green T-shirt, brown sneakers, and jeans so fitted his zipper looked ready to burst. When Mark introduced us, Steve opened his lovely mouth and grinned, his dimples flashing. "Wow, you're really cute for an Asian guy." His teeth were so white, the orange light of sunset just starting to cut the fold of his biceps beneath the... wait, what? I know he meant it as a compliment, but instead it felt like my eyes were rotten teeth I should bring my hands up to cover. My race is not an obstacle I have to overcome. But I guess I should be happy for you that you're able to overlook such obvious deformities to find the beauty around it. Jerk. I plastered on a smile, resigned myself to never see him again, and tried to muster the best thank you I could without punching him in the face.

You'll find the signs all around you. Go on any dating/hook up site and read profile after profile of "No Asians, Blacks, Fats, or Femmes." Count the number of heads that turn away when you try to smile and say hello. Listen to the tittering conversation of the group in the red corner booth as the guy in the cowboy hat proclaims proudly amongst giggles and guffaws that he has *never* dated an Asian guy, how dare they. It doesn't stop. It gets pounded into your bones, tattooed on your skin. You can tell yourself everyday how beautiful you are, but it's hard to believe it's true if you're the only person who seems to think so.

I didn't feel like I deserved much for a long time. But as I've grown older, I've come to realize that trying to change people's minds about you, trying to convince them of your worth, is a sprint up an endless hill. The hardest argument isn't with others, it's with the thoughts that creep on you like a shiver in your spine. It's the moment of doubt before you open your mouth to say hello. It's the inspection of your reflection every morning, turning right, posing left, looking for just the right angle in the dull light of morning. It whispers, again and again, that you're not good enough. It's an addiction, you're not smart enough, not funny enough, not pretty enough, you can't seem to break. So you look for someone to fill in those spaces. Someone else who can make you feel as special as you always dreamed you were. But it's a façade. A hollow casing you won't be able to stand on. When the guy in the office you're hoping for turns away, when you scroll through endless profiles, skipping through all the pages your skin is too dark for, you'll be crushed. You'll feel ugly and unwanted, angry at yourself and the world for setting the values you don't fit into. And you should be angry. Because it is unfair. But when you're done, when you're done lighting the world on fire, crushing fingers and toes, breaking windows, and kicking down metaphorical doors, I hope you'll come to see that the only image that matters is how you see yourself.

There is someone out there who thinks you're ugly. You're not tall enough for them or rich enough or you're too fat or your nose is too big for your face. But you have to believe. Against all reason. You are good enough. You are capable and amazing and beautiful and lovely and you are here, right now, breathing, full of opportunities to change worlds and forge new definitions in your wake. If you can believe that, nobody can touch it, not some headless stranger on the Internet, not some twink in a white braided belt, not blond-haired, blue-eyed lovers desperate to be worshiped. And maybe, just maybe, you'll wake up one day, rub sleep from your eyes, yawn heavily into a foreign air. You'll climb out from the heat of night and find the world immersed in a brave new light. You may find to your surprise, a small sort of knowing on your cheeks, a quiet smile on your lips, that maybe, just maybe, you've learned to love the one thing you didn't know how.

Alone, Outside

G. Winston James

"I must be honest." I begin this way because I know that my method of writing will require that I constantly return to the start of this essay as I attempt to move forward. The first truth I must confess is that this is not an essay I'm immediately inspired to write as its genesis is not "in my heart" as it were, but rather arises from a "Call for Submissions" from a colleague whom I respect. That is to say that this essay emerges somewhat reluctantly from the social compact I yet maintain with others. As such the sentence with which I begin reflects that hesitancy and serves as a repeated reminder to myself, as I revise, that I am pledged finally, here and in my life, to resist the temptation to create work (to live a life) whose principle (if noble) purpose is to affirm others or to inspire, rather than to examine honestly who I am and why, absent as much as possible the considerations of others. This essay then is a metaphor for the life I'm living as I return again and again to where things began and examine what I've wrought in order to best move forward on a project I did not initially devise.

I write here as a Jamaican-born, gay man who indeed strongly considered (and perhaps attempted) suicide early on in his high school career. That I later convinced myself that my unhappiness, my desire to no longer be alive, was due to an ineffective coming to terms with my homosexuality comes as no surprise to me since that is a common enough explanation, one that is oft-repeated, and easy to come across in LGBT circles. It is, in fact, the explanation that my former teacher—a Catholic priest—offered when I determined I would no longer set foot in his apartment or allow him to touch and probe me as he once did soon after my high school graduation. It is an explanation that I would argue borders on the "useful" when one considers the struggle for LGBT rights in which we as a community, nation, and world are still embroiled, needing as we do to have clear, uncomplicated points around which to rally.

What is surprising to me is that until recently I allowed myself to forget the reason I told myself I wanted not so much to die as to "cease to be." According to my uninfluenced, not-yet political, hyper-curious, artistic teenage self I'd considered suicide not because of my unspeakable feelings towards other men (I actually got along quite creatively without announcing them, and escaped my childhood with very little teasing or bullying), but because I felt that life was an endless and exhausting series of decisions—one leading again and again to numerous others—in a sort of game (one I never asked to play) that seemed as impossible to win as to take a break from. I wondered then, much more strongly (or perhaps differently) than I do now, "What is the point?" "Why am I alive?"

I admit that I'm uncertain how much my outlook on life (my conflict with what seemed to be the violation of my birth—ripped from the *guff* as we are and ordered into the confinement of corporeal "reality") is influenced by my sexuality and the accompanying sense (even if unconscious) of LGBT folk being abnormal relative to the majority of society. It's certainly true that my Jamaican family home was not a place in which I was free to share stories about my same sex attractions. The few friends and acquaintances I had who later came to self-identify as LGBT were either questioning at the time and/or were well-practiced at hiding. At the same time, though, there was no shortage of opportunities (generally with men older than myself) to explore aspects (the physical, sexual ones) of my developing sexuality. I positively see in my childhood years the roots of my clandestine, adult erotic behaviors (having been introduced to empty lots, closets, shrubbery, peep shows, and porno theaters before I was sixteen). I saw those activities as adventures though; if anything, they mitigated my greater sense of desolation. I understand also, based on those ways in which I interacted with men in my youth, why it took some time for me to consider men with whom I had sex as viable sources for any type of emotional intimacy or security. That reality at the time, however, did not consciously worry me.

I cannot say with any confidence either how (if at all) causally linked my "unconventional" sexuality is to my (even as a Baptist church-raised adolescent) atavistic, heathen spirituality. Church was a place to go every Sunday. A chance to go to Sunday school with other children and to fall asleep during the main church service—kept awake only by whispering with my friends or listening to the Gospel Choir on those Sundays when its members were singing. Calvary Baptist offered me the opportunity to sing in the youth choir, to volunteer as an usher and to act (once the part of Moses) in Sunday school plays. Looking back now I have to say that I felt in some ways more welcomed, nurtured, and protected in church than I did in grammar school. My issues with the idea of church grew as I got older and had more to do with what I came to see as the display/performance aspect of the ministers and congregation than with any feeling at all of persecution for my homosexuality. Also as I became more educated, inquisitive, and individualistic I began to critique what appeared to be the unquestioning attitude of that same congregation. My problem with the church and religion is what I consider to be their flocking nature that can dull the mind and limit growth even as it provides sanctuary and inspiration.

Of the things that I am certain is that I felt different in ways that set me apart depressingly from other children and that I had parents who (despite clearly loving and caring for me) were not demonstrative, affectionate, or (I felt) progressive or culturally American enough to offer consolation. This difference went well beyond what I lusted for or felt sexual desire or eagerness towards. My sense of otherness involved very much the ways in which I sought and found refuge, inspiration, joy, solace, mystery, and magic. I was a scientist, occultist, and poet seemingly trapped in the bottle of my own mind. Time and again my peculiarity showed itself in the level, range, and manner of sway I allowed my inquisitiveness to have over my actions, often with little regard to moral or ethical implications or values. I was the black, teenage poet in urban Paterson, New Jersey, who clipped cuttings from neighbors' plants to root them, took in stray domestic animals, watched birds with binoculars, bought seeds and sat in the midst of sparrows and starlings to feed them, and volunteered as a candy striper on the one hand, while vivisecting worms, pinning bees to flowers, setting fires, peeping in neighbors' windows, attempting to conjure demons, and casting spells out of curiosity on the other.

Always as a backdrop to my movement and exploration (so often alone since I'd failed to find anyone who shared my vulnerabilities and more private interests) was the question of "God": the desire for an explanation for the breath and energy animating my body. I was a sixteen-year-old begging in various ways, "Earth and sky and sea and rain/Reach out your hands to me…Whisper to me the name of your creator…" Even now, twenty-seven years later, I remember the moment (as I performed the simple act of putting out the garbage on a snowy night) when those words came to my lips. I remember the sense of emptiness with regard to my life, the lack of motivation to continue this thing call "living."

I believe that the question of life's purpose was so pivotal to me as a teenager partially because I hadn't yet begun to (or even consider that I could realistically) live my life contentedly for myself, and even to a large extent by myself. I was still contemplating my own thoughts and actions through the eyes of others, and in so doing either coming up short (not fast enough, not quite smart enough, not aggressive enough, not outgoing enough) or deeming myself unattractively and unacceptably strange. I hadn't begun to take stock of who I was, to establish my own terms on which to carry out my life, nor demonstrate the force of will and confidence in my own existence and personhood required to reject the opinionated, expectant gaze of others. Having hit bottom at some point and survived my own directly suicidal hand, I realized that I did have some control over my life: death. I conceded that if I could (apparently quite easily) end the game that had so wearied me, I could also try to change its parameters.

That moment of seizing control, of having found and for a moment attempted (if half-heartedly) to press the "off" button allowed me to emerge still alive, with parents and siblings who continued to look and comport themselves as they always had, in a house where family dinner was still served that evening. No one was any the wiser in that moment than they had ever been to my despair. I felt foolish for having thought that killing myself would somehow have punished them for conceiving me and for being ill-equipped to recognize my suffering and unable to deliver adequate care. It dawned on me that walls did not talk and neither had I ever spoken to them about my feelings. My expectations (particularly based on the hardworking, focused on providing, generally uncommunicative people my parents are) had been completely unfair. As I watched them all going about their business oblivious to the finality that I'd been close to achieving, I was, perhaps for the first time (despite my failure) "glad to be alive." I had, in effect, without knowing or intending, hit "reset" and grasped that—as I've said elsewhere—at the end of the day "Nothing really matters."

"Nothing really matters" is somewhat Buddhist in its way of warning against attachments. That simple fact, once it became clear to me, was not only acceptable and life altering, but liberating. Once I'd turned my own gaze away from the dark mystery of God and the pressure of determining my shape and fit in some predetermined grand design, the straightforward answer to the question of life that I'd been asking myself became quite simply: living. Curiosity is enough. Experiencing for the sake of experiencing, doing precisely because I want to and can, or at least am able to try to, is more than sufficient, knowing that everything I will do here is associated with some wakening, arousing sensation, regardless of the fact that all of it passes. Life, ultimately, is little more and no less than a chance to do...for a measured while, and to (if I choose) partake in the diversion and career of projecting and plotting the course and results of my actions.

Once I'd set life itself aside as my enemy, though, I recognized that my own nature (tending toward the isolationist, perilous, emotional, and enchanted as I do) and society's expectations of me remained powerful forces ranked sometimes against one another and my peace of mind. In hindsight I assert that the greatest pall and drain on my life has been the perceived social requirement (instilled since earliest childhood) that I please, appease, impress, fit in, get along, and align myself with others—beginning with family (nuclear and extended), then friends, classmates, and endless others—"just because," regardless of any discernable affinity. I feel now that inasmuch as I allow myself to become "known" by these individuals and collectives I risk being kidnapped in a sense by the expectations that attach themselves to that "knowledge," that familiarity, and eventually being seduced into complicity in my own constraint.

This public more of conformity, I suppose, is at the very heart of the notion of "society," wherein individuals contort themselves for the good of the many and the whole, regardless of how perhaps unlike their "true selves" they become in the process. Those who are most successful in society, it turns out, are those who are most flexible (or forceful) and those who are most inured to or unaware of the pain and cost of psychological and spiritual suffering and limitation that they endure. This is not what I want for myself. Having chosen to live, I want to test the boundaries of who I'm becoming without being unduly influenced or restricted by others.

As a teenager I sensed not only that I didn't fit in, but that I would likely always be an outsider. Always galloping to some extent against the herd. Rescuing myself from being trampled now and again as I've found new friends, new groups and communities that I initially believe will be more welcoming, more ample, less confining. In the end, I've learned that herd jumping is not a solution for me and that "community" (no matter how defined, large, or well-meaning), if I'm not careful, vigilant, and protective of my self, my truth, and my evolutionary potential, is quite often a trap, coming as most (including the black LGBT community) do with unwritten and inflexible agendas, lists of guidelines, judgments, and requirements.

I moved to Florida several years ago and found myself outside of New York City's active, engaged, and activist gay community. In some ways it was like a breath of fresh air that allowed me to cogitate about the ways in which my sexuality, politics and identity had been influenced (perhaps in ways I may need to undo) by others, by a sense of community, by the reality of group struggle, and the notion of responsibility. I stood still a moment and accepted a truth that I'd been reluctantly living all along: that standing (being) alone for me is not only okay (despite society's call for the well-adjusted to be social) but desirable and essential for my spiritual, emotional, and psychic strength and health.

It's taken me decades to begin to unapologetically stand up for and defend my personhood, my individuality, my distinctiveness, my journey, and to understand that even my friends (my chosen family) can be (unintentionally, one hopes) repressive, misleading, immuring, and antagonistic towards personal change and transformation, which is ultimately what I believe life is all about. My own brush with depression and thoughts of suicide taught me to accept and, in fact, nurture a sense of mystery and curiosity about where it is that I'm going as an individual, with particular emphasis on originality, integrity, courage, and honesty to myself on my particular odyssey. With few true friends, I've gladly chosen quality over quantity and endeavor to be clear, fair, and realistic about my expectations of others, recognizing that my own actualization and affirmation are solely my responsibility.

"I will lift up mine eyes unto the hills, from whence cometh my help..." (Psalm 121) Nowadays, my help cometh most importantly from within, as I'm learning to celebrate myself and my experiences, and to stand comfortably alone outside of the herd, to walk boldly alongside all of the variously established norms.

When the Strong Grow Weak

Kenyon Farrow

I have read too many stories about lesbian, gay, bisexual, or queer young people who have decided the world was too much for them and took their own lives. Although I was sympathetic to their suffering, I did nothing about it. As a black gay man, all too familiar with the suffocating weight of homophobia, it still did not connect for me.

But then it happened. In mid-October 2010, as I was preparing to shut my computer down for the night, I came across a series of disturbing notices on my Facebook news feed, coming from the page of Joseph Jefferson, a twenty-six-year-old black gay man, who was well known in New York City as an AIDS activist and community leader. People were beginning to post messages expressing their shock and grief, and a phone call to a friend confirmed what his Facebook page hinted: Joseph had committed suicide just a few hours earlier. His Facebook page bore his final words to the world:

"I could not bear the burden of living as a gay man of color in a world grown cold and hateful towards those of us who live and love differently than the so-called 'social mainstream.'"

I had known Joseph for about five years while doing HIV advocacy work in New York City, and he was often the youngest person sitting at many of the tables of advocates representing different organizations. I had always been impressed by his intelligence, and his charisma, and I noticed other young black and brown queer and trans youth were attracted to him and sought his friendship, help, and guidance.

We lived in the same neighborhood, and I often ran into Joseph at the subway station, where we'd hug and kiss hello, and if going the same direction, make small talk on our way to and fro. I thought he would be one of the next generation of leaders of black gay men. He had several friends and mentors, and I wanted to get to know him better, but I never told him because I was fearful he may perceive me as disingenuously looking for a way to sleep with him.

Now that I am a gay man in my mid thirties, I walk a fine line, and as I age, I am becoming more aware of the ageism in our community. Almost any intergenerational relationship or relationship between gay men where there is a significant age gap, be it sexual or platonic, will be perceived as one of potential, if not outright, exploitation of the younger by the older. This dynamic is the sole reason I never reached out to Joseph and said, "I appreciate all that you do, brother, I am invested in you and want to be in your life."

I do not know if my words would have made a difference in whether Joseph chose to live or not. He had attempted suicide at least once before, and after he died it was revealed that he suffered from bouts of depression, especially since the death of his mother some years earlier.

Whatever the outcome, I know that I did not make the effort to extend beyond my fear of rejection to reach out to someone I had some investment in and affection toward. But my discomfort is only part of what I am trying to sort through. I am also trying to understand why I was so shocked and devastated by his suicide.

Though black, gay, and a part of the working poor, Joseph did not, in my mind, fit the "suicide profile." He was one of us. He was a so-called "leader." He was "doing the work." He understood the "isms" and the "intersections." He was a "bridge builder." He was all of the buzzwords we use to describe the people we think should get it and should be able to survive to fight again the next day.

But as I am coming to think through this, I am realizing that the work, and how we go about it, is part of the problem.

I am a writer, always busy writing and blogging about race, class, gender, and politics. My blog has captured many of the murders of people in our community, and the comments often written by friends and family members of the departed become an online epitaph to the lives of many queer and trans people of color who were murdered. The eulogies no one dared utter at their funerals and memorials.

When I served as executive director of Queers for Economic Justice, a small nonprofit organization dedicated to economic justice issues impacting low-income and working-class LGBTQ people in New York City, our staff size fell from five to three due to the economic downturn. I was left as the primary fundraiser and grant writer, in charge of fiscal management and program support, and I was responsible for almost all of our national program work, which required me to spend a lot of time traveling across the country for meetings, panels, and conferences. It was an impossible amount of work for one person to do effectively, but all too often many of us doing grassroots organizing find ourselves in this situation.

While my organization embraced the goals of larger

transformative change, the reality is that the work itself, especially in the nonprofit model, can help produce the same sense of isolation we struggled to battle against. Far too often we mirror depersonalized (and deeply dehumanizing) corporate models, where workers are expected to subsume all other issues, conflicts, traumas, and personal histories for the benefit of being "productive."

As I climbed the nonprofit ladder of success to become an executive director, I found I had fewer options for self-care, for caring for my family and friends, and for personal development that reflected the values we tried to achieve with our work.

To be blunt, I had become a worse friend, a less attentive partner, and a much more hands-off brother, uncle, son, and cousin to a family that I thought of much more often than I spoke to or saw. After all, to be a better friend, partner, brother, uncle, son, or cousin would mean less time to do the work of trying to maintain and build an institution.

Although many of our organizations help to do the work that builds community, the staffs of these organizations are often the worst at being able to take care of themselves, which includes making time for the community outside of our meetings and official "work" spaces. People like Joseph should be a priority for us too.

Admittedly, I have received emails and phone calls from friends inviting me to spend time with them, and many of these requests I have ignored out of sheer exhaustion. At the time, I could only deal with the things that were right in front of my face. But we have to mean more to each other than a political idea or another call to make on a laundry list of things to do for the day.

We also need to take care of ourselves. Based on the outpouring of grief by hundreds of people who turned out for community rallies and memorials to Joseph, he took his role as leader and mentor very seriously, and he made himself available to people who needed his help. But where did he turn for support?

As a nonprofit worker, I have struggled to find a place for support when I needed it. It can be difficult to seek support outside of your organization without potentially damaging the organization's reputation, which can affect fundraising and your own job security. Therefore, many of us bear the burden of our stress by suffering in silence. Silence turned inward often produces depression, migraine headaches, high blood pressure, and insomnia, and can lead to alternative and often self-destructive patterns to manage the stress, like alcohol and substance abuse, overeating, and aggressive or violent behavior.

While I have met some of the most daring, intelligent, sexy, and innovative people working in the movement, I have also met some of the most depressed, self-obsessed, and undermining people who call themselves fighters for social justice.

The outbreak of suicides in our community, including my friend Joseph Jefferson, points to the utter failure of our various movements. For instance, white gay sex-columnist Dan Savage was celebrated for launching the "It Gets Better" campaign, which enabled people to create their own video messages to LGBT youth, telling them to just "hang in there." That makes people feel good, but the campaign makes a range of assumptions about the audience. For young people who are experiencing poverty, racism, HIV, bad public schools, or violence within their homes, it may not "just get better" by virtue of getting older.

These campaigns also allowed politicians like New York Mayor Michael Bloomberg to post videos that make them appear "gay friendly" while simultaneously trying to cut funding for homeless LGBT youth services in the city. In contrast, the Gay Straight Alliance Network created a "Make It Better" campaign, which provided a more useful framework by offering tools to LGBT youth and by showing how real people got engaged in their own healing, even when it did not just "get better" by virtue of time.

While Savage's campaign reflected a white, upper-class male

viewpoint of gay life, the mainstream equality movement has shown even worse support and engagement on issues impacting queer and trans youth.

Most of the national equality organizations use bullying and suicide newspaper headlines as a hook for a fundraising pitch. At the same time, the mainstream movement has bet all of its chips on a legislative strategy of achieving marriage equality, ending "Don't Ask, Don't Tell," and passing civil rights legislation like hate crimes laws and the Employment Non-Discrimination Act. They believe that if LGBT people win legal victories, more LGBT people will be able to participate as full citizens, and that participation will mean that homo/transphobia will largely become a thing of the past.

This strategy is foolhardy, as demonstrated in South Africa, which has written anti-discrimination laws into its constitution but has not reduced the threat of violence, including the targeting of lesbians for so called "corrective rape." Nor has it actually changed the economic conditions that keep black South Africans, including many queer and trans South Africans, desperately poor in a nation where wealth remains largely in the hands of whites. Similarly, we can expect that any LGBT strategy in the US focused primarily on political "inclusion" will fail to deal with the underlying socioeconomic conditions that disproportionately affect queer people of color.

The task before us is huge and will require a different kind of organization and a different kind of organizing. It cannot burn out or isolate those of us who labor in it as workers, nor can it assume legislative or policy wins will positively impact all queer or trans people.

I don't want to hear about another series of suicides that I take in stride because I have grown so comfortable with their occurrence. Nor do I want to be shocked into the gravity of the situation just because one of them happened to be someone I knew personally. I don't want to be too exhausted pushing paper to satisfy someone or some foundation I don't care about to take care of myself and my family and friends. I don't want to lead the so-called movement while too busy to notice the comrades behind me who have dropped dead from the struggle before we crossed the finish line.

I want you to matter. I want me to matter. I want you and me to know, before it is too late, that we matter to each other.

FAITH UNDER FIRE

The Holy Redeemer

Victor Yates

couldn't believe it
still was wondering was it true
he's such a gentleman, the pastor
no one never knew

hope he gets that-there therapy
straightens himself and recovers
this has the church shaken
we can't lose another brother

pastor went to Estabrook Park
just after Sunday service
the word, a taste on his lips, it
wasn't dark but he wasn't nervous

a little bear lured him with his pot
pastor dropped his pants dropped
the bear, a cop, withdrew
said seeing pastor's penis flop was lewd

Coventry, Christ, and Coming of Age

Topher Campbell

It's one thing to come out to your school at fifteen, as I did, but it's another thing to come out in a black-led fundamentalist Pentecostal Church if you are a lay preacher. At fifteen I decided to do both: first to come out at school as a gay teen and second to be born again in the blood of Christ.

It was the 1980s and I was living in Coventry, a small city in the center of England at a time when Elton John, George Michael, Justin Fashanu, and Boy George had yet to come out. Margaret Thatcher was still mashing up things in government and institutionalized homophobia was rampant. A controversial new law, Section 28, supported by the African and Caribbean Evangelical Association, prohibited schools from teaching about homosexuality in the classroom.

But something within me had stirred. I knew I liked guys, and at the time I was dating a girl and a boy, although the boy was in love with a girl who later became pregnant. It wasn't like dating in the States. It was more like quick fumbles and heavy snogs here and there, and then a sort of hanging around each other after school.

I was being mentored by my English teacher, Wes Webb, who had recently come out and was undergoing a separation from his wife. It seemed to me a very brave and courageous act at the time. After the school was scandalized by his self-outing, I somehow managed to tell him about my confused feelings. I remember his less than sensational response, an amused smile, which helped me trust him and continue to seek out his company between classes and after school.

"I think I'm gonna tell the headmaster," I said to Wes one afternoon as I sat in his office. Wes looked at me askance and laughed nervously. "And that would be because…?"

"I don't know, I think it's important to be seen as out. After all, you did it." Wes just groaned and wished me the best. He could hardly argue against me, as he had put his whole career on the line and was struggling to come to terms with his own big life change. More than that, he told me later, he had committed himself to a hands-off approach to me and was willing to support who I was as opposed to how people thought I should be.

The headmaster's office was located on The Bridge, a very big part of the school suspended on concrete stilts that joined one teaching block to another. The Bridge was only open to teachers and to sixth-formers, who were a couple of years older than me but were known as the "Big Boys and Girls" and mysteriously had more freedom and often more facial hair and bigger breasts. Some, like an Asian guy called Jaswant, were also incredibly beautiful and, of course, unobtainable. There were therefore a few good reasons to want to go on The Bridge.

I fearlessly relished the thought of stepping foot on a part of the school rarely allowed visits by mere lowly pupils like me. The headmaster's office was placed at the center, rather like the King's Chamber in Henry VIII's day. As with Henry VIII, this central position seemed to make the occupant more powerful.

One had to travel through several corridors, past the staff room, and around corners to be rewarded by the plain wooden door titled "Mr. Dean."

"Sit here," said the secretary. "Mr. Dean will be with you in a minute."

Actually it was less than a minute before the door swung open and a gracious, charismatic and very handsome man in a cheap suit sat me down.

An ex-Welsh rugby player, Mr. Dean was a big man who I imagined drank heavily and punched people when he was young. I was a tall, skinny, sixty-pound black boy. He stood for a minute behind his desk, and then, as if realizing how intimidating he could be, sat down with a thud.

I had met my match.

"I think you should be doing more for gay pupils in this school," I demanded.

"Yes. Yes, of course, and we will. It's good of you to come see me and I know it must be hard and its great that you are at Stringer and please come back and talk to me about this. We care so much for all our pupils at Stringer, and, well, this cannot be the end of this, and we will do everything we can in the future. My door is always open."

The door closed behind me.

So there I was once again outside the plain wooden door, on The Bridge, but this time trying to find my way back through the corridors and corners. Mr. Dean had talked me out of his office and all my dreams of a "New Gay Dawn" had evaporated. It was as if in his embarrassment and hurried schedule he had decided to say yes to everything while managing to do absolutely nothing. We never spoke about this again, and very soon afterwards Mr. Dean resigned in the middle of a divorce from Mrs. Dean, the head of music.

After my meeting with the headmaster, things got darker. I turned inward and tried to make sense of the powerful emerging emotions I felt. Why couldn't I just be normal? Why am I more interested in the video when Duran Duran's clothes are blown tight across their bodies on that bloody boat? Why is the Incredible Hulk more exciting when he is in the ripped shorts than when he is plain old David Banner? What is in those magazines on the top shelf? And as for the true love cartoons in *The Sun* newspaper, where guys regularly get in and out of bed half dressed, oh Lord. And why, oh why, don't I get to meet those guys in Michael's vids? "Beat it, just beat it, beat it, beat it, beat it, oh, beat it!" Oh, how can I get out of this messy flesh?

I realized with horror that this wasn't a game. It wasn't just a phase, and even though I appeared all grown up making my coming out plans, when I looked around I found myself utterly alone. It was crushing and confusing. How was I supposed to continue living with this? I was stuck with it, and there was no way out.

My big sister Jenny came to the rescue, sort of. Jenny was my best friend. I remember her vaguely when I started at Stringer as being the embarrassing girl who was always snogging some boy in some murky corner. I was twelve and had just returned to my mother's home after spending my entire life in foster care and children's homes, and I was achingly, painfully shy. I kept my distance then. But gradually over the years she took more interest in me. On refection I think I was a good guinea pig for her emerging bossiness and a neat deflection for her obsessiveness. She in turn fulfilled my need for attention and excused me from having to think too hard about anything.

"It would be better if you wore that jumper with that."

"No, a shirt is good."

"Those shoes are nice but need a polishing."

"Where have you been all day? Mum wants you."

"Have you eaten?"

(and my favorite) "Have you washed down there?"

Jenny had also been fostered for a large part of her life by the Taffs. I knew nothing about these people or why they had taken her on, and my mother didn't really explain anything. All I know is that Jenny ended up with two Mums. Mrs. Taff was a great, big woman with a huge, round face, big teeth, big appetite, big eyes and a big lovable chuckle that turned into a big laugh: she was just *big*. She had a warm, seductive, deep voice and a way of looking deep into you. I liked her, but I was scared of her.

Minister Taff, her husband, on the other hand, was like Stan Laurel from Laurel and Hardy. Like Stan, he was socially inept, always bungling things and just never got it right. If there were an item to be forgotten, Minister Taff would forget it. Mrs. Taff would always be rocking back and forth in frustration and rolling her eyes every time he did something off-key. A bit like Hardy, actually, but funnier because it was happening right in front of me every Sunday before, during and after church. Sister Taff and Minister Taff were the Elder Sister and Minister of the United Reformed Pentecostal Church of God.

They instilled religion into Jenny and made it clear that Jesus was about to return any day now—so you better watch out! Jenny had by now stopped snogging any boy she found and started wearing little hats, cute socks, long skirts, and one-piece dresses.

"Why don't you come with me to church tomorrow," Jenny said one Saturday.

"Am I doing anything on Sunday?" I thought to myself, trying to remember if there was anything juicy on the telly.

I was bored and looking for a way out of the sexual fire raging within. By this time I was fantasizing about every boy in my school. First, there were the guys on the basketball team, the teenage boys with man-boy muscles. But I also dreamed of the brainy guys in the chemistry class whose glasses provided a heated distraction. But the ultimate distraction: the guys on the basketball teams we played. The ones I had to mark or bump and bounce off every other bloody week. The ones who changed in front of us when we had to share a locker room. I was on fire.

Guilt and worry also added to the hurricane of emotions

So what harm could a little trip to Jenny's funny church do?

I grew up with white people and had never been amongst many black people until I went to live with my mother and met all my brothers and sister. I had been to church often before, sang carols at Christmas, celebrated Easter, but never had I experienced the wall, the solid concrete mix of emotion, hysteria, and performance that hit me that Sunday on my first visit to an all-black Pentecostal church. People jumped up and down to the point of levitation; people cried frustrating, piecing cries of agony and joy; people spoke in gibberish like they were possessed. The ferocious, enthusiastic way everyone sang full-voiced and clapped in staccato rhythms literally rattled my internal organs. I was hooked! This place would certainly be able to forge a new kind of me.

I submerged myself in this new world, and within weeks I was baptized in the blood of Jesus, totally committed and ready to receive the Holy Ghost. Innocently, I did not think my emerging sexuality was a problem with my religion. I believed that God is Love and that Jesus was more concerned with the idea of Love than of Hell and damnation. I'd found a way out.

This, however, was not the case for the congregation. Time and again their obsession with the evils of homosexuality were duly supported by a reasoned and passionate condemnation from the pulpit. There was, of course, no hatred or even disgust in this condemnation, only arguments that claimed to be about love and forgiveness. After a year or so of soaking up this intense experience, the new me didn't emerge either. Instead I became the "Two Me."

"One Me" was the kid who everybody thought was cute and intelligent, well-behaved and well-mannered. I was going to school and staying in class. I helped around the house. I had a part-time job. I was quiet at home and diligent at church.

"Two Me" masturbated endlessly and looked for every opportunity to meet boys. Two Me hung around in parks and rode buses and sat in the City Centre, waiting, looking, and hoping for that thrill. Sometimes that thrill would come and I'd find myself in his arms again. But then Two Me would drown in heavy guilt and emptiness as I fought my craving for affection and love. Two Me prayed fervently, ardently day and night to be normal. The conflict between my position as a God-fearing lay preacher and my sexual feelings led me to contact the local gay Christian group.

I'd found the number of the gay Christian group in one of those dirty magazines on the top shelf that Two Me had brazenly purchased (okay, stolen, I was too young to buy one). After weeks of procrastination and fear and after numerous attempts at dialing the number, I just picked up the phone and dialed swiftly.

"Hello, Gay Christian Association...Hello...Hello...?"

I swiftly put the phone down again.

Suddenly I knew there might be other gay people. I did this several times just to hear the man's voice. After all, it could have been a mistake.

Eventually, One Me took over and just said, "I am a Christian and need to talk to somebody about being gay." Within a week, after having lied to my Mum about a basketball match, I arranged to meet the man who had answered the phone in Coventry City Centre.

He was a tall man with dark hair and probably twice my age. I got into his car, and we spoke for a short time.

"Are you gay?" I asked hopefully.

"Yes," he said casually.

"Are you a Christian?"

"Yes." He looked at me intently.

I was dying to talk about all my troubles, and even though part of me wasn't sure if this old white guy would understand, I was reassured because he was gay and a Christian. There was silence in the car. He asked a few questions about where I was from and how old I was. He promised we could talk later.

He took me to a boring church recital in Bedworth, a small town outside Coventry, where the formality of the service was so dry it made me thirsty and fidgety; and the people appeared to be made of pure Bakelite compared to the white-hot heat of my own church. The promised talk seemed to have vanished so I sat glumly. We made our way through the badly-lit streets back to Coventry. I hadn't any money to get home so I was at least thankful for the lift, and I'd be home without my mum asking intrusive questions.

I sat in the car, tense and unsure as he drove past my neighborhood.

"My home is that way," I said, worried that I wouldn't be able to explain yet another late night to my mum. Coventry didn't have late-night public transport then, and I'd used all my money just to get across town to meet him. I needed this ginger guy to take me home safely. Instead he was driving farther and farther away form where I lived. I was a hostage.

"Don't worry, I'll get you home," he said. I was worried.

We arrived at a house in a well-off part of town on the other side of Coventry. I'd not been there before, and I had no idea where I was or what was about to happen. I was both curious and anxious. I wondered what the house looked like inside and if I'd ever be able to afford that one day.

"Come in and have some tea and we can talk." It seemed a cool enough suggestion and I was relieved, thinking this will be over in no time and I'll get back home and be in my bedroom busy thinking over the night's events very soon. We had talked earlier but I convinced myself he wanted to give me some more advice and perhaps something that would really help my situation. I really thought there was a solution to getting the demon out of me. Maybe this guy knew. I went into his house full of hope.

I ignored the way he looked at me. Looked into me. I ignored the way he sat next to me on the sofa, close, and the way he touched my hand when he asked, "Are you alright?"

I did not answer; didn't know how to answer. His hand stayed on mine. I hoped that he was going to say something kind, wise, meaningful. He shuffled closer to me. His leg touched mine. His eyes held a steady gaze. I felt very unsettled at this moment and got up and moved away from him, putting as much space between him and me in the large, clean living room, as large as the floor of my mum's whole house.

He got up and followed me. I went behind the sofa. He grabbed me, and I tried to fight him off. He fought back. He was brave. I was a sixteen-year-old boy, nearly seventeen, tall and strong. I'd had a few fights and won them all.

Finally, he stopped and sat down. "Do you want a lift home? Does your mum know where you are?" he whispered.

He looked at me not so much threatening as pleading whilst at the same time gripping my arms and forcing them tight around my back. This time I had to give in. I hated him so much. This old man. I hated myself, too, as I let myself enjoy his closeness. I let him touch me and hold me. Kiss me. His hold was intense, his hands full of authority and trespass. This was not the tentative fumble of the boys I met at the bus stop or the tenderness of my first kiss with my first girlfriend. This was a man who knew what he was doing. His mouth all over me. His hands enjoying every moment. He undressed me, and I started to feel detached. I was just there. I just wanted it to finish so I could get home. I was forced to lie there naked. I felt myself positioned, placed with careful aggression in a way that suited him.

He entered me.

Time

Stood

Still.

I don't remember breathing.

Thankfully, mercifully, my teenage body gave in. I came—but too early for him. Too early for him to do any real harm. My hurt body or some other force made him give up. He stopped suddenly. "I'll take you home."

I so wanted, needed, ached to be home. What made it worse is that I actually enjoyed the experience.

This guy had used threats and the privilege of age and my lack of money to hold me hostage. At one point I had found myself holding him close as he kissed me. My raw emotional needs had turned his ugly behavior into a good thing for my desire. For many years after, I reasoned I had "allowed" it. Invited it. For years I could only blame myself. Then, in a brief moment during a conversation years later with a friend who told me he had been abused time and again, I said, "Nothing like that happened to me, I'm so lucky...but there was this guy and..." I stopped talking. In that moment I slowly realized what that man had done.

I felt no sense of panic or crisis in the days and weeks that followed. Just resolve to rid myself of this peril. I realized I needed to accept myself wholly or forever live in pain.

Wes stayed true to his word of supporting me as I am. I liked being around him. He had let me into his home and opened his life to me. He became a sane and calm counterpoint to the hysteria raging inside.

At eighteen I had moved away from home and was living in Brighton on the South Coast. I had been offered a place at the University of Sussex. Coventry offered no prospects of a future for me. My experiences at University were taking me closer toward an inevitable choice. I was meeting people from all over the world, from different backgrounds, making new friends, and feeling my way through myriad choices of identity.

"What's it like to be black and gay on campus?" Louise, a new friend, asked. It was a naïve question but also one that reflected the way in which I was allowing myself to be seen in the world. Without a defined strategy the true me was emerging anyway.

"Black and gay," I thought. "Yes, I suppose I am." I was coming to terms with the permanence of this thing. It was a deeper sense of identity than the posturing I had tried on Mr. Dean. There were no other black gay people in my life; the only other visible gay people were white and no public figures were openly gay. It was therefore difficult to know how to be who I was. I didn't know it then, but I was to be amongst the first generation of out black people in the UK.

Years later, a boyfriend pointed out to me that the most important decisions in life are made quietly. In the movies and on TV there is always a big drama and lots of loud music that accompanies good or bad news. However, in life, perhaps the most important things we say to ourselves are in those quiet times. Just like the motion of light in water, as Samuel R. Delany put it; moments of clarity flicker into being almost from nowhere. In that gentle conversation with my new friend, I had decided to come to terms with who I was. I was no longer filled with anxiety and guilt.

Then this moment of light, this glimpse of true self became like a beacon of purpose that guided me to write a letter to Jenny explaining that I had been struggling with my sexuality for some time. I explained that despite years of torment and self-hate, I now found myself in a calmer, accepting space. It was important for me to tell my sister because I loved her dearly and saw that she, too, loved me. Then as now, I believe in love.

"It's a dirty nasty sin," she responded. "It's evil. You are going to go to Hell." Her condemnation was so absolute that it shocked me. Unfortunately, she was relying on the full force of the irrational logic of a belief system that ran through her veins, thicker, it seems, than blood. The very thought of her brother being "possessed" by this "demon" drove her to tears. Her words seemed incongruous as we sat high up on the roof of my shared Marine Square flat on the seafront in Brighton. The location allowed for a glorious view of the English Channel and a majestic panorama of the open sky and blazing sun.

Jenny had come to visit me. This was the conclusion of her thoughts after several months of talking back and forth. I had constantly and honestly tried to explain the extent of my feelings and aspirations as a young man. I desperately wanted to keep her and the church in my life, but I was also not prepared to live a lie or repress any part of me anymore.

One Me and Two Me had to become just Me and there was no other way forward.

"If you continue with this behavior, then I will not talk to you ever again," she said. "I can't have anything to do with you. I can't condone evil."

"You really mean that?"

"Yes. Jesus would not allow it and my devotion is to His will."

The brutality, and to be truthful, stupidity, of this is plain to see now, but at the time it was the logic that offended me.

I thought that if my own sister cannot see past the rhetoric of Old Testament sin and damnation and not see that God is really about love and compassion then this whole thing called Christianity is no longer for me. Jenny was my best friend in the family. It was a fierce betrayal that made me leave the church immediately and vow never to return.

It is a heavy thing for black people to loose a connection with family, for often it provides a space that acts as a counter weight to racism in the wider world.

Even so, I didn't stop there. I also came out to my mother around this time, again with a letter. Her reaction: she didn't eat for a week. In later years, before my mother died, we managed to forge a very close relationship. I was also heartened by her robust defense of me over time whenever my siblings, especially my older sister, talked about how disgusting I was and how I was bound for Hell.

I remember coming home late one evening when visiting home. I'd been out exploring Coventry's nightlife. My mum, awoken by my drunken stumbling about the house, opened her bedroom door and said, "Where have you been? How was the gay club?"

It floored me. After all the struggle and all the intense introspection, the humor and simplicity of my mum's words made it all worthwhile. I was home.

The idea of homosexuality in fundamentalist black churches is always treated with hysteria and hyperbole, ridicule and disdain. "God made Adam and Eve, not Adam and Steve" is the not-very-funny joke used often by church leaders. This is said despite the fact that black churches in the UK, just like their US counterparts, are populated by men and women who "praise Jesus" Sunday morning, hours after raving at black gay clubs Saturday night. In a world where black people, especially men, have a lower life expectancy and are subject to so many obstacles, it is strange and dangerous for our communities to ostracize their sons and daughters. Our communities are already full of secrets and lies.

The showdown with my sister helped to resolve the conflict in my life. The Me that I was searching for was discovered in ways I could never have imagined at fifteen. Instead of living in a permanent state of confusion and anxiety, I resolved to live openly, and the places I've seen and the people I have met would not have been accessible to me if I'd denied my true nature.

Of course, some of the Bible-thumping preacher's zeal I picked up from those days remains. That sense of purpose is embedded in my life and work, and like all Holy Rollers, I continue to keep my eye on the prize. Thankfully, too, there have been many times when the quiet flicker of truth has guided me since, which is a good and necessary thing. Now, whenever I find myself striving for a solution, I try to let time pass, so that I can listen to that quiet voice and let it show me the way.

Religious Zombies
Clay Cane

Zombies want to eat your brains. The goal of the walking dead is to colonize the globe and force an irreversible sickness upon others. "There are no survivors. It's just us in here and them out there," is a line from the opening scene of *28 Weeks Later*, the classic zombie apocalypse film. Within seconds of the ominous warning, the zombies attack and ravage everything in sight, passing on their disease of rage. Every day we are surviving a zombie attack in the form of "religious zombies." Brain-dead, maniac, and unconscious; you don't have to go to them, they'll come to you. Whether it's the *700 Club*, Jehovah's Witnesses banging at your door, or religious doctrines thrust into legislation, it's a battlefield. Religious zombies stalk funerals ("God Hates Fags"), colonize the streets with wild rants (Israelite street preachers), plucking at passersby, looking for new victims. Even in the daylight there is always someone trying to eat your brain; nightfall isn't necessary to let the darkness in.

"My mum, my dad—they tried to kill me," a child survivor cried in *28 Weeks Later*. Many have been killed by their parents due to religion. Whether it was a killing of their spirit or a brainwashing of their soul, they were the undead, unable to receive or give love. Religious zombies don't stop to think about what is being said or taught. They explain their hate with rhetoric from the Bible or whatever handbook for the spirit to which they subscribe. Religion often teaches and reinforces otherness, and religious zombies will attack anyone: family, friends, co-workers, and especially themselves.

What has always intrigued me about religion is not its alleged beauty or inspiration, but the characters and the psychodramas who come out of religious institutions. Black or white, when people believe they are doing work in the name of goodness, otherwise known as their God, there is a power they feel they possess. This power can be lethal, especially if held within an oppressed group. But in many ways, religion is meant for the poor and meek to stay quiet and content.

My experiences with religion are not based on Jesus, Allah, Oshun, or Buddha but more on the people who preach. Being a charismatic celebrity with a stage presence can garner millions of dollars at the pulpit. Religion is profitable, which is obvious when the Vatican controls more wealth than Pepsi.

In one of my first experiences with the fever of religion, I was living in Washington State as a child and attended a Christian summer camp with a white church. Far from religious, my mother was hesitant about my participation in the camp. Throughout my childhood my mom insisted I would not be raised with religion. Her family was sadly destroyed when her mother became a devout Jehovah's Witness. Family members weren't allowed to speak to each other, some were "disassociated" for random infractions—even her own mother ended up being disassociated. Her family never reconciled after the attack of the Witnesses. When a Jehovah's Witness randomly knocked on our door, my always-colorful mother would yell, "Get away from my house! Ya'll fucked up my life enough!" Nonetheless, our neighbors assured her the camp was run by Christians, not by fanatical Bible beaters—Bible beaters never think they are fanatical.

My best friend was also attending and his parents paid for me to go, knowing my mother could not afford the pricey fees. A group of twenty kids traveled deep into the woods of Washington State for the camp. I soon realized it was focused less on summer games and more on the vengeance of God, sinful music (especially the Madonna and Prince songs I loved), and anything under the blood-filled sun of Revelations. By night one, those upper-class Christian whites scared the good-golly-Jim-Crow-Jesus hell out of me.

On our last night, we sat on metal folding chairs in a dark, carpeted basement with no windows and a musty smell in the air that reeked like a dungeon. We were encouraged to confess our childhood sins. The adults stood stoically in front of us children. In a monotone yet terrifying voice, they read the most horrific of scriptures. If zombies could talk they would sound like these possessed adults. Fearing we would burn in Hell, the children cried about Jesus and promised never to sin again. Kids reverberated, hollered and trembled with the supposed love of Christ.

When I returned home, I cried to my mom for days about the fear of Hell. I even considered throwing out all of my Prince and Madonna records, threatening to only listen to Amy Grant—now *that* is a true sin.

My mother phoned our "Christian" neighbors and cursed them out so severely that I was banned from speaking to my best friend again. They decided my mother and I were tawdry sinners while they were simply spreading the love of Christ. That was my last experience with religion in the white community.

Upper-class, white religious families have the resources to send their kids to expensive camps to indoctrinate them. In the black community, the resources to brainwash children were not as accessible, but far more creative.

By my early teens I was living in West Philadelphia, strikingly different from Washington State. Before I moved to the City of Brotherly Love, I visited often and was always shocked at the number of churches in the neighborhoods. Almost every corner provided a church along with drug dealers, prostitutes, and alcoholics. I wondered why they would spend so much time around a church. Weren't they embarrassed?

I would soon learn these "degenerates" marked their territory on certain church corners because that was where they could make the most cash. The hookers had plenty of clientele who attended and worked at the church. The drug dealers could always sell their crack, weed, and any other mixtures to members of the congregation. And, the alcohol, well, of course, everyone was getting their drink on. This "place of worship" fit right in with the street urchins—even if pastors would damn them to Hell every Sunday, but lay down with them later that night.

My older cousin became deeply involved in an underground church in Philly, which were all the rage in Philadelphia during the mid-nineties. Someone decided God spoke to her and—abracadabra, she was ready to save souls. I followed my favorite cousin who insisted I attend one of the "services." I had been to black churches before, but I had never attended something as underground as the "event" I witnessed in someone's row house—a far cry from the ritzy Christian camp in Washington State.

Once again, I found myself in a dark room listening to a zombie roaring about the love of Christ. The several girls and few boys, who clearly fit anyone's stereotypical perception of what it means to be gay, packed in a living room. A black woman shrieked the Word, gripping her tattered Bible, shaking it at the ceiling and asking if we wanted to burst into flames. Unlike the monotone voice of the whites at the Christian camp, this "preacher" was filled with rage. "Satan is everywhere! Everywhere!" she hollered, her eyeballs manically bouncing in their sockets. "He's gonna get ya' if ya' don't repent fo' yo' sins! Repent, children, or burn in the furnace of Hell!" Her wild rants continued until one by one everyone got "da' spirit." Teens jumped, screamed, spoke in tongues, and dropped to the dirty, red velvet, carpeted floor.

I scanned the room but remained quiet, in a deep prayer that I wouldn't be forced to throw myself to the filthy carpet. Suddenly, my cousin caught the spirit, too, flung her arms in the air, shrieked from her throat and withered around on the floor. However, she moved her head back and forth ever so softly and I knew why—she just got her hair done and no amount of spirit would ruin her fresh, burgundy finger waves!

I stood still, along with another girl, but I didn't want to be the last one standing. It would be like being picked last at school for the kickball team. I didn't want people to think Christ picked me last!

So, I decided it was time for me to perform. Faking the Holy Ghost, I flew my arms up, spoke in tongues, fell to the floor (scuffing my new white Reeboks) and shook it up like a Patti LaBelle drag queen. My cousin hollered and grabbed onto me because I had finally gotten the spirit, and she held me to her bosom as if we were Jesus and Mary. Everyone was so proud she brought me; I was special. Then we were ordered to pay ten dollars.

I understand the black church is steeped in history and tradition. Having majored in African American Studies in college, I fully comprehend how the black church provided safe spaces for African Americans to gather without the presence of whites. That said, today, I strongly believe many sectors of the black church are losing relevance, compassion, and reality.

I am not an atheist, but I am no Christian either. As Dr. Hubert Harrison, a member of the Socialist/Independent Party during the Harlem Renaissance, once said, "Any black person who accepts orthodox Christianity needs to have his head examined. I refuse to worship a lily-white God and a Jim Crow Jesus." Following Dr. Harrison's line of reasoning, some of these church members need CAT scans.

In the summer of 2005, I landed my first professional writing assignment for a website called BlackPlanet.com, which at the time was the top-ranked site for African Americans. I wrote an article titled "Black, Gay, and Beyond HIV," and I trekked to the soul of Brooklyn for a story on an organization called People of Color in Crisis (POCC), which is now closed.

POCC was one of few organizations in New York City reaching out to African American gay and bisexual men who were infected with HIV/AIDS. Formed in 1988 by African American and West Indian gay men who were deeply concerned about the lack of HIV/AIDS awareness in the black community, POCC provided numerous services, including group meetings, testing, and counseling.

I spoke to Michael Roberson, the director of services, a passionate man who had fought for LGBT rights even in my days as a teenager in Philadelphia. I will never forget what he said during our interview: "We live in a black community that's systematically homophobic. Black gay people live in communities where they operate out of a place of invisibility, which is detrimental to their own growth." He added, "For communities of color that are very God-centered, the most detrimental thing you can tell somebody is that the Supreme Being views you as an abomination. Where can you go from there? If that is the case, then why ask someone to wear a condom to protect a life that they have been told is of no value?" It was a sentiment I always felt but did not know how to put in words.

Then, in November 2006 an acquaintance in my neighborhood suddenly died. He was twenty-nine years old, just a few months away from his thirtieth birthday. A black gay man, he was well known in the club scene with a beautiful smile and always greeted me with warm energy. His death was a shock. We were the same age, and while we were not the best of friends, he lived in my neighborhood and I would see him at least once a week.

I attended his funeral with my best friend. I had some concerns because it was rumored people in his immediate family were getting angry with all the "gay people" calling their home. I never knew how true that was, but I assumed a grieving family would put their differences aside for the untimely passing of a twenty-nine-year-old man. Before I went to the service I told myself I would leave my political beliefs at the beat-up church door. I hadn't been to a church in years, and I was showing my respect for a friend, not joining the church choir.

The "Bishop" began his eulogy in a massive chair that resembled a throne for Marie Antoinette. The image of the pastor seated in the extravagant chair with rhinestones, fake gold, and a hypocritical sparkle posed a stark contrast to the tiny church in shambles. Once that Bishop hit the slippery soapbox, he said everything short of, "All faggots are going to Hell!" He belted out scripture and declared, "If you don't have the key to Jesus, you are going to Hell! I know there are brothers and sisters in here who don't agree, but you will be judged! It ain't too late to save yourself!" He pointed to my friend's shell of a body in the coffin. "He don't have another chance." He yelled the classic, trite line, "If you accept Jesus, you will be washed white as snow!" White as snow?

There was no compassion or sincerity in the Bishop's toxic voice. This man of the church didn't mention my friend's name any more than four times. That wasn't a eulogy; it was a narcissistic sermon to preach his oppressive beliefs as the church queen deacons, seated right behind me, co-signed with a "Well!" "Amen!" "Hallelujah!" I could tell some of them were gay. I know a sloppy, self-hating, cooning church homo when I see one.

My best friend and I sat angrily in the pews. A tear fell from my left eye, not for our friend who passed, but because of the astronomical hatred I heard at the service. A eulogy is to eulogize someone, not damn them to Hell. I've attended funerals for convicted criminals where no one said anything as bad as what I heard that day.

As we sat there for an over twenty-minute sermon, I said to my best friend, "I couldn't imagine hearing this as a child or teen and knowing I was gay." This aggressive display of hate from the deacons nodding their heads in unison to the horrific preacher could damage someone for life. I certainly grappled with my sexuality as a child, but the blatant spiritual violence I witnessed at my friend's funeral was not part of my upbringing.

That experience proved to me that for black folks to move forward we must challenge the black church. It is one of the most poisonous aspects of our community. One would be shocked how much the agenda of the black church shares in common with conservative, racist groups—on issues of sexuality, gender identity, and interracial relationships, the black church has some uncomfortable bedfellows. So don't be appalled the next time your homophobic church stomps off to an anti-gay marriage rally and a good old boy from Alabama is perched right next to the reverend and his wife. Yes, anti-gay beliefs are funded by whites, but there is one thing that links racist whites and homophobic blacks—religion.

This is not an assault on conservative Christians. Instead, this is a call for a panoramic view into the structural underpinnings of the use of religion as a tool of oppression. The faithful Christians and the gays who co-sign are equally a part of this oppressive fabric. However, not everyone who is anti-gay or opposes equal rights for LGBT people is hateful.

The zombies who follow the super-cult of religion have no idea they are fed microwaved soul food. Being religious does not make you a zombie, but following dogma from busty church queens like Bishop Eddie Long, alleged ex-gays like Donnie McClurkin, or your everyday preacher who is not a historian or your therapist can land you a role in *Night of the Living Dead*. Spiritual development unfolds and regenerates itself in many different ways through several different periods of human existence and cultures. The construct of religion is a spiritual mini-mall. Nothing handcrafted, just an assembly line of reversible, matching little outfits for the spirit, creating a shame to the human potential for spiritual ascendance and transcendence.

Almost every black gay man I know who grew up in a religious household is still suffering from the effects of spiritual assaults. However, for me, being gay saved my life. If I were straight, I would probably be dead, incarcerated, or bombarded with out-of-wedlock children like most of the boys I grew up with in West Philadelphia. Being gay made me more introverted as a child and forced me to stay home and study rather than hang out on street corners. I prepared myself for a life I knew was bigger than constantly being bullied or being called a faggot everyday by classmates or some family members. I wouldn't be the writer I am if I were straight. I would not appreciate art, music, and literature in the way I do if I were heterosexual. This is not to suggest that black men must be gay to be creative or to escape our environments, but often times creativity and success are not encouraged among young black men.

I remember walking through Harlem once when a T-shirt in a window stopped me on the street. The black shirt in white letters read, "A real black man is a man who loves God. A real black man is a man who doesn't deal drugs. A real black man is a man who doesn't have sex with men." I was only twenty-one but already secure in my sexual identity at the time, so that shirt didn't hit me in the same way it must have assaulted many others that day. Nonetheless, I realized that engaging in homophobia in the black community equaled becoming a "real man." I rejected that equation. I am black. I am a man. Most importantly, I am free and continue to survive the zombie apocalypse. My sexual orientation is not my damnation, but my saving grace.

Preacher's Kid

Nathan Hale Williams

When comedian Tracy Morgan "joked" he would stab his son if he were gay, it was no laughing matter to me. My father, a Baptist preacher, once made a similar statement to me when I was sixteen years old. He, too, thought he was making a joke: "I would shoot you if you were gay." He laughed, and I chuckled uncomfortably as I sat there knowing good and well I was gay—I even had a boyfriend at the time.

I am fortunate to have two very different parents. My mother, a retired social worker, is the antithesis to my father. If you looked up the definition of supportive, Marcia J. Williams's picture will be there. She is not only supportive but quite progressive for an African American woman from Chicago. If you know anything about black women from the Midwest they tend to be conservative. My mother is not.

My mother is so progressive that we never attended my father's church, even when they were married. My mother didn't believe in many of the antiquated doctrines of the Baptist church; women couldn't be in the pulpit and couldn't even wear pants. Instead, we attended the church she'd grown up in and helped found as a teenager—a United Methodist Church.

Church was important while I was growing up and we went almost every Sunday. It was where I gave my first speech, where I learned how to play the piano and gave my first recital, and where I developed confidence in my abilities to communicate and engage people. I was a member of the youth choir (thankfully they let everyone in) and the junior usher board, and I tag team preached with my friends on Youth Sunday.

In fact, church is where I met two of my lifelong best friends, Andrea and Antonious. Although my United Methodist Church was far more progressive than my father's traditional Baptist church, it still wasn't the most welcoming for homosexuals. For a brief time we had a music director who was clearly gay and the church whispered about it. But, to my church's credit, I never once heard any of our three pastors say anything negative or destructive about gay people in the pulpit. With that said, it was silently clear that being gay was wrong and against God.

My relationship with God at an early age eventually posed a dilemma with my sexual identity as a young teenager. I had always known I was gay. My first memory of being attracted to a boy was in kindergarten, when I was infatuated with a redhead named Jimmy (who turned out to be gay, too). Over the years, I had several encounters with other boys, and I never wanted to do the same with the girls. It was clear I liked boys for as long as I can remember, which is why I think it's laughable when people argue that I somehow made a choice. Tell that to the five-year-old Nathan playing with Jimmy. We didn't know what we were doing, and we certainly didn't have the cognitive ability to make a "choice" about our sexuality. We just knew we liked each other.

As sure as I was that I was gay, I was also sure it was wrong and God hated me because of it. I spent many days and nights trying to pray the gay away. I prayed to God that if He would just change me it would all be better. I didn't want God to hate me, and for that reason I did not want to be gay. Fortunately, that's one prayer God never answered.

I didn't realize it at the time, but I was building up a self-hatred that at thirty-five years old I am still coping with and getting over. I believed something was wrong with me, and the kids in school would talk about me behind my back, calling me "fag" and "sissy." My way of coping with this brewing and growing self-hatred and lack of self-esteem was to become an arrogant and brazen jerk. My thought was, "I'm going to get you before you get me." I became the male version of Regina George (Rachel McAdams's character in the movie *Mean Girls*). It worked, and I got through high school relatively unscathed by bullying.

I started the coming out process in college with my closest friends, who, like my mom, were very supportive. However, I was still dating girls and denying my sexuality to the great majority of the campus. People whispered about me, but my popularity on campus helped deflect the questions.

I soon began to experience inner turmoil as I confronted my sexuality and spirituality head on. When I was eighteen, my mother found a letter I had written to a boyfriend and called me at school. At first she was very upset until I freaked out, dropped the phone, and threatened to kill myself. My terrified mother screamed for me to pick the phone back up, proclaiming, "Everything is going to be alright." She was more concerned about my safety than the discovery that I might be gay.

After I calmed down and promised not to do anything drastic, we hung up. Her last words to me were, "I will love you no matter what and God loves you no matter what." I'm not quite sure if I was genuinely considering suicide, but had my mother disowned me—my rock—I can easily contemplate a scenario where I would have. Instead, her statement struck me the most; she and God would love me no matter what.

After that episode, my mother and I went years without discussing my sexuality again. I went to law school, became an adult, and began to attend church regularly again, as I had stopped while in college. I found a church that seemed progressive and welcoming, but later I heard the minister had publicly spoken out against homosexuality. I must've missed those Sundays.

Although I was older and back in church, I still had not fully reconciled my sexuality and my spirituality. That would happen a few years later, once I had moved to New York to practice law and pursue my dream of becoming a producer. In the process, I fell in love and began a long-term relationship. About a year into the relationship, I realized it was time to come clean about my sexuality with my mother. So, I did the "bravest" thing in the world—I mailed her a letter.

Two days after my twenty-seventh birthday, I got a call in my office. It was my mom. "I got your letter," she said directly. "I hope you don't think it was a surprise. I was just waiting for you to be comfortable enough with it yourself to tell me the truth." Wow! Here I was thinking I was waiting to come out because my mother wouldn't be comfortable with it and the truth was it was my own discomfort preventing me from sharing my truth. Revelation number one.

My mom and I went on to joke about how other members of our family would react. It was a reassuring conversation and reminded me that my mother loved her gay son and always would. But the most important thing she said to me was, "If God loves you more than I do there is no way he could hate you or forsake you. We serve an awesome God who loves us and makes no mistakes. You have always been my gift from God (the meaning of my name) and I know He made you special in so many ways and it was on purpose." Revelations number two to a hundred!

It was the single most liberating moment I have experienced so far in my life. So much so I went in and quit my job at the law firm, which I hated. Trust me, the feeling was mutual. I felt empowered—if God and my mother loved me as I am, who else mattered? I was free to live my best life and go for my dreams. And that's exactly what I did.

I then began a search for a church that fed my spirit and affirmed what my mother had taught me about God's love. It took a lot of visiting different churches, but I was determined not to be bullied, denigrated, or abused from the pulpit. Even in New York, it's difficult to find churches that have moved past the old ways of fire and brimstone. And many of the openly progressive churches didn't give me that down home, black folk church fire I needed—the singing, the spiritual release, and good ol' fashioned worship.

Ironically, I stumbled upon a Baptist church in Harlem one Sunday. A gay friend had recommended the church, and so I decided to try it out. I was skeptical because even though my friend was gay, I know too many gay people who sit up in churches where they are consistently bashed and tormented.

To my pleasant surprise, this church was different. The pastor was young and spoke about the power of God within you. He encouraged the congregation that anything was possible with God. And more importantly, he encouraged us to love each other no matter what and to drop our prejudices, because that truly was what it meant to be Christ-like. I had found my church home, and I have been going ever since.

Ask any of my friends, I am always talking about how great my church is and I invite everyone to attend. I always feel special and powerful when I attend service on Sundays. And I know that God loves me just the way I am—gay and all. My favorite statement from my pastor is, "If God is impressed by you, then who is there left to impress?" It's such a freeing and empowering revelation to believe in that statement; and it's true.

All my life, I had been struggling with what seemed to be two competing aspects of my life—my relationship with God and my sexuality. Having my preacher father threaten to shoot me because of my sexuality taught me I could not have a relationship with God and be gay. The good news is my father was wrong. I am a living testimony that you can have a close relationship with God and be gay. Me and God are cool! It's other people who get His message twisted.

LOVE IS A BATTLEFIELD

I Still Think of You

Jason Haas

Dear Greg,

I hope this finds you
Well.
I'm sorry
It took me so long to write.

I still think of you,
When I see
A dogwood tree in bloom,
Our first time, and
Hear the drum and bass pour out from a nightclub door.
We'd dance 'til dawn on a school night!

I still think of you
When I smell
The lube we used to get off and
My first time and
Taste the metallic dew on another man's skin.
We'd dance 'til dawn on a school night!

You should see me now.
I don't do drugs or cry when my mother drinks.
I don't hurt when folks call me names.
I don't blame others when I'm in the wrong.

You would love me now.
I finished school and have money.
I have muscles and can fight back.
I help those in need.

You broke my fucking heart
When you left town,
Lost hope, and
Checked out.

"But sometimes life ain't always the way…"

I still think of you
And know
You would love me now
And I would love you.

Jason

Bad Romance

Darian Aaron

I should have never opened the door when he knocked on that second Sunday in February. I'd prayed for God to send me a black man to share my life with, someone who would make the loneliness I knew so well leave as quickly as it had come. A man who would provide the unconditional love and support I couldn't seem to get from my own family. My entire body was wrapped in invisible duct tape with the word "fragile" written in bold caps. Within minutes of casual conversation, I found myself sobbing, releasing years of pain in the arms of a stranger, who in an instant had become the answer to my prayers. From his lips to my ears, the script I'd written, rehearsed, and performed in my mind countless times was coming into fruition right in my living room. I never anticipated that he would come with a price or his own re-writes to the script that was my life.

With nothing but the clothes on his back, a garment bag that contained a pair of jeans, a few dress shirts, and a suit, I allowed him to move into my house and my heart. It would only take six months before the tsunami hit, and the truth about who he really was began to unravel.

"It's me and you against the world," he said. "Don't you know I love you? I'll never do anything to hurt you," he assured me.

I liked the idea that I finally had someone to call my own, but his authority over my life and the imposed isolation from friends was beginning to be too much.

"Shut up!" I said to myself in an attempt to silence the voices in my head that said something wasn't right about him and our relationship.

I told myself that this was just a sacrifice I had to be willing to make if I wanted this to work.

And, God, didn't I want it to work. I'd completely given all of myself, including my body, to him and only him. He was my world.

Never mind that I was beginning to lose everything that I'd worked for and treasured, including my dignity.

"It's me and you against the world." I could hear him saying over and over again in my mind. And the crazy thing is I believed him, until the moment I was forced to remove the rose-colored glasses that kept me from seeing the ugly truth.

The ninety-minute commute from work to the San Gabriel Valley we called home was miles away from city life and the friendships I'd formed in Los Angeles, and he liked it this way. The drive on this day had been particularly brutal, and all I wanted to do was rest. I still hadn't gotten over the fact that he'd failed to pay the rent on our—excuse me—*my* North Hollywood apartment two months in a row after I'd given him the money and trusted him to pay it on time as he said he would.

I made my way to the front door of the apartment, inserted the key and went inside, making sure to close the door behind me as our new neighborhood was far from safe. I fully expected to be greeted by him seconds later as this was our routine. It was eerily quiet. I called out his name. No response. I walked towards the bedroom and there was no sign of him there either.

I searched the bathroom. Nothing. Panic began to set in.

"It's not like him to make plans after work without telling me," I said out loud to an audience of none.

I called his cell phone. Voicemail. I tried repeatedly over the next hour until a strange, unfamiliar voice was heard on the other end.

"Hello," the man said.

I immediately knew that something was wrong. The sick feeling in the pit of my stomach alerted me to at least that much.

"This is the sheriff's department. Ned was arrested earlier today."

Instantly, fear and confusion set in. None of what I was hearing was making any sense to me.

"Arrested! On what charges?" I asked.

"Fraud, grand theft, and defrauding an innkeeper," he replied.

In that moment life as I once knew it began to change forever. I was about to learn exactly what I was made of. It's been said that God never gives you more than you can bear, but on this day it felt like the man upstairs was being unusually cruel.

"When can I see him?" I asked.

"Tomorrow after one P.M.," he stated with authority before ending the call.

I couldn't help thinking I would awake from what was clearly a bad dream as I awaited my turn in line to speak with my felonious boyfriend via a videophone in the jail lobby. As I approached the phone with the demeanor of a concerned and loving boyfriend still in tact, I lifted the receiver in anticipation of what was to come. The next five minutes was a blur as Ned rattled off a rap sheet in my ear as long as the distance that now separated his incarceration from my freedom. The stream of tears that began to travel down my face landed in my mouth and left a bitter taste of salt and sweat that forced me to live in the moment. This was not a dream.

"I don't even know who you are anymore," I managed to

shout in between Ned's self-serving statements that were void of an apology. "Is everything we built over the last six months all a lie?"

"No. I love you. There's just some things in my past that are catching up with me," he said. "I was pulled over for speeding. I had no idea there were warrants out for my arrest."

He lied.

"I need you to stay strong and continue believing in us. You have to help me get out of here," he said in a voice now laced with obvious desperation. "Remember, baby, it's me and you against the world," he said as the phone line went silent, bringing our jailhouse visit to an abrupt end.

I knew the first thing I needed to do, in addition to finding a good lawyer, was to contact his job to see if I had any chance of saving it while he was temporarily "away." I thought that it might be a good idea to check his voicemails to see if he'd made contact with anyone on the outside that could potentially help me secure his release. Luckily, both our cell phones were in my name—shit, all the bills were in my name, including the car I'd bought him a month earlier. He was the "man of the house," but I bore all of the financial responsibilities according to the fine print and my dwindling bank account.

I retrieved his password and began to access his voicemails, and just as I thought, his employer was a little less than pleased with his no-call no-show and left multiple messages to vent her frustration. What I heard next stopped me dead in my tracks.

"Yo, 'sup Ned? This da dude you met in Griffith Park the other day. I just wanna know when we can finish what we started; so hit a nigga up, a'ight? Holla."

The homo thug bravado of this stranger, who undoubtedly had an anonymous sexual encounter with Ned in a public park notorious for gay cruising, sent me into a tailspin.

"End of message," the automated voice said into my ear. "New message."

"Ned, baby where are you?" said another male voice that

was not the homo thug from the park or my own. "I haven't heard from you in a few days and I'm worried. I just need you to call me and let me know that you're okay."

My entire body was now burning with anger. How could he? And how could I be so damn naïve not to see what was happening right in front of me? There were red flags all along, but I didn't want to admit it. I had to talk to that guy from the voicemail. I needed to know the extent of their relationship. Thank God for the dial back option. The phone rang only twice before the stranger answered but it seemed like an eternity.

"Hello, Ned?" the man said in a voice that exuded relief after being reunited with a long lost lover.

"No, this isn't Ned," I said. "I'm Ned's boyfriend."

The phone fell silent.

"Well, that's impossible because I'm Ned's boyfriend," he said in a matter-of-fact tone.

"What's your name?" I asked.

"Richard," he said.

I quickly told him mine in order to get the introductions out of the way and to the meat of why I was calling.

"Have you slept with my boyfriend?" I asked, fearing the answer that I already knew was coming.

"Yes," said Richard.

I couldn't believe how forthright this dude was. There wasn't an ounce of shame in his voice. I'm not sure why, but I needed more details. Before I could even muster up the courage to ask, true to form, Richard beat me to the punch. "Are you the guy who was in the pictures on the wall in his apartment?"

"You had sex in my apartment? In my bed!" This was the ultimate betrayal and my voice was now at an octave that even I didn't recognize.

"Look, I'm sorry, man. I had no idea he had a boyfriend, he told me you were his best friend," Richard shot back.

"Damn! I can't believe this shit is happening to me. Did you guys use protection? Please tell me you used protection," I asked as the reality of a new fear gripped my spirit.

"No, we didn't," Richard said in a regretful tone that uncovered his awareness of the potential severity of the situation in which Ned had now placed both of us.

"You need to get tested and I'm doing the same" were the last words I offered to my boyfriend's other boyfriend before I hung up the phone.

As I waited for the results of the OraSure test in the clinic waiting room I frequented for my annual HIV screenings, images of passionate lovemaking between Ned and I danced in my head. I'd loved this man with reckless abandon and slipped up more times than I was even willing to admit to myself. We couldn't get any closer, and I couldn't feel any more loved than I did during those moments when I looked into his eyes as he lay on top of me with nothing but the earth supporting my back. There wasn't an area or object in the house that hadn't been introduced to our lust for each other. But that was then and this is now. I kept telling myself that I'd been here before and it always turned out fine. Before I knew it, the nervous energy had disappeared, and I'd fallen asleep in a chair that had the task of holding up six months of pleasure and pain while I waited for my results.

"Your results came back non-reactive," said the counselor.

I'd just been given a second chance at life. A single tear ran down my left cheek as my battered mind and spirit kept any normal reaction at bay. I'd hit rock bottom, but I was determined not to stay there. In the days and years to come, I'd have to take responsibility for the chaos I allowed Ned to bring into my life. I was immediately faced with the dilemma of whether or not I was going to sit in the driver's seat or passively watch as my life continued to spiral out of control. I had to create an action plan that would result in becoming a whole person capable of providing myself the love I sought from others that got me into this mess. Crying was cleansing, but tears would not lay a solid foundation for my future. Seeking help from a therapist was a no-brainer; I count myself among the minority of African Americans who believe that prayer and therapy can actually co-exist. If I ever needed assistance from a professional to get my life back on track now was the time. It would have been easy to internalize what I was feeling, but at what cost? The unwarranted stigma attached to seeing a shrink was not about to deter me from living my best life.

Although my heart was shattered, I had to believe that what was meant to destroy me could be turned around and used for my good. Becoming bitter and jaded or ruling out other black gay men as viable romantic partners was not an option. I wouldn't give him the satisfaction of being able to dictate my future as a result of his actions. I was going to remain open to finding authentic love from a black man who was looking for nothing more than someone to love and be loved in return. Ned was not going to win.

Thankfully, I never bought the perpetual lie that two black gay men are incapable of having a healthy relationship, even after all that I've experienced. Five years later, the black man I will soon marry walked into my life, bringing with him no ulterior motives other than to be an active participant on our journey through life and love.

Afraid of My Own Reflection

Antron Reshaud Olukayode

Night is growing
Their laughter maturing into insults
My magnetic stance pressures them
And all I'm feeling is swallowed into
Their bellies and fiery conceptions,
I have no identity to them
No face, no voice, no reason being here
Except as a slave to unavailable blessings
Their public jokes and torments.
This wound's deeply penetrative
And I am in love still
With a broken race of men

Just the Two of Us

Curtis Pate III

I woke up like I did every Friday morning, to a mind-piercing alarm that was loud enough to wake even the most hung-over of college students (and my neighbors who were constantly leaving threatening notes on my door about my noisy ass alarm). I jumped out of bed and walked across the room to shut off my strategically placed morning torture device. The previous semester I kept it right next to my bed, in arm's reach. This made it too easy to hit the off button, roll over, and go back to sleep. So easy, in fact, that I missed just about an entire semester of Bio-101. Which is why I was getting up early this morning to take it again.

The day unfolded with no major surprises: class, lunch with my boys, and more class. Every Friday my boys and I met at our apartment to lay down our plan of attack for the weekend. We were Jersey boys, but the weekend always meant we were hitting up NYC. The only question was how hard we were going to hit it. So, there I was in the apartment, deciding on my weekend wardrobe, when both my boys busted through the front door, laughing and yelling. Max came in the bedroom, with Cam right behind him, and said, "Come here and sit down." Cam looked like he was about to explode. As soon as I sat down, Cam said, "We just met the perfect dude for you!" I was like, "What? Where?" They started going on and on about how he's a shorty (under 5'9", cute face, tight waist), he's super cute, and he's coming over!

It was Friday, which meant I had to stop by mom's to grab a plate and then get fresh before we hit the streets of New York. So, about an hour later, I was packing my bag to take to my mom's when the doorbell rang. The "perfect guy for me" was downstairs ringing the bell. I told my boys "I'll go let him in." This way I could see what all the hubbub was about. I went to the door and this dude, about 6'1", my size, maybe bigger, said, "I'm here to see Cam." I said, "Cool I'll get him."

As soon as I got upstairs, I said, "Shorty my ass. That dude is bigger than me!" Cam busts out laughing and says, "No, that's his roommate. He must be outside with him."

I was over it. My superficial twenty-year-old ass had seen enough. Max and Cam both went downstairs to chill with these dudes while I continued pulling together my outfits for the weekend. About twenty minutes later, I finished packing and headed down stairs to throw my bag in the car and head to my mom's.

I got downstairs, said what's up to big dude again, and leaning against a money-green Eagle Talon was the cutest, little chocolate shorty with wavy, jet-black hair I had ever seen. Where in the world did Max and Cam find this cute little guy? And they served him up on a silver platter. I mean, all I had to do was come downstairs and there he was, right there in the parking lot waiting for me. Game plan: I would hit him with a few lines, get his number, and immediately work him into my dating rotation.

I walked up to him and said, "What's up, shorty, I'm Curt." He smiled and I lost all train of thought—all sense of where I was or who I was. Somehow I was bathing in a beauty and an energy that had covered every inch of me and was welcoming me to a place I thought I had been before but obviously was mistaken. For this place was new, and the feeling was like nothing I had ever experienced. Never before had I met someone who immediately drew me into a place where only the two of us mattered, where only the two of us existed, and he made me feel like I could stay there in that place with him forever. Without another want or need, just there, enjoying all that he was and all that he would become.

For the next four months I was wrapped in a love that reassured me and made me strong. People say no one should complete or validate you, but this love had done just that. I was validly complete and completely validated. My walk was more confident; I smiled easier and laughed harder. So this is what Whitney, Luther, and Jill sang about. That "love won't let me wait" kind of love. That "I wanna run to you" kind of love. That "he loves me" kind of love. The love people pray for and wait their whole lives for—and I at twenty years old had found.

After reveling in the greatest love I had ever known for four months, I wanted everyone to know about this magical ride I was on, starting with my parents. Of course, up till then, my parents were used to me bringing home bright, young college girls, but I didn't think twice about telling them about this new love of mine. My parents were always in my corner and since I had fallen this deep for someone, they needed to know so they, too, could share in this great new chapter of my life.

One Saturday, I picked up Carwyn, the love of my life, and said, "Babe, we have to stop by my parents' crib." He said, "Cool." He'd met my parents before so he asked, "Do you have to pick something up?" I said, "No, I'm going to let them know the deal." He turned to me and said, "What deal?" I said, "About us," and started laughing. I spent the rest of the drive calming him down and saying, "You know my parents are cool…especially my dad."

About twenty minutes later we pulled up in front of my parents' house. Carwyn was still nervous, so I said, "Man, just chill. My fam is cool." We walked inside and said what's up to mom, who was in the kitchen wiping down the stove. She smiled and said "Ya' hungry. I just put the food in the fridge. It's still warm." I said, "No, we're good. I need you to come downstairs for a minute." She raised one eyebrow and said, "Come down stairs for what?" I said, "I'll tell you when you come downstairs."

So the three of us headed down stairs where my dad was watching TV. I said what's up to my dad and gave him the usual handshake and half a hug. Before I could say another word, my mom said to my dad, "Honey, Curt has something to talk to us about, and he's looking real serious about it."

Now, I've heard lots of coming out stories and I pretty much knew how this would play out. My dad would crack a few jokes and my mom would say something like, "Boy, please, I'm your mother. I've always known."

I told them to sit down so I could say what I had to say. The room went completely silent. I don't remember my dad turning the TV off, but there was no sound in the room, just my voice as Carwyn, Mom, and Dad sat on the couch staring up at me.

I had the floor. This was going to be my moment, my coming out story: "Mom, Dad, after breaking up with Lisa, I started dating Carwyn and he's the absolute best th..."

Before I could finish, my dad jumped to his feet and yelled, "WHAT!" He was standing so close to me I could feel his breath on my face. He stared me right in my eyes and said, "What did you say?" All I could see was my dad's face getting redder and redder. Then I heard my mom's voice in the background softly saying, "Oh my God" over and over again. Her voice was so soft, it reminded me of when I was a child and she would read me bedtime stories, and then whisper the ending so I would fall asleep. Only this was no bedtime story and what was being whispered was not a happy ending. Carwyn had moved next to her and was saying, "I'm so sorry."

My nephew, who was no more than four years old at the time, had woken up during all the commotion and was making his way down the stairs. Not wanting him to witness all the raw emotion on display, I met him halfway up the stairs and immediately picked him up and took him to his room. He smiled, hugged me tight, and said "Hey, Uncle Curtis! When did you get here? Wanna play my new video game?" I said, "Not now buddy, but later." My four-year-old nephew had innocently and unknowingly been my port in this crazy-ass storm. What the hell had just happened?

As soon as I put down my nephew, I heard my dad say, "Come here, man." But his voice wasn't my dad's voice. It was the voice of that guy on the playground who punched you in the stomach, took your lunch money, and then stood over you and called you faggot. It was the voice of the guys who circled you in the park while you were on your way home from school and took turns pushing you and calling you homo and sissy-boy.

I followed him across the hall into my parents' bedroom. As soon as I stepped foot in the room, that voice returned and hit me like a back handed slap across the face.

"What is this crap you're telling me? You're not gay!"

"I am and Car..."

"You are always stirring things up. You're not gay. You just want attention. You don't dress like a woman. You don't even act feminine."

"Being gay is not acting or dressing like a woman. It's..."

"I don't want to hear about these sick ass feelings you have! I want you and that thing out of my house...NOW!"

I ran downstairs to grab Carwyn, who was crying and still saying, "I'm sorry," while my mom was rubbing his back with one hand and holding her head with the other and saying, "It's okay, baby."

I told Carwyn, "We gotta go now!" I headed out the door, and I didn't look back to see if Carwyn was following me or to see my mom's reaction. I got to the car, opened the door, jumped in, and started the motor all in one motion. Carwyn jumped in the passenger seat and I slammed my foot on the gas.

I sped off with no destination in mind. Still in shock and complete disbelief, my body must've gone into autopilot because the next thing I knew we were at a park about twenty minutes from my parents' house. Neither one of us had said a word during the ride there.

Carwyn looked at me and said, "Are you alright?" I turned to him and said, "What the hell just happened? This is not how it was supposed to go down."

"You and your dad were upstairs for a long time. What happened?"

I began to tell Carwyn what my dad said, word for word. I even described the vicious anger in his voice and how he stared me in the eyes the whole time. Carwyn didn't say a word. He just sat there silently and watched, eyes wide. Then he said, "Are you going back?"

For the first time in my twenty years I didn't know if I could go back. If I could go home—tonight or ever again. And to make matters worse, it was July, school was out for the summer, so I had no dorm room or apartment to retreat to.

We sat in the park, holding hands, not saying a word until the sun went down. I broke the silence and said, "Guess I'll drop you at your mom's and get a room for the night." Carwyn looked at me and said, "No, babe, I'm going to stay with you and make sure you're alright."

So we got a room, ordered a pizza, and watched TV. Now, my mom always called me at 10:00 P.M. on the nose if she didn't know where I was. She'd say, "What's up, son of mine? Are you coming home tonight? Do you want me to leave a plate out for you?" That night, 10:00 P.M. came and went...then 11:00...then 12:00, and no call. No "Where are you?" No "Are you alright?"

Was I on my own? Could I ever go home again? Would my parents ever speak to me again? Those questions filled my head and kept me up the entire night.

The next morning, I took Carwyn home and then waited for both my parents to leave for work. Once they were gone, I went in and got cleaned up for work. I was working as a bank teller around the corner from my parents' house. Little did I know I should've been saving up for my own apartment, because who knew if these locks would be changed by tomorrow or even tonight.

I would go to work and then stay out till the wee hours of the morning and then sneak back into my room when I knew my parents were asleep.

I don't know if I was still in shock or just embarrassed at being treated this way by my own family, but I hadn't breathed one word of any of this to my friends. After my parents' reaction, there was no way I was going to tell my brother or ask him for help—as a matter of fact, I wasn't going to tell anyone anything about my personal life ever again!

After about two weeks of sneaking in and out of my parents' house, my dad called me at work and said, "Son, we need to talk. Make sure you come straight home after work."

That was it. He was going to tell me to get out for good. What was I going to do? I was a full-time student with a part-time job. I was broke.

So after work I headed straight to my parents' house. I wasn't nervous. I wasn't scared. After all, what could my dad say worse than what he had already said?

I pulled up in front my parents' house and realized it could be the last time I ever called that place home. I guessed it would be cheap hotel rooms and pizza until I figured something out.

I walked in the door and headed upstairs to my room. My mom met me in the hallway and said, "Your dad is waiting for you downstairs." She was talking in a whisper again. This time, like the nice, cool girl at school who warns you that her bully boyfriend was waiting for you out front and then helps you sneak out the back door. I didn't say a word. I just turned and headed down the stairs.

My mom followed me, and when I hit the bottom stair, I saw my dad sitting on the couch. He said, "Come sit down." His voice was no longer angry, no longer threatening. His face was calm, not bright red like the last time I had seen him. He looked at me and said, "This whole sneaking in and out the house thing has to stop. This is my house and you are my son and you are always welcome here."

I didn't say a word. I just stared at him and listened as he continued. "Now, I don't want to hear anymore of this gay talk. I don't know if you're going through a phase or what, but I don't want to hear about it anymore."

And from that moment on, he didn't. I never mentioned Carwyn, our relationship, or the love we shared again, but I didn't stop there. My brother, my family, straight friends, new friends, co-workers—I didn't tell anyone. At that moment I became two people living two separate lives. There was the real me, who I shared with close friends; those who would not judge me or think that Carwyn, our love, or I was sick or abnormal. Then there was the façade, the mask, the pretender who delivered to society, and my family, exactly what they wanted and expected. A black man who was educated, with a good job, who owned his own home, and most importantly was straight.

At work, around my family, and in unfamiliar circles, Carwyn became Carla. My pronouns to describe him all followed suit; my partner was now my "girlfriend" and he became "she," his became "hers." This great love I shared with a partner who was handsome, intelligent, and caring, a partner who loved me at my most unlovable and who stood by me when everyone and everything had turned its back and walked away. This man who validated and completed me was now hidden behind this dark veil of secrecy.

For ten years my parents never saw Carwyn or heard his name. They missed birthday parties, anniversary dinners, vacations, and graduations. For ten years they lost a part of me that was so special, so loving, so remarkable. They never witnessed my eyes light up when Carwyn entered a room. They never felt the way our love could fill a room and change the mood of everyone in it, until…

I took a job in Los Angeles that kept me there for about a year. After the job had wrapped I was relocating back East and Carwyn and I had brought our first home together in New Jersey. Although I spoke to both my parents at least twice a week, they had no idea I was moving back to Jersey and they definitely didn't know Carwyn and I had purchased a house about an hour south of them.

My parents were under the impression that I was in New Jersey on a visit. I decided I would stop by and tell them the situation. Unlike ten years earlier, I was no longer a naive young kid. I was a grown man, making my own money, paying my own bills, and making my own decisions. This time I wasn't seeking approval or acceptance. I was simply letting them know what was going on and where I would be. They could take it or leave it. At the end of the day, I was getting in my car and driving to my home that I shared with my partner.

I walked in the house and Mom was in the kitchen preparing food. She smiled and said, "Hey, son of mine!" Then she walked over and gave me a big hug and a kiss on the cheek. I said, "Hey, Mom. Where's Dad?" She said, "Downstairs watching TV." I said, "Come on downstairs." As I headed down the stairs, my mom followed behind me. Suddenly I realized this scene was all too familiar. I said what's up to my dad and gave him the usual handshake and half hug. I said, "I need ya' to sit down for a minute."

They both sat down on the couch, and I sat on the love seat across from them. Again, the room went completely silent and both my parents stared at me, my mom still wearing a big smile.

"I'm moving back to New Jersey." My mom let out a scream and said, "My baby's coming home! Are you staying here?"

I laughed and said, "No, Carwyn and I bought a house in South Jersey." Without missing a beat, Mom said, "Well, what does the house look like? Is it big?"

Before I could answer, Dad said, "Let me know if you and Carwyn need any help getting set up down there. You know I just got a new flatbed."

No screaming and yelling. No ugly confrontation. I was shocked, elated, relieved, excited, all in one. I smiled and said, "Thanks, Dad. I'll let you know. Now let's eat. I'm starving."

As we headed upstairs to the kitchen, Mom turned to me and said, "I made extra for Carwyn."

I looked at her with a slightly confused expression on my face and she said, "Well, you brought him with you last time. I'll make him a plate for you to take home."

Hey, You

Erick Johnson

Hey you, little sissy boy
Playing with the girls
Spending your days
Jumping rope and telling secrets
No father around leaves your mother to do it all
A woman alone can't raise a man

Hey you, yeah you, punk
You think you can hide behind books and glasses?
I know what you are
You know it too
And the shame weighs on your shoulders
And keeps your head pointed towards the ground

Hey you, sinner and sodomite
You are an abomination before God
From the pulpit I see the sin you try to hide
Lost in lust and confusion

The fires of hell are your only reward
There is no place for you in heaven

Hey you, Ms. Thing
I've seen you around
You never smile—never laugh
Life is joy and you can't see it
You need a diva in your life
You're welcome I am here
And there is work to be done

Hey you, my fine black brother
How can you just pass me by with a simple hello?
Don't you see these hips rocking to a rhythm you want to dance to?
Don't you see these…wait…you're one of those brothers
You smile with no apologies
I smile with no expectations
And we continue on our way
In our search for everyday adventures

Hey you, wassup bruh
I recognize that look
The stare that is not a stare
The smile that disappears when I look your way
You got somewhere to go
This don't mean nothing
It's just us feeling good
And you don't need to run your mouth

Hey, you, my baby baby
Talk to me
Tell me what's on your mind
Tell me what I already know
Dry your tears

Lift your head
And I will tell what you already know
That I have loved you since before you took your first
breath
And I love you still

Hey you, familiar soul
You are welcome here
Protestant, Catholic, or Baptist, makes no difference
Forget the words that have been used to pierce you like a
sword
And make your soul bleed
Let us give you the message of unconditional love
Love that is warmth and comfort
Strength and steel
God loves you as you are

Hey you, Mr. Man
Get your lazy ass out of bed
I've had five years of you sleeping late on weekends
And it ends today
All good fags are at the flea market or doing brunch
I know you're not asleep
I reach to pull you out and you pull me in
I look into the brown eyes that I swam in so many nights
ago
And I remember
And I smile
You look into my eyes and say
Hey, you

My Night with the Sun
Mark Corece

I laid there in complete silence, surrounded by white sheets and fumy remnants of the night before. I listened to him in the bathroom as the water from his sink ran and poured out pounds of double hydrogen and oxygen. I imagined a face rag, lathered and balmy, rigorously scrubbing and rinsing away the unwanted residue to clean and restore his dignity to his important parts.

I remained still and, simultaneously, my mind streamed with thoughts of how the birds chirped just before dawn, pleading for a new day to be filled with colorful rays that implied warmth and hopefulness. I listened and agreed with the cardinals and robins that sang patiently. I knew the sun would not rise until he smiled and we exchanged playful gazes, and then, alas, a new day would be before us.

I thought of how we held each other. It was truly intentionally unintentional. His arms were so heavily wrapped in my madness; the entire act was enlightening.

The water continued to pour, my contemplations proceeded. I looked ahead, but a fluffy pillow obstructed my view of the window. The pillow provided a nice contrast between the sun and a shadow.

I could relate to the birds outside full of glee. I laid alone, crowded by memories of how I looked at him throughout the night. His perfectly sculptured torso framed his meticulously groomed chest hair, which I thought was beyond sexy. I was honored to be in his presence.

I shifted myself so I could rest my head and my thoughts on my folded arm. My mind intensified with an unidentifiable velocity. I thought of the passion and zeal we knew. And when I tried to describe it, it moved so far away, my psyche could not pull it close enough. Eventually I decided to halt any attempt to recreate the moment because I didn't want to lose the glory of its improvised perfection; our alignment, in that moment, was blissful.

The water shut off, and I was too frightened to face him again because the night before—which was only hours ago—had been too much. I had been bent in too many ways, in shapes I had never seen since geometry. In the pitch-black room, I could feel a tear inhabit my face. A tear fused with exhaustion and passion, mixed with the safety of our ability and willingness to be vulnerable with each other one last time.

The night proceeded as we pressed our palms against one another. The night we had created was a new echelon, even for us. We didn't verbalize or intellectualize our future together. Our silence and bodies did all the talking. What we had to do was evident. It was clear. His eyes revealed that he truly loved me, but a squint whispered, "You can't take the love with you." His lips pressed against my body bared a secret I couldn't quite hear. The closer I got to him the more I smelled his distinct odor. The indescribable aroma wafted me into reality. It felt like he had plans that didn't include an immediate future with me. I understood.

When I held onto his neck, I wanted him to know that my love was still as strong, if not stronger. When I clasped the sheets, the friction between my fingers and the cotton sang the song, "Your access to me is infinite," but softly, I hummed, "only in my solitary moments."

He walked in and my eyes shifted in his direction. He joined me in bed and eclipsed my view of the window. But it didn't matter because the light illuminated his skin. I slanted my arm across his body, we kissed, and we stared into each other's eyes once more. I wiped the remainder of water from his face. He smiled and I thought, "He and the sun are finally one again."

Love Your Truth

B. Scott

Washington D.C. seemed like the perfect place for me to be… and I quickly found what I thought was the perfect man. He was an extremely charming, established, secure man. I never really had a father figure in my life, and as a twenty-one year old newcomer to the city, he met those needs for me. And truth be told, I've always been a sucker for a man's charm.

It wasn't long before we moved in together and he met my family. I introduced him to my parents as my "mentor." My mom got it, but I don't think she really cared what was going on with us. All she chose to focus on was the fact he had money, and I think she was thinking, "If you are going to be gay, at least be with someone stable." He charmed my parents much like he charmed me.

During the course of our relationship, I began to express my sexuality in new ways. Not only was I expressing my sexuality, I was toying with gender as well. It started with the clothes — I wore more androgynous/feminine clothing — and expanded to other areas of my image. I allowed my hair to grow longer in length, I wore makeup, and so on. At that time I wasn't wearing a full face of makeup. I just did a few things to accentuate my natural look. But he didn't like me doing those things. As time went on I felt as though he was trying to control me. Although he identified himself as gay, he didn't want it "broadcasted" all over the city. Being with me made him feel gayer or more "clockable."

We had totally different ways of conceptualizing being gay. He believed being gay was all about the sexual attraction. I hated when he would say, "Well, you are homosexual," emphasis on sexual because it made my sexuality seem so animalistic, as though who I am was just about sexual interaction. I believe that my spirit is innately gay, regardless of whether it manifests in any sexual way with another man. How I act and how I express myself, whether you call it feminine, flamboyant, or stereotypical, is a reflection of what's on the inside.

One day while we were living together, I went to visit him at his office to talk about our issues. He verbalized for the first time an issue that had been present in our relationship for a while, calling out the pink elephant in the room. "Why can't you just be the person who I met when we first got together?" he asked.

I hadn't realized I was different. Whatever changes I made happened at such a gradual pace that I hardly noticed it, but it clearly made him uncomfortable. Still, his words hurt. It wasn't just about him. For most of my life, people made me feel like I couldn't be who I wanted to be. Society conditioned me to believe that I couldn't express myself in certain ways and to feel that my identity was something to be ashamed of. As he spoke to me, all those emotions resurfaced.

In the course of the argument, he challenged my manhood. "If I wanted to date a woman, I would," he said. "And nowadays I don't really know with you." I do identify myself as a man. I know that I'm gender nonconforming and I don't adhere to the stereotypical guidelines as to how a man or woman should present themselves. However, when he challenged me, it made me realize I still wasn't completely comfortable. He thus continued his questioning.

"What are you trying to be?" he asked. "Why you gotta be all extra? If you wanna be gay, why can't you just be gay? Why do you have to be one of the gays who straightens your hair and puts on makeup and wears women's clothes? Why can't you just be a man?" I got so angry listening to him, it took every bit of restraint to not show him exactly how much of a man I was. That's when I realized I couldn't do it anymore. He ended up crying because he knew he had hurt me emotionally. I started crying because I had almost hurt him physically.

In hindsight, I can say that he loved me the best he knew how. His own limited concept of sexuality and gender expression got the best of him. After that altercation I realized how just extremely unhappy I had become. One day, six months later, I was in the kitchen washing dishes and I began to cry...seemingly out of nowhere. I realized that was not the life for me, that was not my destiny, and that was not where I needed to be. It finally clicked in my head that the relationship was not right for me. I loved him, but he was not the person I needed to be with. I deserved someone who loved me for me, no matter how I chose to express myself. I was still very young and I wanted to explore, and I needed to see what the world had to offer outside of the relationship.

Back in North Carolina, anything dealing with the arts was deemed as being a "sissy." If you wanted to express yourself in dance or theater or media, my parents and the greater community would look down upon it and often assume you were gay. I spent much of my younger life playing sports—including baseball, trying to adhere to social norms, and exhibit masculinity. I knew Los Angeles would be different, and it was.

A week later, I packed three red suitcases and I left D.C. for L.A., a place I had never been. I had always thought as a kid that L.A. was where dreams come true. It was so different from anything I had known. I had already met people from New York so I felt like I knew what that city had to offer, but I had never really met anyone from Los Angeles. I think deep down inside, there was something in me that wanted to explore my creative side and L.A. offered that opportunity.

I've since learned there's much power in walking in your truth. While that man fell out of love with me over my choices to explore my gender as much as my sexuality and chastised me over it, those qualities ultimately made me unique and helped me flourish in my career. By embracing who I am including my gender nonconformity, I've stood out as unique and been able to make strides in the media—and advocate for people like me in the process.

Thankfully, I've come to understand the importance of facing your obstacles, overcoming them, and seeing my truth as the powerful gift that is.

BOYS LIKE GIRLS

The Night Diana Died

Daren J. Fleming

"Ladies and gentlemen, please welcome Sir Faggamuffin himself, singing his new hit single, 'Mr. Skid-Pipe Plumber,' our very own Gay-Man-Walking!" the announcer said as the orchestra began playing.

"Fagga-what?" I said out loud. As the curtain began to rise, I realized two of my male back-up dancers were dressed as minstrel performers in bright neon-colored suits. They began tap dancing around me while glitter sprayed from their twirling wooden canes. Then three female dancers dressed in bugle-beaded mammy costumes began rolling out a hot pink shag carpet for me to walk on.

This wasn't supposed to be happening! After all of the work I had done to get my one-man cabaret show out of my imagination and onto a Broadway stage, I end up being sabotaged! "Skid-Pipe Plumber"?

I began to sweat profusely under the stage lights. If one had stared closely at the scrolling marquee across my forehead, their retinas would have been scorched from the neon lights flashing

"Daren J. Flaming." The audience laughed, and just as I was about to run off the stage I woke up in a cold sweat.

My nightmare always ended the same way. Even as a teenager my imagination was vivid, so I never read too much significance into the sequined Aunt Jemima trio and the minstrel duet that appeared in my dreams. My ridiculous teenage insecurity made me believe a scrolling marquee actually ran across my forehead that read "Homosexual," so I censored myself to deny the world the satisfaction of knowing I was, in fact, gay. Although I was told that my appearance resembled Carlton from *The Fresh Prince of Bel-Air*, I felt everyone saw me as Antoine Merriweather from the *In Living Color* sketches "Men on Film." I was later told that not everyone assumed I was gay. In fact, because of the way I spoke and dressed, people thought I acted like a *white* person.

I learned to dismiss the "acting like a white person" comments, but it took a long time to understand that the perceptions of others don't dictate my reality. I did a lot of soul searching during my teens, and by the time I had turned nineteen, I was finally able to admit to myself that the random infatuations I had developed with men (mainly male soap opera stars) weren't just a phase I would eventually grow out of. My sexuality wasn't something I wanted to hide from people anymore, and I didn't want to live a double life.

I enrolled at Millikin University and after an ego-bruising freshman year, I felt inferior to some of my classmates who were consistently cast in prestigious Main Stage productions while I had only been selected for student-directed shows. I had also been dumped by a boyfriend I'd met while doing summer stock theatre, and my self-esteem needed a boost at the beginning of my sophomore year. Then I landed a role as the Captain in my first Main Stage musical *Anything Goes!* Before I had felt like a homeless person with my nose pressed against the glass in front of Bergdorf Goodman dreaming of a fabulous life. Now, with this leading role and newfound sense of self, I finally felt as though I had stepped inside the store.

One Saturday in August, my friend Dwelvan and I had rehearsal from 9:00 A.M. until 3:00 P.M. We were the only two black people in the show, and on the first day of rehearsal we had made eye contact with each other with the subtext, "Hey, only other black man in this fifty-person show, come sit by me," as we found our way through the crowded auditorium to one another.

When rehearsal ended on this day, I called my friend Gabe, also a musical theatre major, and told him to meet us at the coffee shop on the first floor of my dorm. Gabe was a skinny, light-skinned black guy with a look very similar to a young Little Richard. I often joked that his permed hair resembled Anita Baker's hairstyle during her "Rapture" years. While I found his flamboyance amusing, there were a few times I had to stop him from ruining a pair of jeans because he was in a mood to show off his legs in a pair of Daisy Dukes. He was a lot to handle sometimes, but he was my friend.

Gabe met us at an outdoor table at the coffee shop, and the strange aroma of gourmet dog food mixed with maple syrup emanated from the factory that helped establish Decatur, Illinois, as the soybean capital of the world.

"Daren J, I'm going to need you to get that long face lost quick-fast-and-in-a-hurry! We are celebrating my nineteenth birthday all weekend," Gabe said to me. "There is fresh 'Milli-Meat' to be had on this campus." He cheered me up and we held court at the coffee shop, singing our favorite show tunes and acting out scenes from our favorite movies. We were admittedly the epitome of every "musical theatre" kid stereotype there is.

Afterwards, we followed Gabe to a Payless shoe store so he could buy himself a birthday present and our buddy Antonio, a commercial music major, joined us. His short hair was dyed platinum blond like Sisqo from the singing group Dru Hill, and his pierced eyebrows were arched before it was fashionable for men to do so. We were the only openly gay black men on campus, and our behavior, personal style, and taste made the four of us stand out from the other lethargic white students who wore baseball caps, sweat shirts, and pajama pants to class.

Despite disapproving stares from the blue-collar customers at Payless that day, I purchased a pair of sandals, Antonio bought a pair of black dress shoes with an elevated sole, and Dwelvan became frustrated because the store didn't carry a men's size fifteen. Gabe, on the other hand, somehow found a way to squeeze his long but narrow feet into a pair of size twelve women's boots, which he referred to as his "bitch kickers." Although the boots had a unisex look to them in a Prince sort of way, the spike heel made it obvious they were made for women. We never questioned Gabe's choices in clothing or anything else; we just went with it and gave each other side-eye glances every now and then.

Gabe insisted on wearing his bitch kickers home from the store and began carelessly prancing down Main Street like Naomi Campbell in a Gianni Versace fashion show. Antonio, Dwelvan, and I were content to walk a bit more leisurely as we chuckled to ourselves how "extra" Gabe was acting. I saw the look of amusement on Dwelvan's face quickly turn to disgust as Gabe continued to sashay down his imaginary catwalk. In Dwelvan's view, "The world sees us as Black Men. What sexuality we are comes later. Man up, gentlemen." He always commanded attention when he walked into a room, whether he wanted it or not, because he had a regal aura about him, and at 6'4" and 250 pounds he towered over most people. Dwelvan saw Gabe's "everyone look at me" behavior as excessive.

We arrived at a "don't walk" sign at the intersection of Main Street and Oakland Avenue, where Gabe lit a cigarette and tapped his foot impatiently. Behind us I heard someone in a vehicle repeatedly revving his engine. I turned around and saw a blue Ford pickup truck carrying three white men in their early twenties. The driver had a scruffy brown beard and wore a green baseball cap and a plain white T-shirt. The other two guys were typical non-descript white residents of Decatur, or "townies" as most of the students and faculty called them. As soon as I made eye contact with the driver, the light changed. That's when he put his foot on the gas and charged toward us; he was trying to run us over!

"Gentlemen, haul ass!" I screamed as we ran down the empty sidewalk trying to get behind a tree or bush for protection. "Sizzling hot faggot-queens!" one of them yelled as the other two laughed and made "yee-haw" noises. They showered us with a barrage of beer bottles. "Sissy-nigger-fags!" they howled as they high-fived each other and spit chewing tobacco at us. Finally they skidded around a corner and away from us. The whole scene was redneckery at its finest.

Fearing they would return, we ran back to campus as fast as we could in a state of shock. I retreated to my room to watch a bootleg VHS tape of *Diana Ross Live at Caesar's Palace*. Antonio rambled about needing a shower and a "Vision of Love" all the way up the elevator and into his dorm room. Dwelvan remained silent and stoic. It was as if an internal boiling rage had ignited inside of him as he walked back to his room and began blasting Leontyne Price's recording of *Cleopatra*. Gabe always had a flair for melodrama and gave an Academy Award-winning reenactment for all of our friends the moment we got back.

When his dramatics were done, someone drove him back to his home in The Woods, a brand new student apartment complex. He later called to tell me some kids in the theatre department were having a joint-apartment party and our friend Margot was having a pre-party at her place. The last thing I wanted to do was go to a party but if I missed his birthday weekend, Gabe would've never let me hear the end of it.

Getting dressed was a production for Gabe so I grabbed a pre-assembled outfit off a hanger in my closet, got dressed early, and went over to his apartment to help speed up his process. The first order of business was to give his "new-growth" a "touch-up" so all his hair would be straight and not just the tips. Next, we trifled though Gabe's closet but nothing was jovial enough for the evening's festivities.

Gabe improvised by raiding Margot's closets. Margot, the self-proclaimed queen of bargain shopping, had more designer clothes and accessories than anyone else on campus. She's only 4',11" tall so I'm still confused how someone as tall as Gabe successfully got into a pair of her black, stretchy bell bottoms, but he did. He then found a black sparkling Lycra T-shirt that Margot wore as a regular length shirt. On Gabe, the shirt stopped just under his nipples, creating a makeshift midriff.

Apparently that was the look he was going for that night because the moment he checked himself out in the mirror, his face lit up. He then grabbed Margot's body glitter and covered his arms and mid-section with it. Next, he applied some brown glittery eye shadow over his eyelids, and topped things off with heavy mascara on both his eyelashes and his mustache.

"I'm going to *look like a faggot* tonight," he said as he placed a hand on his right hip and admired himself in the mirror.

"I'm going to *look like a faggot*," was code for "I'm in *heat* so I'm going to wear something skin tight that shows off as much of my body as possible. If I flirt with everyone maybe I'll get laid." Usually this plan failed, and he would spend the night making love to a bag of Steak 'n Shake cheeseburgers at 2:00 A.M.

After having a drink at Margot's, we decided we were fashionably late enough to make a noticeable entrance into the party, three buildings over. The party was just like any other theatre party; a bunch of silly, under-aged drinking debauchery. Some allowed the alcohol to serve as an excuse for a sudden interest in someone of the same sex and vice-versa. The stoners, who had gotten high before they arrived, sat together in a corner and stared at the drunks with looks of THC-induced judgment on their faces.

I was on the patio having a conversation with my future

boyfriend, Kevin, when Gabe, who had been flouncing around the men all night like a cat in heat, came running up to me shortly after midnight. "I just heard on the radio, Diana's dead," he whispered in my ear.

"What?" I screamed so loudly that everyone around me stopped talking and began staring.

"She was in some sort of car accident. I don't have all of the details but Diana is gone, Daren."

I was well into my eighth or ninth vodka-based cocktail, and I instantly started crying. "No, she *can't* be dead. This is terrible! She was on my list of people to meet before I die!" I screamed. Antonio and Dwelvan came over and began consoling me.

I was crying so hard I had begun to see black spots as I tasted my own salty tears and screamed, "Why, damn it, why? She *cannot* be dead!"

Gabe had now begun alerting the other partygoers of Diana's death like Paul Revere on his Midnight Ride. When he realized I was having a breakdown, he ran over to me and asked, "Are you going to be okay?"

"I never got to meet her," I sobbed. "What about her children? Oh my God, her sons are too young to understand all of this!"

"Daren, I didn't know you cared so much for the Lady Di."

"Huh?" I looked him squarely in the eyes.

"I just meant, I didn't realize that Princess Diana's death was going to affect you this much or I would have waited to tell you," he said.

"*Princess* Diana?" I asked, wiping the tears from my face.

"She's gone, she was so young." Gabe squeezed out some crocodile tears as he sat down and tried to put his arm around me.

"Wait, wait, *wait*," I said and jumped up. "So Diana Ross is alive?"

"As far as I know," he said, looking puzzled.

"Man! You can't come up to me talking about Diana is dead

and not clarify *which* Diana it is," I said. My tears had dried up almost instantly. "Why would you think that I would cry over some bulimic British bitch with a gym-teacher dyke haircut?"

"Jesus, Daren," Gabe choked on his freshly lit cigarette. "You don't have the sense that God gave a chicken!"

"Say whatever you want, but as long as *Miss Ross* is alive, 'Someday, we'll be together...' I began singing as I wafted into the apartment to refresh my cocktail. "Mmm, yes we will, yes we will."

Antonio, Dwelvan, and Kevin erupted into laughter. I didn't wish Princess Diana any harm, and as an adult I later realized what an impact her life and death had on the world, but on that August night in 1997, the only Diana I was concerned about was the Queen of Motown Records: Diana Ross.

When I came back outside, I found more people in mourning. They held hands, passed around candles, and cried a lot, and they had begun throwing daggers at me with their eyes as I chanted the lyrics to the song "Ain't No Mountain High Enough." It was after my third request for someone to turn off the somber John Lennon music and play "I'm Coming Out" that our friend Theresa came up to me and pulled me aside.

Theresa, a costume design major, was my next-door neighbor in our dorm. At twenty-three years old, she was *ancient* to us, but she was the "mature" one who often took care of us on emotional nights. I knew she was going to chastise me for my insensitivity to Princess Diana's death. What she said to me, though, was more sobering than a large cup of black coffee with a turbo shot of espresso.

"Daren, just act like we're having a regular conversation and don't make any big gestures," she said. "When you get ready to leave, make sure someone straight is with you."

"What?" I asked.

"You aren't safe," her eyes shifted. "There are townies at this party who want to hurt you."

"Townies? Theresa what are you talking about?" I asked.

Theresa had noticed some guys who looked out of place at the party. After approaching them, asking if they were freshmen and why she had never seen them around the theatre department, she was able to pry out of them that they were townies who had heard that the school was full of "real-live homos." They hated "faggots" and were looking to "kick some faggot-ass and let them know that we don't go for that *fag-shit* here in Decatur."

"Theresa, how did you get them to tell you all of this?" I asked.

"I told them that I didn't like gay people either, but I have to put up with you guys because of my major," she lit a cigarette. "Then they sang like birds."

"How do I know who the townies are and who are just students who I don't know?" I asked.

"Do not turn around but there's a bearded guy with a green baseball cap in the corner behind you," she explained. "He's also got two friends next door on the lookout for gay people, too. Those are the ringleaders but they also have people surrounding this complex with weapons. Don't trust anyone who tells you that they are lost or need directions back to campus; it's a set-up."

I surveyed my surroundings and realized the same person who had tried to run us over earlier on the sidewalk was now at the party ready for round two. Then I noticed Antonio being eyeballed from the apartment next door; Gabe was on everyone's radar or "gaydar" for that matter. Dwelvan's size and stature made us believe it was very unlikely anyone would try to jump him but after the events from earlier that day, even he was scared to walk back to the dorm. Although The Woods was technically still on campus, the complex was a good ten-minute walk from our dorms and far enough away that some serious bodily harm could be done to us if we weren't careful.

By that point, I no longer cared about celebrating Diana Ross's life or not grieving over Princess Diana's death, I was concerned for *my* own life. Theresa and I began walking up to gay people at the party, warning them about the townies. We told Gabe last because I knew his reaction would be dramatic. Sure enough, Gabe had to all but be medically sedated. "No, ma'am! This can't happen on a campus where I pay tuition to go to! No ma'am," he swooned and clutched his imaginary pearl necklace.

"Man, you can't let on that you know," I warned. "Act as if you are upset about Princess Diana and find your way back to your apartment immediately." Even though Gabe lived in the complex, we still thought it would be a smart idea to have a few of the huskier guys from the department escort him and some of the other gay students back to their apartments.

The party was crowded, so it was easy to warn our friends without looking obvious. Every time I looked, though, I saw a townie hovering in my area. Theresa had rounded up some of the other student car owners at the party and explained the situation to them. Without exception, everyone who was sober agreed to drive some others back to the dorms.

"I'm parked in the Winery parking lot right across the street from the entrance to The Woods," Theresa said.

"How are we going to get out to your car?" I asked.

"Easy, give Antonio your hat to put on so that he can cover up that blond hair. When we leave, I'm going to take my hair down and put my sweatshirt on over my T-shirt. I'll hold Kevin's hand as if we are a couple and the four of us are going to just walk right out of here. I guarantee you that they won't recognize us, they're not that bright and they have been drinking."

Everyone had to leave in shifts, as to not make the escape too obvious. Gabe's roommate drove a pickup truck and hauled Dwelvan and several other kids back to the dorms on the flatbed. Antonio, Kevin, Theresa, and I made it to the car without a problem, but to say we were power walking would be an understatement. Theresa kept whispering to me, "Slow down, it's going to be fine. We are walking boys. We are not running."

Once we were safely in the locked car, I looked out the window and sure enough, there were four more townies loitering in front of the main entrance to the complex, as if they were waiting for a signal. These guys were of college age so Millikin's security wouldn't have necessarily thought them odd or out of place. One had a large backpack, and they were all drinking something from glass bottles that could be easily bashed against the sidewalk and turned into weapons.

No one was injured that night but from then on I never set foot off campus unless I was driving my car and stashed my wooden baseball bat underneath the driver's seat. I was always ready to defend myself when I left campus. What I wasn't ready for was the series of vicious anti-gay and anti-black hate crimes that began exploding on campus between other students. These violent episodes even erupted in our own dorms, apartments, and at school-sponsored events.

The school's administrators denied our repeated requests for protection and implied that if we didn't dress or *act* a certain way, people wouldn't bother us. There were days where I found myself too afraid, too angry, or too depressed to even leave my dorm room for fear that a glass Snapple bottle would drop from an upstairs dorm room window as people shouted "faggots below" at us. By the end of my sophomore year, I had developed a chip on my shoulder that would take years to lose.

Time took its toll on my nerves, and I fled the sleepy soybean capital in search of clarity, positive energy, and most of all, safety. I vowed to chase after all of my dreams and never again allow the ignorance of small minds to force me to feel any sort of shame for being myself. I transferred to and graduated from a New York acting conservatory and later earned my bachelor's degree in creative writing at The New School in New York. Some of my Millikin friends, unfortunately, dropped out altogether. If becoming a victim of multiple hate crimes is what it takes to get a degree, they would rather not have one, they said. As a matter of fact, Dwelvan was the only one of us who was able to stick it out in Decatur and actually graduate with a degree from Millikin.

Years later he told me there is finally a hate crimes policy at Millikin that formally recognizes the verbal and physical harassment of gay and lesbian students as a hate crime. For me, though, that news was bittersweet. I'm relieved to know that no other students will have to be treated as though they deserved to be attacked if they become the victim of a bias-related crime. At the same time, I'll never know why it took a year and a half of harassment and physical violence and the departures of several students before the adults took what was happening to us seriously.

I know Theresa saved someone's life that night. The night Princess Diana died I realized a person's life can end in the blink of an eye. The night Princess Diana died I realized we live in a world filled with more hate than I could fathom. The night Princess Diana died was only a mere preview of what was to come.

Many Rivers to Cross
André St. Clair Thompson

When my grandfather first held me in his arms, he said to my daddy, "Dis bwoy ah go be special an great." When Daddy told me that, it was the biggest gift he ever gave me.

In the winter of 1990, Air Jamaica flew my mother, my five-year-old sister, and seven-year-old me to the US to live with Daddy. My sister and I ran into his arms when we saw him at JFK International Airport. He and Mommy kissed. It snowed the next day, and Daddy woke us up to take our first look. I was happy we were finally able to live together as a family. But Ervine, the father I had previously known mostly through phone conversations and his periodic visits from the States to Jamaica, would soon turn into a monster.

Throughout my childhood, my father verbally and physically abused my mother. As the damaged and poorly educated product of childhood abuse, abandonment, and neglect, my mother adapted to the violence but felt trapped in the relationship. She would never press charges the many times police were called to the house. Each year passed with new promises that things would get better but they only got worse.

I grew to hate my father so much that I began wishing for his demise, even cursing God for saving his life when he was critically injured while working as a construction worker at the World Trade Center following its 1993 bombing. The sight and sound of him made me sick. He so repulsed me that I spat into lemonade he made me make for him one hot summer day. I enjoyed watching him swallow every drop.

The turning point for me came one night in 1996 during my freshman year of high school. He and Mommy had gotten into an argument while I sat watching the television amidst the commotion. The next thing I knew, a butt naked and dripping-wet Ervine stormed from the bathroom to the kitchen. Enraged, he pinned my mother between the opening of the refrigerator and the wall, and wailed on her as my siblings and I yelled, cried, and tried to pull him off, even taking some of the blows ourselves.

Feeling powerless, I grabbed a knife, "thinking of committing some dreadful crime," and threatened to stab him with it. He was undeterred. All I wanted to do was rid our world of him, but as I grazed his arm with the blade, the live-in tenant in our house dislodged the knife from my hand. Finally, Ervine stopped and returned to the bathroom. That was the last time he tried to beat my mom in my presence.

I wanted to rescue my mother and my siblings from Ervine forever, but I had rivers of my own to cross. By the time I was five years old, I knew I was gay. Many days I even wished I had been born a girl. Sometimes I simply wished I had never been born. As an effeminate boy living in New York City with Jamaican parents, everyday life posed challenges.

When the song "Boom Bye Bye" was released in 1988 by then-fifteen-year-old dancehall reggae superstar Buju Banton, I was five years old and still living in Jamaica. Though it was a major hit, I do not remember the song from that period. What I do remember is having my first homosexual encounter at that age with a friend who was only a couple of years older than me. One day we played house. I was mommy and he was daddy and our younger siblings played the roles of our children. I enjoyed the role of "woman" and I used a shirt to give me long hair. As strict parents, my "husband" and I sent the children to bed and we made love in private. We kissed and I put "it" in my mouth and sucked it. Our imaginations ran wild. The experience only happened once, but I liked it. Fortunately we were not caught, and neither one of us told anyone.

Banton's song was re-released when I was nine years old, while my family was living in East New York, Brooklyn. Life in America had not turned out as I expected. My father had let me down, and the kids at school and in my community were bullying me for being foreign. It became difficult for me to form friendships, but what affected me most were my developing feelings of attraction to boys that I tried to hide. What I could not hide, however, was my effeminate nature. Perhaps I could hide it from my family but not from my peers. To a group of boys in my school and in my neighborhood I was a "batty boy" that needed to be shot, as Buju himself had urged in "Boom Bye Bye."

"The world is in trouble/Anytime Buju Banton come/ Batty boy get up and run/ ah gunshot in ah head man/Tell dem crew…it's like/ Boom bye bye, in a batty boy head, rude boy nah promote no nasty man, them hafi dead."

The average member of the reggae dancehall culture knows the message that song is sending to its listeners. Translated, the lyrics read: *"The world is in trouble/When Buju Banton arrives/ Faggots have to run/Or get a bullet in the head/Bang-bang, in a faggot's head/Homeboys don't condone nasty men/They must die."*[1]

By 1994, the message of "Boom Bye Bye" was well ingrained in my childhood psyche. The song received continuous play in

---

1. Melissa Henry, "'Boom Bye-Bye in a Batty Boy Head': Reggae Icons, Jamaican Culture, and Homophobia," Paper delivered at the Fourth Annual Composition and Cultural Studies Conference for Student Writers at George Washington University, 2001

my mostly poor and working-class black neighborhood heavily influenced by Caribbean culture. The penalty for homosexuality was clear, but one specific episode that summer stuck with me.

Every summer, the neighbors put on a block party that all the kids looked forward to attending. At the 1994 block party, I was enjoying the festivities while riding my bicycle up and down the block. But the fun stopped abruptly when "Boom Bye Bye" came blasting through the sound speakers, and like a Greek chorus, block members, children, and adults alike, recited its lyrics.

I was positioned at one end of the block with my house more than half the block away towards the other end. My body temperature rose dramatically and I felt lightheaded. I wanted to get home immediately, but I would have to pass one of the burned out abandoned buildings on the block that had become a congregation post for the "boy's boys" of my neighborhood. As I pedaled past them, they all pointed, laughed, and hurled the lyrics at me. It was one of the most embarrassing moments of my life.

Before the song had ended, I parked my bicycle and ran inside to my bedroom, crying in solitude, and eventually falling asleep, robbed of the opportunity to enjoy the rest of the festivities.

Over the years, some intellectuals have tried to rationalize Banton's song. Jamaica's own Carolyn Cooper, for example, suggests the controversy over "Boom Bye Bye" is overblown, as Melissa Henry explains:

> Carolyn Cooper, a well-known Jamaican literary and cultural critic, has insisted that Buju's gun is essentially a "lyrical" one that is meant to illustrate the function of metaphor and role-play in contemporary Jamaican dancehall culture. Consequently, Cooper argues that critics who are unfamiliar with the metaphorical qualities of the Jamaican vernacular have misread Buju's

song by taking his words all too literally. Thus, taken out of context, the popular Jamaican Creole declaration, 'all battyman hafi dead,' may be misunderstood as an unequivocal, literal death-sentence: 'all homosexuals must die.' In contrast, Cooper suggests that Buju's "lyrical gun" should be understood primarily as a "symbolic penis" and, therefore, in the final analysis, the song can be seen as a symbolic celebration of the vaunted potency of heterosexual men who know how to use their "gun" to satisfy their women.[2]

As a Jamaican myself, I feel I have a strong grasp of the Jamaican metaphorical vernacular. And at only nine years old when "Boom Bye Bye" was re-released, I was made very aware of what the lyrics meant. The song is heterosexist and homophobic. It put me in check and reminded me that Jamaica could reach beyond its borders and reclaim me. Cooper's so-called "lyrical gun" is able to fire shots at very real queer lives in order to remedy the supposed emasculation of the black male under colonialism. The message clearly states that the black queer as object needs to be exterminated. The black gay male might as well be the white man without any protection of his inherent skin privilege. That is the message that followed me to the States and continually reasserted itself in the slew of songs with similar messages that succeeded "Boom Bye Bye."

By the fall of 2001, I was attending Brown University, considered the most liberal of the eight Ivy League schools, and for the first time I was surrounded by out gays who were thriving. I began to go through a multi-stage coming out process. First I was "bisexual." Then I was "gay." But as quickly as I started to embrace my sexuality, the collective voice of the melodic Jamaican male dancehall reggae group T.O.K. came to torment me.

2. Henry, *Boom Bye-Bye.*

T.O.K.'s 2001 hit song "Chi Chi Man" provided a new voice of admonition. Now, in addition to the gunshots that Banton threatened, gay men like myself had to worry about being torched by fire. In T.O.K.'s words:

> *Every chi chi man dem haffi get flat*
> *Get flat, mi and my niggas ago mek a pack*
> *Chi chi man fi dead and dat's a fact*
> *Blaze di fire mek we bun dem!!!! (Bun dem!!!!)*

Line for line, the translation is:

> *Every gay man must get killed*
> *Get killed, me and my niggas are going to make a pact*
> *Gay man must die and that is a fact*
> *Blaze the fire let us burn them!! (Burn them!!!)*

The addition of the backup (Burn them) gives the feeling of a true following of people. In fact, during the 2002 elections for Prime Minister, Jamaica Labour Party Leader "Edward Seaga adopted T.O.K's "Chi Chi Man" as his campaign theme song and strongly implied in speeches that the Prime Minister [P.J. Patterson] is gay."[3] This was a national political leader's campaign song as he vied for the highest office in the land, and there was no outcry about it. When T.O.K was criticized abroad about the music, Carolyn Cooper's metaphorical bullshit resurfaced. "Chi Chi" means termite in Jamaican patois, and therefore the lyrics were said to refer to driving away those folks who eat away at the foundation of society. But for Jamaicans and others, gay and straight, who know the meaning behind the metaphors: The termite is the battyman is the gay.

"Chi Chi Man" got great play in the US and many a gay man was caught dancing to its infectious rhythms in gay nightclubs. Hell, I was one of those people dancing to the tunes that advocated for my death. I danced because I liked the beat. It

3. Elena Oumnao

hooked me and I forgot about politics. I was just eighteen years old and only cared about having a good time. However, when I stepped outside of queer safe spaces, I felt eyes on my queer body as the song roared over my liberal college campus. It was silencing, bringing me back to the day of that 1994 block party.

T.O.K became a phenomenon amongst not only reggae fans, but also hip-hop lovers. As a cultural crossover, T.O.K was able to reach an American audience that had already accepted the conception of black male sexual outlaws accompanied by their black female whores. A homophobic celebration feeds that conception. Misconceptions of blackness sell here in America. Dancehall reggae is similar to gangsta rap as they both boast vulgar rhetorical traditions. With this similarity, it makes sense that Jamaica's form would carve out a place in the American market, especially given the strong West Indian population, reggae's global success, and its contribution to early hip-hop culture.

As "Chi Chi Man" blazed on during freshman year, I fell into deep depression. Up until then, education provided an escape from my inner torments, but I was living my life as an "out" gay man to my college community while living a lie outside of that community. Originally a pre-med, neuroscience concentrator, my studies took a back seat to the pain I was grappling with for the very first time. By second semester, my escape from the pain became a first boyfriend who came in tandem with excessive partying and experimenting with drugs.

Next, I began exploring my gender expression. I began dressing as a girl on a regular basis, both day and night, with the intention of passing. *Yet another river.* Could I become a woman? During the hardest days of my childhood, my imagination had played out how life would have been if I had been born a girl. My spirit would be congruent with my body. I would have been beautiful and ultra femme. I would have been able to express myself as a whole person. I would be accepted as a whole person. I would not feel so alone. I would grow up to have a rich and handsome husband with whom I would live happily ever after.

The first time I cross-dressed I was mesmerized by my own transformation. With my tight and small frame and a big behind, I made a convincing woman when I added breasts, hair, and makeup. My girl Tahirah hooked me up. As months passed on the Brown campus, female friends reported to me that some of their guy friends swore I was the hottest girl they had ever seen until they were informed of my "status." I was feeling myself. But just like my childhood fantasies, these moments would not last. I began to contemplate gender reassignment.

When I returned home from campus for semester breaks, I had to shed completely the person I was becoming. Finally, in March 2002, I had a severe emotional breakdown on the day I was scheduled to return home for spring break. With my roommate already gone, I woke up anxious and crying in the fetal position. I did not want to go home. Alone in my bedroom, I missed my train from Providence to New York and phoned my mother just an hour before the train's scheduled arrival. She immediately knew something was wrong from the tone of my voice and pleaded with me to explain. I did not say much, so she asked questions.

"Did you get a girl pregnant?"

To this I laughed for the first time that day and informed her that was the last thing to worry about.

To that she came back with, "Are you gay?"

Silence.

"It's okay. You can tell me. Mommy will always love you."

"Yes," I replied.

My mother promised to be there for me, and reminded me I will always be her son, but she also admitted this was not the life she dreamt for me. I felt like a disappointment to her. Knowing that my father would respond negatively, we agreed to keep it as our secret. My mother was now in the closet with me.

After spring break, I returned to my out college life where I had a better support system. At the urging of Professor Elmo

Terry-Morgan, I attended an event with a visiting lecturer named Keith Boykin. As an eighteen-year-old college freshman, I was completely smitten by him, and I bought a copy of his book, *One More River to Cross: Black & Gay In America*, which he signed: "To André, Enjoy the book. I hope it serves as an oar to cross the rivers in your own life. Keith Boykin." Little did I know that *One More River to Cross* would lead me to another river.

Although I spent the summer taking classes at Brown, mostly to avoid going home, I had to return to New York because of a death in the family. I went home with *One More River to Cross* and found moments to sneak away and read it. Then one morning my father woke me up and told me to come to the dining room. As I entered, I saw him holding the book in hand, and I realized I had left it on the table where I had been reading it before going to bed. In that moment, I experienced the same bodily sensation as the eleven-year-old André assaulted by the rhythms of "Boom Bye Bye."

My father immediately asked what I was doing reading such a book. The only thing I could think of telling him was that I was reading it for class. The man who never went to college replied, "No way a school would permit di reading about no battyman" and that I was reading it because I must be a "battyman." Angrily, he went on to question the way Boykin signed the book. Why would this book serve as oar in my life if I was not a battyman? I explained that there are lessons that anyone could learn from the book. This, of course, incensed him more as he could not fathom what anyone could learn from the likes of a battyman like Boykin.

Our escalating conversation woke everyone in the house, including my mother. He showed the book to her, and I repeated the lies I told him. I needed the book to write a report, I said. My mother, thank God, was able to convince him to believe me. Finally, reluctantly, he returned the book to me. Several days later I returned to Brown.

Upon my return I met and accepted the mentorship of an older female-to-male transsexual visiting scholar and activist who understood that I felt like a woman trapped in a man's body. He was deeply involved in a personal training and development company called Landmark Education. Feeling I could benefit from the company's services, my mentor urged me to participate in its weekend introductory "Landmark Forum" course. I was skeptical of the company's work as mere "brainwashing," but less than two months after the book incident with my father, I found myself in the Forum's intense environment of what felt like proselytizing. Allowing myself to be "coachable," I experienced a weekend of consuming self-examination where many of my walls fell and in group session I was encouraged to come out to my father.

Exercising a newfound sense of freedom and power I called Ervine from my cell phone. He was watching a soccer match when he picked up the phone. Without delay, I explained that I lied to him about the meaning of Boykin's book in my life.

"I am gay, Daddy."

Translated from his Jamaican patois into English, what he said to me in response was this: "If you were still in Jamaica, I would have somebody kill you, you see, boy." My father then disowned me and told me not to step foot back in his house ever again.

Ten years have passed since that phone conversation, and I have not seen Ervine once. I have not even a clue what he looks like today without so much as a picture as a reference. He is still married to my mom who feels trapped in a loveless marriage. I have not yet been able to reach my goal of rescuing her and my siblings.

"Your father loves you; it's just your lifestyle he doesn't like."

I am now twenty-eight years old, and this is the message I recently received from a distant relative. My father, who disowned me, threatened to kill me, and hasn't called me in ten years, professes to love me. I am his great disappointment, he tells others, but my freedom from his tyranny is what really bothers him.

The "lifestyle" my father dislikes is not one I chose. I have only chosen to take advantage of the opportunity I have in the United States to live out of the closet. As a Jamaican, I was fed cultural cues that described my feelings as unnatural, and I learned early in life how to keep my sexual feelings and gender issues to myself. Although I have vivid memories of the island's beauty and majesty, today she scares me. Remaining in Jamaica, for me, would have been a death sentence unless I could hide my sexual orientation and gender identity.

I am proud to see my nation's culture enter into mainstream America, a celebration of my Jamaican roots. But with this national pride comes a feeling of exclusion and a sense that I am betraying my own being. Now I cannot help but to disidentify with my culture.[4] Unquestioned Christianity, used as a nation-building tool, has resulted in the unrelenting proliferation of homophobia in the streets, music, and most influentially, a government with no separation between church and state. Jamaica has more churches per square mile than anywhere else on earth, according to the Guinness Book of World Records. Fortunately, through Jamaica's active participation in globalization, that nation is encountering resistance to homophobia that will one day shape a new future for my country of origin.

I will always be Jamaican and I will always be my father's son, but I will no longer give up a part of myself to belong. Today, I accept what my father called my "lifestyle" as I embrace its potential for nourishing a life of advocacy. My presence as an out gay and cross-dressing male Jamaican could make all the difference to some queer Jamaican youth facing his own

---

[4] According to José Estaban Moñoz, disidentification is meant to be descriptive of the survival strategies the minority subject practices in order to negotiate a phobic majoritarian public sphere that continuously elides or punishes the existence of subjects who do not conform to the phantasm of normative citizenship.

adversity. Of course, my journey of reclamation has put me at war with nation and family. As with any war, people get hurt. This is real hurt that takes the war out of the metaphorical sphere and places it squarely in the midst of reality. But I am no longer at war with myself.

I have chosen to live my life in the body of a male. It took years to realize that the incongruity I felt between my body and mind was the product of social dictates and cultural roots. I do still question whether or not I traverse the "right" path, particularly when I consider the extent to which a full transition could positively impact my life. As a gender nonconformist, gay Jamaican-American, I yearn for change in my home country, I yearn for peace for my family, and I yearn for peace for myself.

Becoming Jessica Wild

José David Sierra

Since I was a kid, I always knew I was attracted to guys. I was also attracted to feminine things, and people near to me would say, "What are you doing?" or "That's girl's stuff?" or "Why do you have a doll in your hand?"

I was doing girlie things, but when I was six, I was also in love with another kid from school, and I was always dreaming that one day he would be my boyfriend. But I thought what I felt inside of me was not normal because I was attacked all the time for the way I expressed myself with my body or my words or the way I moved, so I started to control the real person that I was.

The kids from school and some of the people from my family, some aunts and cousins, called me *pato* or *maricón* or *loca* or *nena*, and they treated me differently, like I was a girl or something out of the world. It felt like "you are here but you are not welcome." That's why I would just wait to be with my mom, because she was the only one who always treated me right. I felt safe with her all the time.

I hated school for that reason, too, because of the things the kids said. So at one point when I was thirteen I said to myself, "You need to act differently," so I started spending more time with the bad boys and trying to be another person because I was thinking I needed to survive. It's not the real me, but it's what the world wants.

Then one day my favorite cousin told my mom something from my uncle that hurt me. My cousin and I were always laughing and joking and having fun and maybe that was too much for my uncle. My cousin was supposed to stay with us during the summer but wasn't allowed, so my mom asked, "Why are you not going to stay with us?"

"Because my dad said that David is a faggot, and he thinks that that may make me a faggot." But then my cousin added, "I love my cousin, and I know he's not a faggot. But if he is a faggot, I love him anyway."

I was thinking to myself, "Oh my God, I want to die right now." He was talking about that in front of my mom. She was so quiet, just listening. I was always trying not to be in trouble because I didn't want to hurt my mom. But I was so embarrassed, and my mom acted like nothing happened. Right there in front of me. I was quiet also but I was dying inside.

I kept in touch with my cousin after that because I loved him, but I started not being in my uncle's world anymore. He was my favorite uncle and everything changed from that day, not with my cousin but with him.

I realized I didn't want to live a gay life because I was going to be in trouble with God or my family, so I never had a typical sex life when I was a teenager, like a first kiss or something, because I was scared that this was not good. I started doing things with boys when I was nine, but when I realized it was bad I quit. I was in Puerto Rico and things there are different. Latinos are very masculine, and it was the 80s and 90s and we were told boys need to find a girl.

Sometimes gay people don't express that they are gay, so I

started thinking I was the only one. And at that point, I didn't realize that a masculine guy could be gay. Or if you have a girlfriend, you can like guys, too. So I felt I was alone. I did not want to live the gay life and live in my own world, but I was always creating things, dancing, drawing, and creating music.

Since I was a kid, I expressed myself by drawing and creating things with the materials I had for play. I have an aunt who was like my nanny, and she was so creative that she was kind of crazy to other people, but she was fun. And she was always making things; if she had a flower, she would create something special to put the flower inside. For Christmas, she created her own ornaments. And when I was with her, I was in a place where I could create a lot. I was in my own world, and I felt "Oh, I like this, I love to create, to paint." That was my first sign of an artistic side, and people thought I was going to be a painter because I was drawing a lot of great things, but I realized I wanted something else.

When I was sixteen my mom let me start dancing class. I started thinking I wanted to be a dancer, I want to be a singer, I want to be a rock star. Dance classes were her idea. If I had asked her to take dancing class, then for sure she would've thought I was gay, because in Puerto Rico it's like, "Why you wanna be a dancer? That's for girls or for gays."

I was high in my own world, creating shows in my head, and always in my imagination I was in front of a big crowd. I started going late to school, just living my dreams—daydreams. I was going to bed sometimes at 5:00 A.M. and going to school at 7:00 A.M. so I was very tired most of the time. I remember one night I went to sleep and the telephone rang, and I answered the phone and it was a friend. When I put my head back on the pillow, I felt my bed was spinning. I was not on drugs or anything, and I wondered what the hell had happened to me.

I got up and went to the bathroom, and the bathroom was spinning. I started talking to God and thought nothing bad can happen to me because I had never really touched a guy, so I went to bed again and I started thinking about beautiful things, and I finally fell asleep.

When I woke up the next morning, I remembered what had happened the night before and I felt it again. Soon all my days started to be a nightmare. I was just thinking about my fears. I was having panic attacks.

I stopped dancing because I was so scared that my life began to be a nightmare. I wasn't scared of anything in particular. I was just scared of this feeling of being scared. My mom took me to a doctor, but he didn't know what was happening; I thought maybe I was becoming crazy. My mom was desperate and crying. She took me to church but I was still panicked. At home she prayed next to me and put a Bible on my chest and told me I was going to be okay. And I took the Bible off and said, "Mom, I need to talk to you."

"You know that boys are supposed to like girls, and girls are supposed to like boys," I began. "I don't like girls. I'm different."

"You know that I love you no matter what," Mom said. "I just want you to feel good."

I felt a little bit better, but later I started to feel bad again. I spoke to my sister about my feelings, and then I spoke to my brother, who had studied for the priesthood before he joined the Army. I remember my brother's words clearly. "You are my brother. If you are going to be gay, just be a respectful one. It's not about straight or gay, it's about respect," he said.

My brother told me a story he hadn't shared before. "You never realized why I quit the priesthood," he said. "Mom never let me be in the Army, but I used to love the church. And you remember all the friends I had when I was going to be a priest, right? One day they had to do a confession and all the guys who confessed that they were gay got kicked out, and so I quit, too. I'm straight," my brother said, "and I like girls, I love girls, but if I can quit sex because I want to be a priest, then they can quit the gay life to be a priest, too. They are not supposed to quit being gay. They're supposed to quit living a worldly life so they can give their life to God. And when I saw how the church treated them, I thought, 'This is what I'm going to be a part of?' My brother then looked at me and gave me some serious advice. "*Nunca renuncies a quien tu eres*," he told me. Never give up who you are. "People need to respect you for who you are," he said, "and if you respect yourself, people are going to respect you."

Some time later, I started going out to gay nightclubs and bars. One night the music stopped at a club, and I turned around; "Oh, the drag queens," I thought. "Why are people looking at that?" But as I watched the show, I changed. I realized I actually loved it. Well, I loved the first drag queen, but the other ones were boring. I started paying more attention to drag queens, and then one day I realized I could do a great job as a drag queen because everybody has a purpose in life, and I believed mine was to entertain.

I was afraid people would think I am a girl, so I started doing it at parties just for fun. My friends thought I made a cute girl but that was it. One day my dance company and I were supposed to perform in a dance contest, and the principal character was a girl who couldn't make it because she was sick. My friend said, "You are going to be the girl." I said, "No, no, no. In a club? With all those people?" But they encouraged me to do it. They helped me buy a wig, which was horrible; we thought I was gorgeous when really I was a hot mess.

When the show started I was inside a rope and I opened the rope and came out, and people were looking at me and cheering as they would for a dancer-performer. They weren't looking at me like a pretty contest girl, because in Puerto Rico at that point the drag scene was more about gorgeous outfits and less about performing. But when they saw me with ten dancers and heels and dancing hard and the wig never fell off, the crowd started screaming and cheering. At the end of the show I felt amazing, I felt something great.

Nina Flowers, a famous drag queen, saw me and said I could be a great Latin drag queen but needed to change some things.

I said I was just doing it for fun, but she told me what to do anyway; to get some pads and work on my makeup. "You are going to be in my show in two weeks," she insisted. I performed at her show with the dance group and all the gays were crazy in love with me. I started doing it more and more until one day I was ready to present my first live concert at the biggest gay club in San Juan, Puerto Rico, in 2001. The show was called "Sobrevivire" inspired by the singer Monica Naranjo. People started to realize I was talented and spread the word throughout the island. That's how I won a space among the drag divas in Puerto Rico.

I picked the name Jessica Wild because one of my best friends in school was named Jessica. For me, Jessica was a sexy name and easy to pronounce. And I chose Wild because I'm wild on stage, so I put them both together. Soon I realized I didn't need the dancers to hide that I'm a drag queen. I was just Jessica Wild. Before I used to finish a show and immediately take off everything because I didn't want anybody to realize that David and Jessica were the same person. But I realized that gays love drag. Straight guys loved me in drag. Girls loved me in drag. So I started to love my character more and take it more seriously. I won the fight for people to respect me because I'm gay. Now people need to respect that I'm gay and I'm a drag queen.

One day RuPaul had a concert in Puerto Rico, and the producer of the concert, who knew me from a club I had worked at, asked me to be in the opening for her. I agreed. He told me that RuPaul couldn't do all the local interviews because she was coming late, but he asked if I could help promote it, and of course I said yes. It was going to be my first time on TV as a drag queen, and I was just twenty-three years old.

I went to an interview for a TV show, and it happened to be a show that my father used to watch all the time. At this point, my mother knew I was doing drag because one of my cousins told her, but she never told my father and he and I never talked about it. I told my mom that if my father was watching TV that day, she should talk to him or distract him because I didn't want him to see it, even though I would be disguised in drag.

The next day my mom called and told me that my father watched the show with my cousin who was visiting from Alaska. My cousin was surprised that the drag queens on the show were guys, and he pointed out one he thought was cute. Without missing a beat, my father replied, "*Ah, sí, y el es tu primo.*"

My mom started laughing because she realized my father could see right through the makeup and knew it was me all along. "*El es mi hijo. No importa lo que haga lo voy a reconocer*," he said. "It's my son. I'm going to know my son no matter what."

My father never changed. He acted the same with me. Nothing changed in our relationship. So I realized I had the support of my mom and my dad.

I was doing Jessica for some time, but I still worked for an art school. Then I quit the art school and I started working for a store because I wanted to have a normal job. I was there three years, but Jessica was always my first focus. People at work would tell me, "I don't know what you are doing here. You are a very talented person, and you have a world waiting for you." But I had a good-paying job and I wasn't going to quit, so I was there but unhappy. Finally, I got fired from the job, and I started wondering what would I do with my life. I had no other job, so I started doing more drag full-time and took another part-time job to support me.

By the time I got to the part-time job, I realized that people think about what works for them, like the store would think about what's best for the store. So I needed to think about me. My boss was upset that I was thinking about other things, but I didn't feel it. I was just doing it for the money. I started wondering if I was ever going to have my moment to live my artistic dream or if I was going to die waiting for that. I slowly learned that I needed to be in drag if I wanted to pay my bills. But being a drag queen is not easy. It's a lot of pain, a lot of money to spend, and it's hard work when you do it professionally.

When I saw *RuPaul's Drag Race*, Season 1, I thought it was an impossible dream. But when Season 2 auditions started, I said no again. I didn't speak English, I didn't sew, and I didn't want to go. But my friends convinced me to audition, and I tried to be cast just for fun, but I was sure they were not going to pick me.

When they called and told me they were interested, I was still struggling with my English and scared, but once the casting finished and they said, "Congratulations, you are part of *RuPaul's Drag Race*," they said, adding, "You can scream." I said, "I'm at work," so I didn't scream. But I was more scared than ever. I was ready to quit before I started. They had my plane ticket, and I wasn't going to take it because I was so scared. But my friend told me, "If you do that, I'm going to kick your ass. You won a lot of fights in your life. This is another one." I knew that was true, so I put my ass on that airplane and flew to L.A., and *Drag Race* changed my life completely. It opened a lot of doors to me and gave people a chance to see and respect me as an artist. Now people know me around the world because *RuPaul's Drag Race* is an international show and my season was a big one.

People used to look at me like the gay or the faggot of the family. And now they look at me like the star of the family. I'm from the mountains in the forest. I'm not from the city or the glamorous life. So they see their cousin from a small town traveling around the world with his own CD, but he's still the same person to them. That's the attention I wanted as a kid, but now I realize I don't need it to believe in myself.

I'm doing what I love, I get paid for what I love, and I believe more in my business. It's not about trying to be a girl or trying to be a diva. It's just about doing what I love and making your dreams come true. I love to do makeup, I love to dance, I love to sing, and I love to entertain—with Jessica Wild I get to do all that. As a drag queen, as an artist, and performer, I increased my income so I don't need my old job. My work for me now is my music and my passion for the arts. Jessica Wild is my business, it's my company, my trademark that I created, and I worked hard for that. I became Jessica Wild because I was waiting to be a rock star, and she is the star I was waiting to become. Now I'm a public figure in the gay community and a lot of people follow my work.

As David I still get to keep my privacy. But people love me with or without makeup. I have a voice now as a gay man. And now I can inspire others to live their dreams or to fight for the things that they want. Because in the end, you are going to be a winner.

IN SICKNESS AND HEALTH

Umm...Okay

Tim'm T. West

he said:
"...umm...okay
I'm okay with you being
...umm...positive"
like I'm okay
with him being negative.
please, spare me the negation
cloaked in pitying self-congratulation
for I have always
had to be my own savior.

today and tomorrow
and...
swallow these pills
that are hard to swallow
twice daily
not to live for an Other
but because

I enjoy the love preparing itself today
for tomorrow
the splendor and wonderment
of blushing and butterflies
and not...
"umm...okay"
so spare me!
This
ain't one of the deep poems, yo.
put simply
my living
deserves better.

need to know
the one I choose to love
and who chooses me
is not afraid
to fall, kiss, sex
yes safely...
yes bravely...
I love me enough to protect
myself
and my better whole
hold fast to the care
those who care enough to care
care to give.

I be that caregiver
not the "gift" some joke about
under whispers in dim-lit bars
nor the House in Virginia
or other stigmatizing thorns
that kill the dying
while they are still living
when we are all dying

if killing, even softly,
one among us who, too,
is of God.
so who you calling sick?

I be better
than the whispers
that seek to indict me
as sick
not healthy
for being honest
am not ashamed.
I have saved lives
for living honestly
the life God gave me
so I'm better
than the scapegoat some hide behind
the DL skeleton-filled closet
protected by pink elephants
how very...umm...tough
how very...masculine...
umm...okay?

I did not break down
one closet door
to enter another
and neither will my lover
whatever his or her status
test results will be
a positive result

in bravery,
we all non-reactive
we trust God, the universe
to keep and hold us

positive or negative.

so I need to know
when family and friends
ask
why you'd "risk your life"
to be with me
that you believe
you'd risk your life
not fulfilling your desire
to build a life with a good man
with a good heart
positively
want no shame in our bedroom
or out of it
for shameful loving
is a most crude disease
kills us faster
than AIDS.
a T-cell fails
with each self-rebuke
and joy is restored
with each Thank God!
that loving has kept me going this long
so must continue
to be the drive
for this BMW
this Black Male Warrior
is over ya' "umm...okays"

now I be a joy snatcher
warmed by the sunshine of my own smile
need it when I cloud
now I unshackle my dreams
so they appear in full color

accept joy only
in 3D and high-def
now I romance in stereo
so love looks so much brighter than
"umm...okay."

so no...
I'm okay.
and it's okay that you're okay
with being with a positive guy
okay?
but I'm not that guy to see and try
just to try and see.

see I am no longer okay
with being anyone's
okay.
I am a diamond
nestling in earth
to shine for the one who finds
and claims
my he-art.

and about that
I'm absolutely positive...
ummm...okay?

Thank You, CNN

David Malebranche

There are times in your life when you are reminded what is really important. Thursday, May 26, 2011 was one such time.

I arrived early to the busy public HIV clinic, where I work every Thursday morning, to make sure I was ahead of schedule and prepared for my patients, for that afternoon I had an important engagement—an interview with Sanjay Gupta, the medical correspondent from CNN, for a special marking the thirtieth anniversary of the first report of what was to be the beginning of the AIDS epidemic. As with most media productions, the planning for this interview had been hectic and insanely chaotic, consisting of a flurry of rapid-fire emails back and forth from the CNN representative, our clinic's public relations person, and the doctors and staff who were to be involved in the interviews. CNN was planning to not only interview staff at our clinic, but also several patients about the racial disparity in the South, which proved particularly problematic, as they were having a difficult time finding young, black, same gender loving male patients to agree to be interviewed and "identified" on camera. They were getting a quick refresher course on the continued stigma of HIV in the South, just in case they had forgotten.

So there I was, rolling through a typical clinic day full with the usual complicated and rewarding interactions with my patients, some of whom I've been seeing for almost ten years. They came to me that morning one after another, each with a different narrative: some dealing with difficult to control blood pressure, kidney disease, or painful nerves in the feet, others just recovering from bouts of pneumonia or severe depression, and a couple of men doing so well that instead of talking about HIV, we spent most of the visit discussing their families, new love interests, and exciting school ventures. Amidst all of this, I was sure to be even more meticulously careful in my chart documentation and addressing their concerns in a thorough and time-efficient manner. It's not every day you get to sit down with CNN and discuss your work, passion, and bring attention to the severely neglected issue of the HIV racial disparity in the South for an international television network special. I felt honored and humbled to participate in such an undertaking that could potentially reach so many people.

I finished up with all my patients around noon, went to my weekly lunch meeting across town, and returned to the clinic at 1:00 P.M. The CNN crew had told us they would be interviewing patients first, then another staff member before my turn. Since I wasn't seeing patients that afternoon, I decided to make good use of the time and catch up on calling various patients to let them know about lab results and other clinical matters. By 2:00 P.M. I received a text from a patient, a young man I will call "Kyle," whom I had seen while he had been admitted to the hospital a week before, but wasn't supposed to see me as a new patient at the clinic for another two weeks.

"Dr. Malebranche, I got your message—I'm at the clinic now. Where should I meet you?"

I had called Kyle the day before to tell him to come into

clinic that day, as one of his medical complications from HIV required him to start his medications immediately once he left the hospital. But in my rush to tell him to come in to see me, I forgot about all the other patients I had to see, plus the CNN interview, so I didn't know exactly how much time I would have for this man who represented the current face of the HIV epidemic in this country—a young, gifted, black, same gender loving male.

I rushed out the main hall of the clinic to find him, bright-eyed and bushy-tailed, glowing with a youthful exuberance that wasn't there when I had seen him in the hospital. He had already gone through the clinic enrollment process and had taken my instructions to heart about coming in early to get the process started, so I promptly arranged for him to see our nurse who does HIV medication counseling. She was now taking him to see our financial counselors to figure out how we could provide him these life-saving medications. I told him to text me again when he was finished and we'd sit down to talk. I figured the interview would be over by then, so I went back to my office to continue my work. There was a knock on the door from one of the nurse practitioners that was being interviewed earlier— CNN and Sanjay were ready for me. I gathered my things and made my way down the hall, only to be stopped by the clinic public relations person, who informed me that they were going to interview two other patients first, and I would be last before they wrapped up filming for the day. I went back to my office and kept working until Kyle texted me again.

"Okay, Doc, I'm ready."

I brought him in my office so we could talk. He had gained back about eight pounds already from when he was admitted, and even though he had been reluctant to take medications for years, the progression of his illness and a brief course in the hospital had changed all that. I told him I had to do the CNN interview soon, which he understood, but that we could discuss his health in the meantime. So we sat down, two black same gender loving men, doctor and patient, and discussed the types of medications he could take, potential benefits and side effects to all of them, and reviewed his labs from while he was in the hospital. It was a rare moment in clinic where I didn't feel rushed, had no interruptions, and felt like we could talk not only about Kyle's medical issues, but also angles of his personal life I hadn't heard before. And it was a good thing that we did take the time to review his labs from his hospital admission, as we found out that one of the tests had come back positive for another infection that required the urgent starting of his HIV meds.

I was glad to have been afforded the time to sit with Kyle as long as I did, so when the knock came on my door announcing that CNN was now ready for me, I think we were both disappointed. Kyle and I walked back to my nurse's office, where I informed her of our discovery of the other infection requiring a more pressing need for us to prioritize getting quick approval on his medications. She agreed and took his prescriptions so they could be filled at our pharmacy. I shook Kyle's hand, gave him a hug, and told him I'd see him in a couple of weeks for his follow-up appointment. My interaction with him that afternoon had inspired me for the CNN interview, and I was ready to talk about stories like Kyle's and other men like him—their resiliency, their strength, and the hope for their future in the face of adversity.

When I got to the interview site, I saw Sanjay, our public relations person, and some crewmembers, who were breaking down the cameras and the equipment. I introduced myself to Sanjay, ready at long last to do this interview that had been emailed, discussed, and delayed for the better part of the past couple of weeks and surely through that afternoon. Suddenly our public relations person spoke up.

"So we actually don't need to interview you today. Sanjay has to leave."

I'm sure the surprised look on my face gave me away, as everyone else seemed to know already what I was just finding out. One of the CNN representatives continued the thought.

"Oh, didn't anyone tell you? Yeah, he's not going to interview you today, but we still plan to come back next week and film your visit with one of your patients for the special. Sound good?"

All I could mutter was a confused "Okay," shook hands with everyone, and walked out.

As I strolled down the clinic hallway that I've passed through a million times during my ten years working there, I wasn't fraught with disappointment about not doing the interview, but was overcome with a profound sense of gratitude for what had transpired during the course of that day. When the media wants to do a story, it is often on their time, their schedule, and often compromises and imposes upon the schedules of the people they are interviewing. For them, it doesn't always register what your day-to-day routine is—you just have to be prepared to drop whatever you are doing to accommodate them. And then, at the end of it all, they may just decide to cancel the whole thing without the slightest consideration of any imposition to the individuals upon whose schedules they had imposed themselves. But that wasn't important now.

What was important was that I had seen my usual panel of patients that morning, but in my waiting for the CNN interview, I had also followed up on another fifteen patients who needed lab results, and I was able to be physically present when Kyle had arrived to enroll in our clinic. In that moment, the fickle, unpredictable, and ever-changing scheduling world of television media had unknowingly done me a huge favor—it had reminded me that while getting a broader message out for this commemorative special was important, that wasn't the "real story." The real story was happening without the attention of bright lights and cameras, and told of Kyle's courage to begin a new chapter of his life. In fact, in order to appreciate the millions worldwide who are living with HIV and the thousands whose lives and work are dedicated to combating this epidemic, it is important to note that the vast majority of them will never be featured on a CNN special, probably because they are too busy dealing with the very issues on which Sanjay Gupta will be reporting. And that is exactly what was happening that day for me, Kyle, and the many other patients and staff who comprise the fabric of our clinic and carried on with mundane daily activities. While the film crew was preoccupied with choosing the right location, context, and people on which to base "a good story," the rest of us were handling business as usual.

So I thank you, CNN, for giving me insight on the typically unpredictable, sometimes self-absorbed and narcissistic, and often disrespectful of others' time approach the media takes in pursuit of the next headline. Long after you have moved on from the fanfare of recognizing "Thirty Years of HIV" to feature the latest episode in the war on terror, the most recent hurricane or tornado destruction of a small town, or any catastrophic life event that you deem as worthwhile news, we will still be here. As it turns out, you helped remind me that in order to do the work we do, we don't need you to interview us either.

The Test

Charles Stephens

John and I work together. He is newer than I am, and younger, too. I've taken him on as a kind of guide, telling him what to watch out for, who to watch out for. I feel responsible for him. Along the way we've become friends.

 We are in the break room when he asks me to do it. I think but don't say to him, "Sure, you should both be negative anyway." Believing that it would be easy, thinking that he and his boyfriend, Josh, are both low-risk, I agree as casually as if he asked me for a stick of gum. I also think they are young and beautiful and intelligent and in love, and they should be fine. They are kids. In my mind love is a shield. But I don't realize that I believe this until this situation. How could the gods of fate not look favorably upon them? They are college students. They are shielded from the world. This can't happen to them. And I'm ashamed of myself for thinking this, reminding myself HIV can happen to anyone. I recite this to myself like a Bible verse. In this work you never want to steer too clear of certain thoughts.

I say to John, "Okay, just send me an email letting me know when."

I am trained to provide HIV tests and counseling, like a mechanic fixes cars, even though these are people's lives, not cars. Sometimes in the routine of things it feels the same.

John doesn't perform HIV tests; he hasn't been trained yet. If he were trained, he would probably do his own, like the rest of us.

He is very bright. He has a romantic sensibility peculiar for someone his age. An aesthete. He is the kind of boy who people fall in love with easily, and he had the fortune to fall in love with another boy just like himself. Josh is a science student who also loves languages, but decided to take a more pragmatic approach to life. Two beautiful and intelligent young black men together, in love. When I see them together, I think, "This is a sight." And I imagine the perfect life they will share. And I am sometimes jealous of the perfect life they will share.

Even for us who know better, it's hard not to develop ideas about who gets HIV and who doesn't. Not that we believe HIV is a judgment or only "bad" people get it. It's more based on the assumptions about their risk, the things they tell us, perhaps demographic. If they report low-risk behavior, such as, say, having only used condoms or not having anal sex, then we might think, "They are going to be negative."

I've tested John before, in my office, door closed. He is always negative. Each time he is scared. His eyes soften. His face vulnerable and anxious. My voice, the voice of reason, is calm and knowing. I'm in control.

I give him the test and later the results; "You're negative," I say. He always wants me to reassure him, "Yes you are negative, the test is over ninety-nine percent accurate."

"But, what if…?"

"You are negative John. One line. See?" I would turn the test toward him. "Look at the test. One line."

This time he is more calm. More sure. So he wants me to

test him and his boyfriend. They have been together a month or so. They met at a party. John has not told me he is in love, but he is in love. I can tell. The way he talks about Josh. The way he looks at him, with that mixture of excitement and vulnerability. The attentiveness. He sees Josh as a mirror image of himself, a complement. What is romantic love other than an intense desire for someone who represents something for us?

He eventually sends the email and we set a date. We talk some more about the test. His voice is sincere, not a trace of concern. No hint of doubt dangling behind his words. No shadow of anxiety subtly sweeping across a glance. Nothing in his eyes. No aloofness or ambivalence. He is confident and sure in the way that being naive can make you confident and sure. He is so sure that he makes me sure. I suspend my professional judgment.

There are narratives that we in the helping professions develop about people. And no matter how aware we become, we still have our blind spots. No matter how many diversity trainings, anti-oppression trainings, client-centered trainings, cultural competence trainings, there are these narratives. This becomes worse with friends. With friends our blind spots become oceans of denial. They are a reflection of us after all, and the things we couldn't imagine happening to us, we don't imagine happening to them. It doesn't occur to me that there are things that John does not know, would not know. I think John is likely negative and thus Josh will probably be, too. I see Josh through John's eyes.

In HIV prevention we communicate two messages: 1-everyone is at risk anytime you have sex, and 2-mostly gay men, the poor, and the marginalized are at risk. We deploy those messages based on our audience and our intent. Mostly we deploy them based on our funders. In my entire professional life in HIV prevention, I've witnessed both discourses tossed around, used cleverly, strategically. At times, manipulatively. I am flattered that John trusts me in this. That he wants me to share this experience with him, bringing me into their relationship in that way.

Those of us who do HIV prevention are sometimes priests. What we call "counseling" sometimes feels like confession. We are the collectors of secrets. Those who we test look to us to provide comfort. They think we hold their destiny. For some of us it's a power trip. We judge.

A friend told me a story once. He was tested at our agency. One of my co-workers, he wouldn't say who, asked while delivering the test result, "What if I said your test was positive?" The test was not positive. The counselor was trying to get through to him. He did not tell me who it was, and I did not ask.

Usually I can remember things, so I don't use a calendar. I think I will remember the HIV test date, but I don't. It's not until I'm on my way to a meeting that John calls me to tell me they are coming in. "For what?" I ask, remembering but not wanting to remember, that I had set an appointment with them.

"You know, the test."

I pause for a moment, as if I'm trying to remember, and then say, "Oh, I'm sorry, it slipped my mind. I'm offsite."

"Who else can I get to do it?" he asks.

"Get Greg to do it."

Greg is my boss, but we were friends before we started working together. Not friend in the sense that we are each other's emergency contacts. More that we've known each other for a long time, a very long time, and we share experiences together. We share stories. We share secrets. And can gossip and laugh together and defend each other if we are in mixed company and someone says something bad about the other.

Greg is nearly fifty and charismatic. He is tall and lean and dresses well, and he's good looking. He has a head full of neat and stunning dreadlocks that come down to his back. He always smells good. He makes people feel safe around him. You want to be in his presence. Women and men are both attracted to him. Everyone wants some of him. He is easy to like. He is charming and attractive and you believe whatever he tells you. He is the kind of man who everyone at some point has at least a little crush on.

A few minutes later he calls me back. "Greg can't do it today, but he can do it next week. I'm just going to do it with him."

I am simultaneously relieved and disappointed that he puts it all in Greg's hands. I like to feel trusted, but I don't always want the responsibility. "If that's what you want. Let me know if I can help," I say to him. I'm ambivalent about him not needing me anymore.

The day of the test, I think nothing of it. Everything around the office is the same. It's amazing when things happen, good or bad, how normal everything can seem right before. In hindsight we might try to look for clues or hints. We might see little omens all around us.

They come in together, John and Josh. They come by my office, smiling and in love. They are not holding hands, but seem as if they are. They are bubbly and not embarrassed by it. Perhaps that's how you know two people are in love.

I feel like a parent. Like I should reach in my wallet and pull out a five-dollar bill and tell them to go see a movie. You would think they were going to the prom together, not getting an HIV test, and yet this is how they are. I am the parent snapping pictures and wiping crumbs off their face with my spit. But I am reminded they are really just getting an HIV test.

They go upstairs to get tested, John and Josh. I think nothing of it. Greg is testing them. I work. Doing reports. Focused on reports. Pushing myself through the tedious reports. Time goes by. Thinking, "What's taking so long?" Still working. Still not thinking it could be anything other than what's expected. Perhaps I think the three of them are just chatting. They completed the test, and Greg is talking them up. More time passes. I start thinking they left. I start thinking they left without saying bye. I create a story in my head about how insensitive they are. How inconsiderate. How consumed they are with each other, that they don't say good-bye to me. They could have at least told me bye. But I work. Steadily I work.

I see Greg come downstairs for a moment to pick up something, and then he heads back upstairs. I think nothing of it.

I am taking a box of file folders out of the supply closet when John comes up to me. Suddenly. Silently. His eyes are red and puffy. He is crying. It takes me a minute to process what's going on, for the situation to symbolize into thoughts. This is too unexpected and my mind refuses it for a moment. Just a moment. And then I know what happened. It occurs to me. What he is about to say. But there is a pause. An ugly pregnant pause. In that pause, the tenderness, horror, fear, and concern rush to the surface immediately.

But we are silent at first. I've never seen him cry before. He starts to talk, but before the words come out I consider grabbing him in my arms; instead I say, "Come with me." We go into my office and I shut the door. We both sit down. John cries to himself for a while. Cries into his hands. Time goes by between his sobs. I watch him. He is so into his grief that it's as if I'm not there. He does not seem aware of me at all. And I am all too aware of him.

I watch him curiously and yet sorrowfully. "Tell me what happened," I finally ask. My voice gentle, delicate, purposeful. As purposeful as a stream. I'm trying to contain myself. I fear my words could break him if spoken incorrectly. "Tell me what happened," the voice rings in my ear. I feel like a therapist instead of a friend. I feel so artificial. So fake. So insufficient. I feel like I should touch him, but don't know how to. I debate with myself about hugging him while I wait for him to respond. Am I a professional or am I a friend? Professional or friend? It doesn't occur to me until that moment that I never learned how to be both. I'm also in another space. I start playing everything back in my mind about Josh. All of what I know about him. I had assumed he was HIV-negative. But then how could I be sure?

Because he and John were so cute together and bad things could not possibly happen to people like them? Another contradiction in HIV prevention. On one hand we say, "You can live a normal life" or "It's just like any other chronic illness" or "It's not a death sentence." But then we tell people, "Whatever you do, don't get it." Social marketing like any other marketing is a lie.

There are things you project your fantasies on to, like a projector to a screen: an irrational desire to be optimistic, even when being optimistic goes against everything you know about the world and believe.

John struggles to talk. He cries into a crumpled piece of tissue. The tissue is torn and ragged from use, tissue crumbs litter his hands and then the floor. Evidence of his grief and stress. Solemnly, voice cracked, eyes fire red, he forces it out, "Josh is positive. Greg is still talking to him."

In this moment it occurs to me what I told Greg, that Josh would be negative. Even joked about it. "The test will be easy, Greg. You have nothing to worry about."

It's Greg's first positive. I feel like I set him up. He is upstairs with Josh, and it's his first time delivering a positive. Sure he has been trained. Trained and certified. He is a professional. He has tested before. But never a positive. We all make judgments about people, especially those of us in the helping profession. Snap decisions. The medical model, which has colonized the field, necessitates control and consequently prediction. We say we don't, but we do. And certainly we have our diversity classes and cultural competence classes and everything else. We are taught humility. But even though we know better, do we still on some level deep down, expect certain things to happen to some people and not others? In the unpredictable world of HIV prevention, the emotional turmoil of giving positive test results to people not old enough to vote or drink or go to war, barely able to drive, it is seductive to try and exercise some control through assumption. We create profiles of people, try to guess their fate, but how can we?

"I should go upstairs to help Greg." I say.

"Test me first. I didn't get tested with Josh. But now I need to get a test."

"You sure you want it now?"

"Yes," he sounds clearer, the crying stops, he is focused on getting the test. His eyes intense, sure. His face becomes composed. He clears his throat, "Please Charles, I need to do this now."

I get up out of my office and grab a test from the closet. "You sure you want to do this now?" I ask once more as I sit back down.

"Yes," he says.

My hands are trembling slightly as I try to open the test kit. I don't get it the first time, but I keep pulling. Eventually I am relieved by feeling the tear, and I remove the test as if it were a precious metal. I place it on the test stand and pull out the stick. I explain the test to him like a Marine reciting the rules of combat, dutifully and patriotically. I know he knows the directions: "Insert the wand in your mouth. Make sure you swipe across your gums, front and back, top and bottom." After he's done, I insert the test stick into the test. I prepare myself for his potential positive result. What it would mean. How I would talk him through it. I ask if he wants to go for a walk, and he tells me no.

The twenty minutes pass slowly. Painfully. We sit in my office, looking at each other, awkward and silent. The silence punctuated by sudden spurts of conversation. Stop and start. Forced, polite, mundane conversation. I face the test toward me, not wanting him to see it, but not looking down either, as not to alarm him. As I talk to him I also think about what I would say if the test is positive. What I would do? And then I look at the clock on the wall. The twenty minutes it takes for the test to process are over.

John's test is negative.

He is relieved at first. "I'll need to get tested again in a few more months, right?"

"Yes, yes, you will. It should be three months after the last time you were potentially exposed." I want to hug him and tell him it will be okay. To hold him. But there has already been so much vulnerability. Though we are friends, we are usually guarded. And now we are in this new emotional terrain. We are both lost here in this place of tears and fear and unwanted rites of passage. Masks are off now. Guards are down now. We are both afraid and moved by the moment. I resist touching him for fear I would not be able to remain strong for him. I would crack. I figure he wants me strong more than he wants me open.

John and I walk upstairs together. It is a dreaded trip. I have never become good at telling people they are positive. Is anyone?

We get to the room. The door is closed. I open it and go in first. The distance from the door to where Greg and Josh are sitting isn't very far, but for some reason it seems far. Greg is still talking to Josh. I'm silent. John walks up behind Josh and puts his hand on his shoulder. Josh is reclining in a chair, slumping.

His body limp with pain. He is crying, a cry I've never seen before or since. He is sobbing. In front of him on the table is the test, my eyes rest on it for a moment, until the sound of his crying forces my eyes back to him. Usually when I tell people they are positive for HIV they are detached and steely. Their eyes glaze over. A tear, a single tear might stream their face. They are silent either because it's exactly what they were expecting or they are in complete shock. Josh is different. His response, raw in it's emotion, jarring in it's intensity, suggests something else. He is responding to it how you think everyone would, but never does. To this day I don't know if he knew or did not. Was the test and result the reality he faced after running from it? Something he suspected but denied to himself? His superego bursting free of the repression? I sit down near him.

Greg is talking to him in his best Social Worker voice. Calmly. He is probably thinking, "This is me de-escalating him." I am there but not there. Even though I am close enough to touch Josh, I resist. I disconnect. The weight of his emotion is unbearable for me, it rushes through me.

There is nothing like seeing a beautiful man cry, one with a cute and goofy smile, someone who usually appears happy, being in pain. His glasses are in his lap. The sight is breathtaking. Like watching a magnificent building collapse. Whenever I hear people say that the young don't take HIV seriously, that they are casual about it, that it's not a big deal, I think of this moment.

Greg leaves and I agree to sit with Josh. John leaves too, to get something. I am there, and it's just him and me. There is an intimacy to watching him cry. He apologizes for his response. Constantly apologizing. Even now he is sweet and considerate. There is a politeness to him. But it seems like he is almost apologizing for something more. He has snot in his nose. In his state, he seems so fragile he might break if I come to close. "We are here for you Josh. You don't have to go through this alone. I am here for you. Me, John, and Greg, we all care about you very much. We are your brothers."

"I'm sorry, Charles."

"Don't be. This is no one's fault."

I don't know if I'm believable. I feel like a fraud. I know it won't be okay. I know the road he has ahead of him. It will be hard. But I have to give him comfort. I believe he can make it. But he is so young. Such an extraordinary thing to face at such a young age. He will have to be strong in ways he never had before. This is the thing that will define his early adulthood.

"I'm so sorry to put you all through this," he whispers, his throat weakened from the crying.

"Please, Josh, don't apologize. You have done nothing wrong."

It's evening and everything is quiet around the agency. It only occurs to me now that we are the last ones in the building. There is silence, the dim light of the room, the plush, white carpet that our agency generously invested in for situations like this, and there is Josh and me. I have never experienced this so I don't know what to say. Usually my voice, my tone, is to bring calm and containment to the situation. It also allows me to keep order. That is out the window. Josh's response does not lend itself to that. He is in control, even as he is out of control. I consider touching his hand. I don't know how he will interpret that so I resist. I think to myself, "What does he need in this situation?" I start turning the situation over in my head, and I come up with nothing. He is devastated. Falling apart. In a soothing voice I keep telling him it will be okay. He pauses for a second to cough a little and continues crying. Time goes by, but I don't know how much time passes. I am uncomfortable with his display of emotion, even as I am moved by it. John returns with more tissue. And then Greg. I ask if the confirmatory test was performed. I am back to my professional self, the thing about me that makes people accuse me sometimes of being too cold but rely on me because I am taking charge.

Greg walks out with me. I feel my own build up releasing. After holding it all in. Being strong for Josh and John, I feel myself coming apart. The flood bursting through. I am John and Josh's big brother. Greg will now have to be my big brother.

"I'm so sorry, Greg," I say, my voice cracking as I unravel. I'm now apologizing. "I didn't know he was going to be positive, I didn't know," as if I'm apologizing that he has HIV. I hold on to the counter in the clinic right outside the room. "If I had known...I didn't know, Greg."

My voice is quiet. The tears are forming. Greg has never performed a positive test before, and I felt like I put him in a bind. "I'm sorry," I keep saying as I walk past him, walking, my voice cracking each time I say, sobs caught in my throat threatening to be released, but I catch them just in time. "I didn't know," I say like a mantra. "I didn't know." I'm walking away, walking fast so he does not see me break down. He calls out to me, "I'm here for you, too." I hear the door close behind me, his voice faint but piercing. I don't want him to touch me, to hold me, but I do. I do want someone to tell me it will be all right, not for me, but for John and Josh. "I'm here for you, too," I still hear. But what does that mean? What does "being here" for me mean? I know he will not and cannot. I am alone in this moment. I want to crash into his arms like a tidal wave. To once let go. But I can't. I trust him. But I can't. I'm afraid to let go. I'm afraid I won't be able to reassemble.

After a few minutes, I come back upstairs. I am composed. I am myself again. We perform the lab test. This is to confirm the positive result. The lab results will be back in two weeks. John takes Josh out of the room. He is still emotional. John and I check-in periodically with glances, and "are you okays." We hug Josh. It's easier to hug Josh than each other for some reason. He is so fragile. A wind could blow him away. "You will be okay," we each tell him. "We are each here for you," we assure him.

After they leave, it's only me and Greg in the room, the two adults. Even though Greg is twenty years older than me and I am ten years older than John and Josh, I feel the same age as Greg in this moment.

"I'm so sorry, Greg, I didn't know."

"It's okay."

"If I had known, or even thought, I would have…"

"I was prepared, I am trained, it's okay."

"If I had known..."

"Things happened the best way they could have. I was prepared."

And then the beauty of the moment hits me. Three generations of black gay men there to support one another. All of us changed forever. Telling Josh that wherever he goes, he will have us. That he will not be alone. This was what I always thought my life would be like.

"I'm glad we are all here together like this. That we could be here for Josh."

"Me too."

Greg and I start collecting materials to pack up the room,

as we collect ourselves. We move about with the cautious embarrassment of two people who might have shown too much too soon. We move about as if it's the morning after drunken sex, embarrassed, picking clothes up off the floor and trying not to look at each other. Our bodies careful not to touch.

There is not so much a quietness but a stillness in the room. After all of the crying, with Josh's sobs still ringing in our ears, with just the two of us remaining, there is an eerie quiet that leaves us somewhat awkward. Greg turns to me and asks "Now what?"

"Now we wait," I respond back, not looking at him, answering the question for myself as much for him, "and be there for John and Josh."

The Voice

Ron Simmons

My first experience hearing the Voice was at the age of thirteen when I was planning my suicide; not contemplating but planning my suicide. I had been contemplating for months. I was tired of being the sissy on the block, tired of the name calling, tired of being teased in the day by boys who would kiss me secretly at night. I knew what they were saying was true. I liked boys rather than girls. Something about a boy stirred feelings in me I couldn't describe. I wanted their touch, their embrace.

For years I thought my feelings were the result of an encounter I had had with my cousin Charlie. I was five years old and he was seven. His family had been evicted so he was staying with us and sharing my bed, a twin bed. My older sister slept in the other.

One night he said, "You wanna do what the grownups do?"

"What do they do?" I asked, having no idea what he was talking about. So he showed me. He hugged me and kissed me and we slept in each other's arms. Since I didn't have any brothers, I assumed that that was what boys did with each other.

It didn't feel wrong. That was the beginning and it is a night I will never forget. I haven't seen him since then.

I had my first boyfriend, Larry, in the second grade; he was a cute, light-skinned kid with curly, sandy hair. We were in the same class and became best friends. During the summer we would play outdoors like most eight-year-olds. But indoors, we played house—serious house. We would tie a blanket over the twin beds and the tent became our home. I would welcome him from a hard day at work with a kiss and prepare dinner, just like my parents did. I remember having a child for him, putting my sister's doll under my shirt, pretending I was pregnant. We didn't know about sex, just hugging and kissing and playing house.

After Larry, I fooled around with other boys. We would ride our bicycles, play tag, and grab each other's dicks underwater in the neighborhood swimming pool. Everything was fine until they reached puberty and started chasing girls, and I realized I didn't want to. I wanted things to remain the same but my friends didn't. I learned that the things I wanted to do were bad. Only sissies and faggots did that. Then the name-calling started.

We lived in a fourteen-story housing project in Brooklyn with more than a hundred families. I couldn't avoid the other kids and their teasing. So I withdrew and read books all day, which made matters worse because I became the nerdy outsider with no friends. Other than going to school, I stayed indoors, and my mother never knew why I hated running errands to the store.

Eventually I decided to kill myself. I didn't want my parents to freak out so I told them of my plan. They freaked out and took me to the family doctor. I remember hoping that the visit to the doctor would fix things and make me like girls. The big day came and my father took me to the doctor's office. When we were alone, the doctor asked me what the problem was.

"I like guys," I told him.

"Don't do that," he said. "You'll get in trouble." The visit was over.

The next day I resumed planning my suicide. I thought of different ways to kill myself. Jumping off a fourteen-story building seemed too painful. There were no guns in the house to shoot myself. I didn't know enough about drugs to overdose. Maybe walking into speeding traffic could do it. That's when the Voice spoke to me. It was the first time I heard a voice in my head that was not my own.

"Don't do it," It said. "Wait until you get older. Things will be different."

So I decided to wait another thirteen years until I was twenty-six, and if things weren't better, I would kill myself then. In the mind of a child, such logic seemed quite rational.

In the sixth grade, my mother insisted that I be bussed to a "good" junior high school in a white neighborhood. There I met new friends who didn't know my secret. Staying indoors and reading books paid off academically. I did well in high school and received a scholarship to go away to college, the State University of New York at Albany. In my freshman year, I met a new friend who took me to my first gay bar. Knowing I was not the only boy who liked guys made things different. By the time I turned twenty-six, contemplating suicide was a forgotten memory. I was having too much fun dancing at the Better Days and cruising piers in Manhattan on Christopher Street.

The second time I heard the Voice was fourteen years after I had graduated. I had moved to Washington, D.C., to pursue a doctorate at Howard University. I finished the course work in 1983 and started writing my dissertation. By then everyone knew of this new disease, the "gay cancer," that was eventually called AIDS. First my white gay friends then my black gay friends began dying. Fear was everywhere. Doctors were afraid to touch you. Nurses were afraid to feed you. On television, the image of someone with AIDS was a skeleton in a hospital bed connected to tubes and machines, suffering a slow, lingering death. When scientists discovered the disease was sexually transmitted, I remembered cruising the piers, the parks, and the bathhouses; participating in orgies with no condoms.

I probably have this disease, I thought to myself. When the HIV test first came out—before any treatments were available—I called the local gay clinic and asked if I should take it. The response was: "What would you do if you were positive? And what would you do if you were negative?" I told them I would do the same thing either way: safer sex. "Then why get tested?" was the reply. So I didn't, but I still worried about my future.

At the time, people with AIDS only had six months to live. Why was I getting a doctorate? I should get a job, buy a car, and enjoy my life while I still can. The indecision between completing the doctorate and enjoying the remainder of my life led to procrastination, and after three years I had only written three chapters of the dissertation.

One night when riding my bike I was hit by a car. I never saw it coming. One moment I was on my bicycle, the next moment I was waking up in a hospital bed surrounded by white walls, white sheets, and a white doctor. He told me I was lucky to be alive and that the last case like mine was in a coma for six months. The car had hit me from the side and my body cracked its windshield. I had lain unconscious on the hood until an ambulance brought me to the hospital. I had a broken collarbone, cuts, and bruises. It was like waking from a dream in pain.

"How's your head?" the doctor asked.

"Frankly my head is the only thing that doesn't hurt," I replied.

"That's strange," he said, "You must have hit it because you were knocked unconscious." Then he left.

I was alone and tried to comprehend what had happened. One minute I was on my bike and in the snap of the fingers I was in the hospital. Why did the doctor say I had to have hit my head when my head had no bruises? That's when the Voice again spoke to me.

"I have work for you to do," It said, "and you need a Ph.D. to do it. And don't worry about a slow, lingering death because if I want you, I will take you like that." (Snap.)

I heeded the message and finished the dissertation in six months. The University hired me as an assistant professor, and I taught there for another five years. I enjoyed teaching and empowering young black minds, but somehow I knew that that was not the work I was destined to do. I never forgot what the Voice told me, and I wondered what my mission was. What work did the Voice want me to do?

In 1990, I came down with shingles and my doctor suggested that it may be the result of a weak immune system, so I got tested. I was diagnosed as HIV-positive, and a friend told me about this black organization that was starting a support group for gay men living with HIV/AIDS. The organization was called Us Helping Us, People Into Living. The first meeting would be Saturday, March 2 at 3:00 P.M., my birthday.

"That Saturday is my birthday," I told him. "I don't want to spend it at a meeting."

Two weeks later, I saw a flyer about the support group and ignored it. I was going to enjoy my birthday.

March 2, I was lying in bed and thinking about how I was going to celebrate the big day. The phone rang. It was another friend, Gary, calling to ask if I had heard about the support group starting that day.

"Yes," I told him, "but today is my birthday and I want to do something special." After he hung up, I continued lying in bed and looked up at the ceiling.

"Okay, God," I said. "It's obvious that you want me to attend this meeting. I will go to the meeting."

I attended the meeting and it was life changing. There were twenty-two HIV-positive black gay men in the group, and for the next twelve weeks the facilitators, Rainey Cheeks and Prem Deben, taught us holistic traditional methods to live with HIV. No one else was saying you could live with this disease. After the group sessions ended, I became more involved in the organization. A few of us were trained to facilitate support groups in our homes. Rainey and I became close friends. We would do forty-two day liquid fasts together and telephone each other sometimes several times a day. In the spring of 1992, Rainey asked me if I would volunteer to be the executive director of Us Helping Us.

"No," I told him, surprised that he thought I would. "I am Dr. Simmons, an assistant professor at Howard University. You have no money. Why would I give that up?"

Rainey said, "I'll pray on it."

"You can pray all you want," I thought to myself. "The answer is still no."

Two months later, my chairman called me into her office and told me the University was not going to renew my contract. After twelve years at Howard, I would be unemployed in thirty days. I was devastated and needed a shoulder to cry on, so I called Rainey.

"That's horrible," he said. Then he paused. "Maybe now you can be the executive director of Us Helping Us."

I held the phone away from my ear and looked at it in disbelief. This is a setup, I thought to myself. Eventually, I agreed to volunteer as the executive director until my unemployment insurance ran out. Then I would have to seek a paying job.

In the years since that time, Us Helping Us grew from a support group of HIV-positive black gay men meeting in their living rooms to one of the largest gay-identified black AIDS service organizations in the country. Writing a dissertation helps you to write successful grant proposals. In 2001, Us Helping Us purchased a building for our new headquarters and service facility, becoming the first black gay AIDS organization in the nation to do so.

Looking back on the thoughts of suicide, the bike accident,

that fateful birthday, and losing my job at Howard, I am convinced this is the work I was destined for. And there may be more work to do. I'm just waiting for the Voice and fate to guide me.

It's Only Love That Gets You Through

Robert E. Penn

I had my first special friend when I was four. He lived across the street and my mother recalls I "couldn't get enough of him." Of course, she did not realize he was my first boyfriend, or at least she hasn't let on to that.

We lived in the Midwestern Bible Belt and my father pastored a Baptist Church. No one ever mentioned "terrible" things like alcohol, gambling, and homosexuality. I knew early on I was not supposed to feel the way I felt and that I'd better do everything I could to conceal my real romantic feelings. I figured out a solution: I would find a beautiful, kind, intelligent girl my age, woo her, and get married so that no one would bother me about that aspect of my life. I also knew there would be a boy my age in my life.

I spent my young adult years chasing the "perfect love triangle" to fulfill my natural-born needs without ruffling any family feathers—one man and one woman both in love with me—the ideal nucleus of the unit. I invested many of my adult years trying to figure out how to juggle making babies with a woman and maintaining the kind of loving relationship I wanted with a man. I alternately dated women and men.

In college, I found my first young adult love. There were only twenty other young black men in my class of 1,200 and I didn't get the sense that any of them was interested. Bob's red hair and alabaster skin shone like a beacon of hope amidst the ninety-eight percent majority. He never mistook me for a servant or challenged my right to be at the prestigious institution, as so many others—including employees—had done. He saw me as I was, or at least a very liberal Midwestern German-American's view of me, which at the time was better than the view I had of myself. I fell in love, but he wasn't ready in 1968 to make a commitment.

I fell in love again in 1973 while living and studying abroad. He was Swiss and painted seascapes. He was bisexual. At the time, so was I. That fit well with the triangle paradigm, sort of, until he asked my permission to make a baby with a woman who meant more to him than sexual gratification. (We had experimented with three ways with both male and female third partners.) I was pleased to know he cared enough about my opinion to ask, and she was a fantastic woman, but the arrangement left me feeling like someone else got the triangle! Karma?

Love arrived again in 1980 at the Paradise Garage. He was beautifully handsome and black. It was with William that I first learned to share a small Manhattan apartment—a very different challenge from dorm rooms in college or an artist's garret in Geneva. We bumped up against each other's baggage—and those steamer trunks have sharp edges. We grew close enough that when he worked late and I went to sleep, I could sense when he was a block away from our apartment and my body would wake up so I could greet him and say good night.

In 1986, I met a woman who wanted to have my babies and whose offspring I was certain to love. The only problem was she couldn't hear me when I talked about sexual variation. Either she was in denial or my approach was too timid. She was a world-class swimmer with broad arms and a strong kick, and our relationship proved my plumbing still worked. I'm attracted to physical traits generally associated with athleticism, in other words, the masculine. (She fit that part of the bill.) I decided against marrying her for her ova after a lusty dream. We were on vacation in Tunisia. One night sleeping in bed together, I had my most erotic dream to that date: I was with an extremely handsome Tunisian man who adored me for me rather than for my US passport. I felt his warmth beside me; his charm drew me to him; I moved closer and spooned him. I was just about to intone his name when I opened my eyes and saw my girlfriend. I was frightened of what almost happened and happy I had not spoken. I was also shaken and shocked into reality—if she married me, she would have a good father for her children and a loveless partnership with me. I would always have a man relationship "on the side" or resent her from keeping me from one.

Shortly after that "burst" of same-gender-loving light, I re-energized my focus on the LGBT community and got more involved in HIV/AIDS prevention and social/cultural activism—the kind that pushed gay cultural gatekeepers to recognize that gay art is not always white art and that black gay stories are not all set in a poverty-stricken areas. (Editors used to tell me my work wasn't black enough! Marlon Riggs said it best: Black Is/Black Ain't.) When I moved from volunteer to employee at Gay Men's Health Crisis in 1990, some staff still claimed that AIDS had not spread into the black community yet. What game were they playing? I thought. How misinformed could they be? I told them two things. First, I tested HIV-positive in December 1985, so it had already spread, and second, the first man I knew to die of AIDS in 1983 was, you guessed it, black. Someone quipped, "But that's only because he slept with white guys." What?

As the only son of the last son of the first freeborn black Virginia Penn and Dickerson (circa 1872), I still wanted an heir. It was up to me to procreate and continue the name and reputation my father had established and I had continued, albeit in different circles. I considered adoption, but I really wanted a blood child. In the early 1990s, I explored co-parenting with a lesbian friend. She was a colleague at GMHC. We researched artificial insemination, co-parenting legalities, Rh factors, and sexual history disclosure, which included my coming out to her as a PLA—person living with AIDS. She didn't run away immediately. She did further research about rates of infection from a turkey-baster insemination with the sperm of an HIV-positive donor and made her decision.

In 1993, shortly after that lesbian friend decided against artificial insemination with my sperm due to the two to four percent risk of her being infected with HIV during the process, a young man introduced himself to me as a fan of my writing. I was flattered not only that someone outside New York had read one of my essays, but also that the twenty-three-years younger man seemed intent on seeing me on an ongoing basis. As our relationship developed, it became apparent to us both that we were becoming surrogate father and son.

A similar incident happened in 1994. A GMHC intern donated his time during the summer between his junior and senior years at Harvard College. Twenty-five-years my junior, he helped revise a prevention module targeting gay and bisexual men of color. At the end of the summer, he told me I had given him more support during his short time there than his biological father had done in a lifetime.

Of course, in both cases my gay-positive attitude made me more accessible to them. More importantly, as a publicly out gay man writing about and working in gay communities, I was an elder.

My third child-of-choice is a young woman. I never expected a lesbian or bisexual young woman to ask me to temporarily fill the role of father, but one did and I accepted. We enjoyed several years of loving closeness. Although our paths diverged some years ago, that relationship helped restore my ability to relate to women in a richer way than ever before, and I had the chance to support her through a very difficult diagnosis of breast cancer when she was only twenty-nine. That led to radical mastectomy. I accompanied her to a battery of tests when it would have been inconvenient or impossible for her biological father to get to New York frequently enough to help her. He calls me "younger brother" because he sees me as his brother. In their extended blood family, a peer of a father is also a parent—a father in function if not blood. Similarly, in the LGBT community, those without children of their own may have time and ability to fulfill a parenting role for succeeding generations of sexual minority people.

These various intergenerational relationships have changed and continue to enhance my life. I encourage all gay and bisexual men to develop strong ties with biological family members who are able to accept our sexual realities, but also to find close friends, companions, and sexual minority members from previous and following generations with whom to build vibrant and rewarding relationships. And, of course, this need not deter us from finding a life partner or partners of our own.

I am currently in love for the fourth time, but it feels as though it is the first. We are mature and approach getting to know one another more consciously. Yet thirty minutes into our first date, I told him I really enjoyed "his energy"—his being, his smile, his face, his fingertips, his voice, and his ability to form thoughts into words he shares with me. On our fifth date, I asked him to be my boyfriend. I felt what I imagine my straight high school friends might have felt when they realized, "Oh my goodness, my life companion is right here in front of me and this is the time to ask." Sitting on the F train heading downtown after a performance by the Alvin Ailey American Dance Theater—how Christmas in New York City, how black, how gay is that! —Harold accepted immediately. Wow! Love again and so many connections still remain alive from my past and await me in the future.

I still keep in touch with Bob. Though he lives in the Midwest, we remain in contact. He's got a boyfriend here in New York now, and I've even heard him refer to himself as gay. Whew! Finally. We spent the afternoon together in December 2010 when he visited the City. I took them to lunch when Bob visited his man for Valentine's Day in 2011.

My Swiss painter, his wife, and their young adult daughter visited New York in 2009. It was great to see them. I owe them a visit to Geneva.

I frequently see my former partner William—we ended in 1992—and he is still beautiful, both inside and out. He's family and I trust him completely. His current partner of seventeen years is cool with our unique and inalienable relationship.

Now is the best time of my life: in love and maintaining all my other relationships.

POWER TO THE PEOPLE

We Cannot Forget

Victor Yates

fire, fire, burn them, the fags
the man in back said, head down

the two South American boys ignored him
the bus seat under me warmed

fire, fire, burn them, the fags
I heard an African accent

the two South American boys ignored him
the smell of burning flesh swallowed the air

fire, fire, burn them, the fags
the man jumped up and off the bus

we, black people, were hung up in poplar trees
and burned-black for being black

we cannot forget that
we cannot forget

Poetry of the Flesh

Lorenzo Herrera y Lozano

(Note: *All poetry excerpts by Lorenzo Herrera y Lozano.*)
As a queer Xicano poet, I have long been obsessively interested in exploring the intersections of identities, desires, and survival strategies that stem from, are informed by, and contest the various—and often conflicting—political and cultural ideologies that collide within our embodied multiplicity. For many of us whose identities are gender and sexually expansive, we are well aware of the intersections we sit in. Whether you're a Xicana lesbian mother, an HIV-positive immigrant *joto*, a bi-identified trans professor, or any manifestation of these and other identities and experiences, poetry can surely be found in the crevices created by the caresses and struggles of our tectonic realities. Poetry is a site for realization.

> Jotos build movements in each other's arms
> craft manifestos, recite them in the dark
> We are ceremony in back alleys

We are the angels under each other's feet
("Jotos," excerpt)

In 2001, I was a young *joto* graduate student attending San José State University's Mexican American Studies program. It was the first year I attended the National Association for Chicana and Chicano Studies (NACCS) Conference. It was the year Cherríe Moraga received the Scholar Award, and it was the first time I was surrounded by people who not only looked like me, but also desired and loved like me.

In her speech, Moraga honored the queer brown men we lost due to a pandemic that attempted to decimate generations and admonished their non-queer brothers who saw it happen— calling on them to turn to the young *jotos* in the room and recognize us as their brothers. It was during this speech that I learned my lineage. In that moment, I realized what the poet Marvin K. White says, "we don't just appear, we come from somewhere." It was in Moraga's words that I came to understand that these queer brown men are my forefathers.

The week following the 2001 NACCS Conference, I was diagnosed with HIV. As the testing counselor read her routine and lifeless speech, I began to think of Moraga's words. I realized that as I sat in the audience in Tucson, my veins were carrying the very virus that flowed through the veins of the generations of queer brown men Moraga spoke of. I was the receptacle, not of death but of opportunity and legacy. I am the descendant of men who were left to die under the shadow of merciless flags, men who were buried by the silence of confused and agonizing families.

I come from a long line of *jotos*. They are my lineage.

I am the couch to their *sarape*
they are the *atole* that raises me

the velvet Jesus hanging over my bed
I am orphan to their souls
the carrier of pillaged dreams
the son of men who died for love—
love airbrushed on the walls inside my veins
("Children of Wilted Suns," excerpt)

Poetry is a site for remembrance. Through poetry, we scribe the story of those who have transitioned into spirit. We mourn the absence of their touch. We conjure their scent through our words. We make sense of our loss. We refuse to forget.

Poetry is a site for memory. It is the kitchen counter where, like a freshly harvested onion, we begin to peel the layers of our complex desires. It is where, in our thirst, we fervently dig for the emanating waters of the love(s) we manifest.

Metaphors are more than pretty substitutes for us to hide behind. They are nude articulations of truths birthed in the vulnerability that is our story on a page. They are the sharp thorns, *espinas de huizache*, lodged in our throats, waiting to be exhumed and planted into yours.

there is no way of choking
the faggot out of our throats
no way of flooding this drought—
a life thought without
spiritual meaning

there is no god for us
the fallen saints
virgins of tainted veins
martyrs of human faith
prophets of our survival
("Fallen Saints," excerpt)

Poetry taught me how to make love to a man. The opening lines of Sandra Cisneros' "Dulzura"[1] and María Salazar's poetic "Panza to Panza" homage to her love, Jo Ann, Virginia Grise and Irma Mayorga's *Panza Monologues*[2] have all shaped the craft of my lovemaking. The poetry of these *mujeres*, along with Cherríe Moraga's "Theory in the Flesh"[3], and the lessons of black and Tejana butches taught me that making love is an art form, a kinetic expression, and the manifestation of metaphorized articulations of desire. *Hacer el amor es crear poesía con la herramienta de dos—quizás más—cuerpos entrelazados. Es el hilvanar sabanas con mudas frases de lujuriosa ceremonia.* Poems are sex on the page.

> when your toes curl up in prayer
> the second heartbeat in you is mine
> my breath leaves hickies on your neck
> trails to find my way back
> I leave drawings on your wall
> remnants for the one who follows
>   ("Chicharrón of Your Inhibitions," excerpt)

I make love to a man with the fear, vulnerability, and irreverent devotion with which I forge a poem. His neck is my opening stanza. My tongue mines his thighs for abandoned desires left behind by previous lovers. As the late miners in my family, picking and diving into the depths of the San Francisco del Oro Mountains, I exploit the mountains of his body,

1. Cisneros, Sandra, "Dulzura," in *Loose Woman* (New York: Vintage Books, 1994)

2. Moraga, Cherríe L. & Anzaldúa, Gloria E., "Theory in the Flesh," in *This Bridge Called My Back: Writings by Radical Women of Color* (San Francisco: Aunt Lute Press, 1981).

3. Grise, Virginia & Mayorga, Irma, "Panza to Panza," in *The Panza Monologues* (Austin: allgo/Evelyn Street Press, 2004).

searching for the hairline of metaphors glistening between the stones that line his tunnel. My muse is not mythical.

> the fault line of your mountain range
> draws my mouth as morning pulls the sun
> as the moon tugs the sea
> my tongue a ravage wave
> beating you with every dive
>   ("Home to My Wandering Appetite," excerpt)

Chances are you have fucked a poem out of a poet before. And in your erotic incantation, the poet captures the beads of sweat from your lips and adds the story of your lovemaking to an ink-drenched canvas. Perhaps, decades from now, a young *joto* will lay hands on the poem you ignited and taste the desire you fed your poet. For poets create artifacts.

Poetry is a site for revolution. The poem that fingers trace across your back is not void of politic. The poem carries the weight of crimes committed against the shades of our skin, the girth of our bodies and the threat of our minds. *La carne* of the poem knows your lovemaking is an act of resistance. The poem bears witness to the uprising of brown bodies—peaceful civil disobedience to carnal dictatorships. This is poetry of the flesh.

> among the panting of my thrust
> the stroking of your kisses
> the tattooed bites along your back
> this son of brown gods
> returns joyful, scarred and free
> to the valleys of his people
>   ("Ode to a Brown Nude," excerpt)

During my coming out years, I searched relentlessly for the works of queer Xicano men. I found some hidden in anthologies, others floating around journals, and a few written in the memory of patrons of San Francisco's Esta Noche nightclub. Little was accessible for the young Xicano working with a dial-up modem, rudimentary computer skills, and a fear of homophobic libraries.

There are many theories attempting to explain the fact that so few publications exist by queer brown men. Among these, the theory that they were simply too busy "fucking in the bushes."

I refuse to believe my ancestors did not write. Yes, they may have been fucking in the bushes, but I know for a fact that poetry is written behind bushes, in bathhouses, in *cantinas* and in our *abuela's* backyard. That publishing could not or refused to catch up with their writings is not an indication of their poetic silence. There were poets among them. There are poets among us. A publisher does not make a poet.

> I am medley of unanswered *plegarias*
> a novena for AIDS-related deaths
> novena for my own
> for the generation who shared my bed
> I recite *Hail Papis*, for us
>
>   ("Chimera," excerpt)

Poetry is a site for documentation. In our poetry, we leave hints, signs of our struggles. We leave sketches of our tragedies, our hopes, our romantic and political breakthroughs. We leave proof that we were here. That we desired and fought and created and imagined a new way of loving. That we wrote. *Que siempre hemos escrito.*

Poetry is a site for audacity. A site for political *putos* to scribe our manifestos. A site for our *gente* to imagine ourselves possible, to recognize each other as necessary, to present ourselves whole.

Poetry is a site for unlocking, dismantling, and eradicating the legislation of our bodies. Poetry is a site for social justice. *La poesía es justica.*

I am the fire of suns on *campesino* backs
eclipsed in the shadow of your heart in my hands
dancing *venado*, sweat down my chest
where men come to rest
where I come to die

                    ("Venado Dreams," excerpt)

Casualties of War

L. Michael Gipson

From the third grade until my sophomore year of high school
I was bullied. Actually, I find "bullied" too genteel, maybe
even too conversely muscular, a word for what it conveys. It
reductively conjures discrete episodes that can be brushed off
proud survivor shoulders rather than the hauntingly prolonged
campaigns of childhood terror endured. After all, world wars
have begun and ended in shorter durations than my time in
the "bullying" trenches. No, I believe "terrorism" is the more
accurate depiction of what I, and others like me, experienced
during those holy wars on schoolyard battlefields. These training
grounds are after all the precursors to the left-right adult
political warfare we see today, of church ex-communications,
anti-gay referendums, constitutional amendments, and fence-
crucifixions along Western plains—the rowdy soldiers just grow
up.

Though such allusions are melodramatically weighty, I do
not use this inflammatory, geo-political word "terrorism" to
draw undue sympathy for my plight. Truthfully, in the lives of

youth worldwide, my experience is frightfully ordinary. Call it an aspect of humanity that has yet to fully experience the distillation of civilization. In the absence of such refinement is the omnipresent fear of one's own premature demise at the "accidental" hands of another's reckless child (solider-in-training?). To be "bullied" is to fear one's own murder being played out against a sweetly ironic backdrop of everyday childhood.

I think something of the psychological profundity of bullying gets lost in our sanitizing national dialogue of inequitably enforced zero-tolerance policies and surface-scratching anti-bullying workshops; the sheer psychic weight of what domestic terror campaigns has wrought upon their survivors. I think when one usually thinks of bullying they imagine unequal, but relatively fair fistfights that may end in bruised skin, loosened teeth, maybe a broken nose. Those who imagine such ABC *After School Specials* have not been bullied. The post-terrorized among you once thought often of murder, ours at the attacker's hands in an act gone further than intended and theirs at ours in a vigilante act of retributive justice. The readiness of murder was so thick in our daily atmosphere, it even stalked our dreams. Conversely, no one ever died "in a very special episode of…"

If murder walked in my dreams, self-consciousness dogged the footsteps of my days. On the surface, I was bullied for being effeminate, articulate, overweight, well-read, interested in recreations and matters non-traditional for black boys or even black people—essentially for being myself. To be hounded for merely existing in one's own skin is not unique to blacks, but at least during Jim Crow we could turn to one another. In modern-day terrorism, we turn *on* one another, with limited options for sanctuary. Always the glutton, my selected sanctuaries only kept the cycles of abuse turning (something about Harlequin romance and musical theater just begs for a beat down, you know?). Refuge could not be found among adults, many of whom viewed bullying as a character-building rite of passage, naïve to the escalation of medieval violence that had leap-frogged ancestral generations to our own. This left very few external, truly understanding sanctuaries. With cyber-bullying, today's targets cannot even depend on the sanctuary of their bedroom.

The main refuge one loses when being bullied is one's own body. In the body's difference and expressed proclivities, it is the ultimate betrayer. This mistrust promoted constant self-checks: to hold schoolbooks to my sides rather than the more comfortable nook of my chest, the artificial bass shakily infused in my faux barbershop banter to try to mask the appropriate contralto of my pre-pubescent voice, the awkward sex jokes and strained pimp-walking—feeble attempts to fit in that made my difference that much more pronounced and transparent to my abusers. I see grownup versions of this in the vastly more studied overcompensation of gay brothers determined not to experience the desolation of being the outsider, the "loser," ever again—be it by physical might, education, profession, or bank account. It still doesn't mean the trauma-sewn masks fit any more comfortably on adult cheeks than the cherubs of old; it just hangs differently.

No, it's not the actual violence that is the worst part of being at the mercy of feral children's raging prejudices. It's the happenings in between the relatively episodic moments of physical assault that most cannibalize the soul. It's the waiting hours staring at tyrannous clocks ushering trembling bodies toward certain doom. The nervous rhythm of your bouncing knee under desks drumming a metronomic beat to match the propulsive pains pounding against anciently scarred ribs. It's the stomach-plunging daily navigation of halls littered with furtive, pitying glances from the compassionate and the maliciously dancing glee from those you know will celebrate each well-placed heel and fist, crooked smiles you see watering for the running of your blood. But most of all it's the interior dialogue with yourself, one vacillating between self-flagellation and bottomless despair and the withering seeds of hope and anxious prayers for some act of God that will preserve your face and integrity, if only for a day.

It's the oppression-bred words and thoughts bullying victims say to and think of themselves that can be far more corrosive than what is spat during the seemingly endless seconds of hard knuckles assaulting tissue and bone. Even worse than the complicit crowds of fellow students, neighbor children, churchgoing peers that one has to later sit knee-to-knee to in polite, adult-monitored settings, weakly smiling and performing as though theirs wasn't the ringing laughter, the acidic catcalls salting your open wounds, or the backs turned, afraid of association with the carcass being carried off to slaughter. These performances are a kind of training, too, readying people for a potential lifetime of abusive exploitation and teaching them to endure it with a polite smile.

Worse than the beatings is the stomach-churning knowledge that despite all the thieving blackness these peers deliver, you still envy them their privilege, still partially desire a place at their table, breath in their breezy Madison Avenue-ready atmosphere, if only as a respite from the daily disrespect. Yes, you know they aren't better than you, *in theory*. Yes, you've heard that they will "get theirs" in time, through some karmic force or universal law that surely wouldn't allow them to sport those effortless smiles for life. Of course, you know that the evil they so casually commit *actually* makes them worse people than you and your wounded kin, and yet…Yes, it's the solitary terrorism of the mind, born from a handful of episodes writ large that makes bullying a 24/7 experience worthy of Dante's poetry. Indeed, in comparison, the beatings are easy.

The beatings may be even easier than the rolling humiliations. To paraphrase Oprah: "There is nothing worse than humiliation. It rips at the core of one's soul." The constant belittling of one's faith and passions; the degradation of one's body, movements, and voice; the devaluing of one's interests and offerings; and the ubiquitous threat of something ominous waiting around life's corners—all hallmarks of humiliation, be it in war, in intimate partner violence, or a classroom.

It doesn't even take a particularly creative mind to cultivate a humiliation campaign. Instructions abound in our popular culture, from any number of reality TV shows to *Mean Girls* flicks, where the evil-doers are only undone in the last reel, after an hour of celebrating their beauty, privilege, and enviable lifestyles. Locker rigs, toilet head, and 3:00 P.M. deadlines have been supplemented by far more sophisticated technological warfare including: tweets, Facebook posts, Photoshopped pics, or, as in the case of terrorized Rutgers suicide victim, Tyler Clementi, hidden video. Humiliation 2.0, combined with tactical run-of-the-mill hallway pushes, gym class rough-housing, and fishing homework out of grimy trashcans, marks round-the-clock coverage of an ongoing one-person national disaster with plenty of spectators tuning-in to add insult to injury.

Those who tortured me in the '80s weren't white jocks with trust funds and video cams. Mine carried guns and pocketknives, a few carried well-worn knuckles. Some were frequenters of juvy, some gang members, others where just higher on our block's social totem pole, if destined to reside on the lower rungs of life. They were the victims of poverty, fatherlessness, crack homes, patriarchal values, hyper-masculinity and their own abuse stories, and they were angry about the dawning realizations that they'd been set-up for a hard climb, if not outright failure. Some were just sociopaths. None were preordained to be domestic terrorists. They chose to be, but it wasn't without environmental supports. They had co-signs from the complicit, be they apathetic teachers, homophobic Christian principals, or crowds determined not to trade places with me and mine. Misdirected anger, faith, and fear all colluding on the terrorism campaigns to make me and mine victims—no, survivors—for those of us who did. As any soldier knows, not all of us survive war.

Which brings me to what to do for the nearly two-thirds of

students who once reported to the Gay, Lesbian and Straight Educator Network that they felt unsafe in school because of their sexual orientation and the thirty-nine percent who reported they felt unsafe because of their gender expression. They feel unsafe because they know they are in a silent war, but underarmed for battle. Twenty years after my own tours, there's still blood, fear, and murderous thoughts plaguing our young. The best we seem to offer so far for this new crop of targets—and these flaccid prescriptions only intermittently—are: zero-tolerance for those already flirting with prison and who still live in the targets' neighborhood post-expulsion, anti-bullying trainings for ever-faithful educators who themselves may believe LGBT children are an abomination in need of "correction," and "It Gets Better" social marketing campaigns of hope for tomorrow. But how does one hang on today? How does one endure terror campaigns that can last up to a decade long? Who's doing *that video* and making *that policy*?

Ensuring legal recourse for the afflicted is a just cause, but it is only a Band-Aid, not a cure. Life and terror exist off the school grid and protection in the streets is guaranteed for none. Besides, many of these policies require youth or witnesses to snitch, an act against the cultural beliefs of some of these very victims (remember training for exploitation begins early). What our youth need is not aspirations that their tour of duty will end at graduation, but sustainable armor. What they need is hope to win now, survival strategies now, self-defense classes now, maps to navigate the landmines littering their block now, guiding hands in the dark pulling them through today, not a far off hope for retribution through class achievement tomorrow (one whose realization really isn't guaranteed for all). Without hope, without training to survive the continuing war against difference, many more than the thirty percent of students who considered suicide will lose heart; they just may do so later in life, when they realize that some of those bullies become bosses, judges, politicians, and pastors—not all of them are pumping gas. Injustice doesn't end at graduation but is a lifelong condition worth fighting.

The stakes were high twenty years ago; they are higher still. As with national anti-terrorism campaigns, nothing less than a counterinsurgency striving to attack the roots, the very foundation of the problem, will do to protect our future. The cures are muscular anti-oppression campaigns that look at the relationships between all the "isms," including anti-individualism, that bring abusers together to commit collective acts of war against us all. A "heart and mind" campaign that understands the origins of abuse and offers reform avenues for abusers to become the allying redeemed. A training campaign that gets our youth prepared to be more than thought and policy activists, but able to physically and psychically defend themselves, too, for the long haul. Unarmed children often become unarmed adults vulnerable to abuse for life by pillagers who fear, disdain, and exploit their specialness. Yes, there is a war going on, its victims falling younger and younger.

It's time we prepared them for battle.

How Do You Start a Revolution?

Keith Boykin

How do you start a revolution?
Does it begin in the dark,
furtive glances
in a dusky city park?

Or on the street
with a tweet
with a cast of characters
to send and repeat?

Does it start on the phone
with a call to the bank
for a loan?
Or with a stone?

If a politician
on his third wife
tried to cut your rights

with a legislative knife
would you heed a plea
to dump some tea
into the sea?

If a captious bishop
with a gold-embossed cross
allowed his church
to take a financial loss
so he could screw
the boys in the pew,
would you continue to offer
your hard-earned tithes
to his silk-lined coffer,
or orchestrate a coup?

If a closeted basketball star,
and yeah, we know who you are,
told a reporter
that queers were bizarre
then smoked a cigar
got drunk at a bar
and sped off in a red sports car,
would you go to his house
and tell his spouse
or is that a bit too far?

If Che Guevara
appeared to you in drag,
If Marx and Lenin
said they were fags,
If Malcolm and Martin
held hands for your rights,
Would that be enough
to get you to fight?

If the CDC
released a report
that your life was endangered
and needed support,
would that be the jolt
to start a revolt
to fight for your rights
to the highest of courts?

If Marlon and Essex
arose from the dead,
If Marie Antoinette
said let them eat bread,
if a guillotine's blade
hung over your head,
would that be the shake
to get you to wake,
Or would ten million slaves
have to turn in their graves
and the earth
begin to quake?

Was Gil Scott-Heron
wrong?
Does it start with
Chairman Mao
on a gong?
With Tracy Chapman
and a folk singer
playing an acoustic guitar
in a sarong?
With sandaled hippies
singing a Beatles song?
Or with Bob Marley

smoking ganja
from a bong?

Does it start with
a poem,
a rhyme,
a riddle,
a rose,
or with prose?

How many licks
and sticks
and stones
bricks
and broken bones
does it take
to get to the center
of your soul,
with love
over fear
to help your own?

Does it start with a rally
at city hall?
With an assassination
at a shopping mall?
With two men
in a shower stall?
With a female soldier
in the mess hall?
With a holy warrior
in a prayer shawl?
When a Wall Street trader
makes a margin call?
With a ninety-minute

conference call?
A flash mob
that becomes a brawl?
Or a bright young kid
leaves suburban sprawl
and a suicide note
in his residence hall?

Or maybe a stone wall?

Do we have to wait
for some imaginary date
When Gandhi and Jesus congregate
When Jimmy Baldwin turns straight
When Audre and Bayard agree to mate
or Madiba made license plates,
before we can create
an army of our own?

Can we write a check,
send a text,
or hold a strike?
Or will some exec
with a smooth silk tie
commodify
our tongues untied,
then undermine
our battle cry,
repackage
and securitize
our rage,
and sell it back to us
for general consumption
as we age?

Does it start
in the course of human events,
two lovers engaged
in an argument,
from childhood games
of robbers and cops,
or grownup games
of bottoms and tops,
while we pose shirtless
for photo ops
for the backs of magazines?

Or perhaps on a computer screen,
when a size queen
with a measuring stick
finds an online trick
from a porno flick,
and a thugged out dude
with a twelve inch dick
walks in with swagger
but hides his dagger?

Will it take a sign
from the divine,
the ghost of Sylvester
turning water to wine,
or just a shrine
hung with twine
to all the victims
of our benign
neglect?

Are you waiting for
a fork in the road,
the reformation

of the penal code,
a gospel choir
singing Beethoven's ode,
a 1960s
segregated commode,
or a first-class ticket
to the underground railroad?

Would you drop your sign
at the picket line
an acre short
of the goal line
and settle for thirty-nine?
Or would it be cruel
to demand a mule
and an extra acre
for a troublemaker
to dismantle
the master's tools?

Could it possibly
be so crass
to come from the kid
in the back of the class,
while holding up
a magnifying glass
to our ass
as we deconstruct
plutocracies
theocracies
and democracies
in the safety of
the bureaucracy
of our ivory towers?

Or must it be so evident
as a little boy in discontent
staring down with a quiver
at Langston's cool-faced river?

Will it start at a book club in Harlem,
when a literary gem
triggers a brain stem
for a guy who's smart
with a bleeding heart
but for some
is just too femme?

Or will it pop with a riot in Harare,
when the police invade
with a hand grenade
to stop the planning
of a pride parade?

Or maybe a stool at Hartsfield
when an old maid
with a hearing aid
looking for trade
is caught and jailed
in a bathroom raid?

Will we stand for the boys
who crushed on each other
and the guys with the dolls
who were told they were wrong?

Will we dance to the beats
that kill us softly,
or demand an end
to the murder songs?

Will we fight the bullies
hiding their pain,
every blow of their fists
disguising their shame?

Will we help the boys
who walk with a twist
or extinguish their flame
and their right to exist?

Will we love the men
who were raped on a date
led to believe
it was just their fate?

And what of the teens
down on their luck
forced on the streets
and paid to fuck?

Will the revolution start
with shock and awe,
a declaration,
of martial law,
a forbidden dance,
a furtive glance?
don't ask, don't tell,
an HIV cell,
or maybe a magic spell?
Or perhaps a spark
plugged into a text
with a friend request
for a not-so-peaceful corps
recruiting for a war?

Do you accept
or do you ignore?

Yes, how do you start a revolution?

With a civil war between the states
of consciousness and conscience,
seeking regime change
with acts of sedition
as ammunition
against our programmed minds?

Or a stomach twisted into a knot?
A conspirator's plot?
With a shot
heard 'round the world,
flags unfurled
in the morning mist?

Or with a kiss?

Acknowledgments

This book would not have been possible without the assistance of hundreds of people, who responded to the call for submissions and took time out of their lives to write and share their stories of confronting serious personal obstacles and challenges. I thank you all.

I would also like to thank the published contributors who worked diligently and patiently to write, rewrite, and revise their work over the course of six months from August 2011 until January 2012.

I could not have selected the final contributors for the book without the skillful assistance of the four submission review editors—La Marr Jurelle Bruce, Clay Cane, Mark Corece, and Frank Roberts—who read through hundreds of essays, poems, and short stories to recommend the most appropriate pieces to include in this collection. And my apologies to Brian Reeves, Doug Cooper Spencer, Dwayne Yates, Stefano Patton, and several others who wrote beautiful, brilliant pieces that we could not include only because they were fiction.

Creating a cover design for this book was a long and complicated team effort between the publisher, the designer, myself, and several others, but I have to thank several people for their help along the way. Aerol Leonard, Meghan Clohessy, Kehinde Wiley, Richard Maldonado, Reggie Miller, Maurice Franklin, Duane Cramer, and several others provided invaluable assistance and feedback throughout the process, even if it didn't necessarily impact the final design.

Nathan Williams and Alphonso Morgan get credit for pushing me to do this book when I wasn't sure about it myself. A very special thank you goes to Jeremy Graves for inspiring me. I must thank Neil Stanley, Allen Orr, Denvil Saine, Krystal Adams, and Shirley Parker for their support. I want to thank Flo McAfee, Rashad Robinson, James Grooms, Dustin Jones, Joaquin Aslan, Jussie Smollett, Lorin Brown, and Cheryl Jones-Samuels for their encouragement. And I thank Rod McCullom and David Blasher for their assistance above and beyond the call of duty. And, of course, every book I write is designed to make the world a better place for Brandon Adams, Jardin Douglas and Cameron Jones.

Last but not least, thanks to my editor and publisher, Don Weise, who immediately believed in this project from the very first email I sent to him in the fall of 2010.

Contributors

Darian Aaron is the author of *When Love Takes Over: A Celebration of SGL Couples of Color*. His work has appeared in *The Advocate*, *The Daily Voice*, the *Los Angeles Times*, and *CLIK Magazine* to name a few. He is also the creator of the award-winning urban gay blog *Living OutLoud with Darian*.

Chaz Barracks graduated from the University of Richmond in 2011, where he majored in criminal justice and fulfilled an interest in theater and dance by writing and starring in a play about his life story. Since college, he has have traveled the world, worked in Japan, and fulfilled his passion to work with ex-offenders and children dealing with adversity.

Hassan Beyah, a native son of Brooklyn and former Marine, is a self-taught writer and photographer. "To Colored Boys..." is his first published poem. He is currently working on pursuing a master's degree in education, as well as completing a larger collection of poetry and writing a children's book. An avid music lover, he attributes much of his artistic inspiration to Lauryn Hill and Nina Simone, in addition to the literary works of Langston Hughes, Ralph Ellison, and Junot Diaz and the photography of Gordon Parks. He occupies a small piece of Internet real estate at blackboyblues.blogspot.com.

Keith Boykin (Contributor/Editor) is an author of four books, including the *New York Times* bestseller, *Beyond The Down Low: Sex, Lies & Denial in Black America*. Educated at Dartmouth and Harvard, Keith attended law school with President Barack Obama and served in the White House as a special assistant to President Bill Clinton. Since 2008, he has served as a political commentator for CNN, MSNBC, and CNBC.

Phill Branch is a graduate of the American Film Institute (MFA, Screenwriting) and an Assistant Professor of English and Film Studies at his undergraduate alma mater Hampton University. Branch is a recent National Association of Television Program Executives (NATPE) Diversity Producing Fellow. In 2007, he was awarded a Screenwriting Fellowship from the National Association for Multi-Ethnicity in Communications (NAMIC). Branch created and serves as a writer-producer on the award-winning web series *The PuNanny Diaries*.

David Bridgeforth is a communicator, writer, television personality, and poet. Raised in a poor neighborhood in Indianapolis, David's speaking career began at the age of sixteen with the help of his mentor and friend, world-renowned communicator Les Brown. In 2009, Maya Angelou affirmed his status as a poet after he presented her with a celebration poem for her eighty-first birthday. David is the publisher and editorial director of *DBQ Magazine*, a new quarterly LGBT lifestyle publication. He speaks nationally, holds personal empowerment workshops, writes poetry, and coaches clients on speaking professionally. He lives and attends college in Indianapolis.

Antonio Brown holds a Ph.D. from the University of Michigan-Ann Arbor, and is an honored recipient of numerous academic awards and fellowships. Brown has been a featured speaker at various conferences around the world and serves on boards of directors and consults with social justice and community-based organizations. Brown also is the award-winning independent producer of the feature films *Tru Loved* and *Coffee Date*, popular with LGBT audiences.

Jamal Brown serves as a Confidential Assistant in the Obama White House. He previously served as the Senior Legal Assistant at Gay & Lesbian Advocates & Defenders and on the Board of Directors of MassEquality. Educated at Dartmouth, Jamal has spoken to audiences about the intersections of race and sexuality and LGBT issues in sports. A former D1 sprinter, Jamal was featured on *ABC World News Tonight* as a part of Jeff Sheng's "Fearless" photography exhibit to combat anti-LGBT prejudice in sports. In 2008, Jamal was named to *Out Magazine*'s "Out 100" list.

La Marr Jurelle Bruce (Editor) is a doctoral candidate in the Department of African American Studies and Program in American Studies at Yale University. Recently inducted as Carter G. Woodson fellow at the University of Virginia, he is completing a dissertation on madness and twentieth-century African American art. Among his hobbies are time travel, nature documentaries, freedom fighting, self-parody, and portable love.

Clay Cane (Contributor/Editor) is an award-winning writer whose work has appeared in a variety of outlets from urban to mainstream press: *The Advocate*, TheGrio.com, *Men's Fitness*, *The Root*, AOL Music, and Essence.com. An honors graduate of Rutgers University, Clay has interviewed various celebrities, including Denzel Washington, Beyoncé Knowles, Janet

Jackson, and Hilary Swank. He has provided commentary for BET Networks and TV One, and is a member of the New York Film Critics Online and the Broadcast Television Journalists Association. You can read more of his work at claycane.net.

Mark Corece (Contributor/Editor) is a graduate assistant for the Men of Color Initiative at DePaul University in Chicago. Mark studied film and movie directing at DePaul, where he graduated in 2010. Originally from Saint Louis, Missouri, Mark currently lives in Chicago.

Wade Davis played professional football in the NFL with the Tennessee Titans, Seattle Seahawks, and Washington Redskins. He is currently the assistant director of job readiness and career exploration at the Hetrick-Martin Institute, where he heads their youth advisory board and teaches a male empowerment class. He is also on the sports advisory board of GLSEN.

Kenyon Farrow is a black gay activist and writer living in Brooklyn, NY. He is the former Executive Director of Queers for Economic Justice, and the co-editor of two anthologies, *Letters From Young Activists: Today's Rebels Speak Out* (Nation Books 2005) and *Stand Up! The Shifting Politics of Racial Uplift* (South End Press 2012). His work has appeared in *Alternet*, *Colorlines*, *The Huffington Post*, and *Black Commentator*, and he blogs at Kenyonfarrow.com.

Daren J. Fleming is a classically trained actor who began appearing in commercials, catalogues and theatrical productions at the age of nine. He starred as Terry in Logo's first original feature-film *The Ski Trip*. Fleming has also been known to dazzle audiences on the New York drag/cabaret scene as Miss Grenadine Ross. Daren graduated from the American Musical and Dramatic Academy in New York and earned a Bachelor of Science degree from The New School, where he majored in creative writing and graduated magna cum laude. For more information visit www.DarenFleming.com.

L. Michael Gipson, an award-winning writer, public health, and youth advocate, has worked on HIV/AIDS, youth and community development programming on the local, state, and national level since 1992. His short stories, speeches, public health and socio-political essays have also been published in three recent anthologies: *Poverty & Race in America: The Emerging Agendas* (Lexington Books), *Health Issues Confronting Minority Men Who Have Sex with Men* (Springer), and *Mighty Real: Anthological Works By African American SGLBT People*. Michael holds a BFA in Writing from Goddard College and resides in Washington, D.C.

Jason Haas is a digital media consultant and human rights activist. In 1996, his landmark case—represented by the Gay and Lesbian Advocates & Defenders—won critical resources for LGBT students in the Boston Public School System. A graduate of Hamilton College, Jason received his BA in Government and Communications and was awarded scholarships by the Posse Foundation and the Jackie Robinson Foundation.

James Earl Hardy is the author of the popular B-Boy Blues series, which includes: *B-Boy Blues*, *2nd Time Around*, and *If Only for One Nite*. An honors graduate of the Columbia University School of Journalism, he is co-author of the book *Visible Lives: Three Stories in Tribute to E. Lynn Harris*.

Indie Harper was raised in the great state of Minnesota where he learned how to shoot, skin, and cook a variety of animals that used to be alive. Growing up, he wanted to be an ice cream truck 'cause he thought that's where all the popsicles came from. He spent two years in Los Angeles before moving back to Minneapolis to finish his studies in English with an emphasis in twentieth-century American Literature and Creative Writing. He now lives and works in New York City.

Lorenzo Herrera y Lozano is a queer Xicano writer of Rarámuri descent born in San José, California, and raised in Estación Adela, Chihuahua. A St. Edward's University Master of Liberal Arts graduate, he is the author of the Lambda Literary Award-nominated *Santo de la Pata Alzada: Poems from the Queer/Xicano/Positive Pen* (Evelyn Street Press), co-author of *Tragic Bitches: An Experiment in Queer Xicana & Xicano Performance Poetry* (Kórima Press), editor of *Queer Codex: Chile Love* and *Queer Codex: ROOTED!* (allgo/Evelyn Street Press), as well as the forthcoming *Joto: An Anthology of Queer Xicano & Chicano Poetry* (Kórima Press).

G. Winston James is a Jamaican-born poet, short fiction writer, essayist, and editor. A former fellow of the Millay Colony for the Arts, he holds an MFA in Fiction from Brooklyn College, City University of New York, and is the author of the poetry collection *The Damaged Good: Poems Around Love* and the Lambda Literary Award finalist collection *Lyric: Poems Along a Broken Road*.

Erick Johnson was born in Jacksonville, Florida, in August 1967. For the past fifteen years, he's worked in the event management industry on events all across the country as well as in Sydney, Australia, Doha, Qatar, Kingston, and Montego Bay, Jamaica and Vancouver BC. He currently manages a restaurant in Jacksonville, Florida, is openly gay, and attends Christ Church of Peace in Jacksonville.

Jonathan Kidd earned his bachelor's degree with honors from The University of Michigan (1997) in African Studies, African American Studies, and English. He received his Master's of Art, Master's of Philosophy (2002), and doctoral degree from Yale University in African American Studies and English Literature in 2004. As a Hollywood writer, his credits include ABC's *The Whole Truth* and TNT's *Memphis Beat*. Dr. Kidd is currently penning a biopic of Shirley Chisholm.

Rodney Terich Leonard is the founder of The Harlem Artists Salon, a series showcasing the talent of poets, writers, visual artists, musicians and scholars. Rodney served four years in the US Air Force and holds degrees from the New School University and NYU Tisch School of the Arts. His poems, articles, interviews and profiles have appeared in the *New York Times*, the *New York Amsterdam News*, the *Margie Review*, *Callaloo*, the *Red River Review*, *Clean Sheets*, the *Grand Forks Herald*, and other publications. Born in Coosa County, Alabama, Rodney currently lives in Harlem.

Shaun Lockhart is president and CEO of Shaun Lockhart Apparel & Promotions (SLAP), a marketing communications company located in Louisville, Kentucky. His marketing career began more than a decade ago with an internship in the Tennessean newspaper's advertising and copywriting department. He holds a Bachelor of Science in Management with a concentration in Sales and Marketing from Kaplan University.

DeMarco Majors came from humble and tumultuous beginnings in Evansville, Indiana, to captain of the gold-medal winning San Francisco Rockdogs at the 2006 Chicago Gay Games. After winning gold, DeMarco went on to become the first pro-men's basketball player (ABA) to come out while still playing, and was selected by *Out Magazine* for its "Out 100" list.

David J. Malebranche, MD, MPH, is an Assistant Professor of Medicine at Emory University's School of Medicine and has a joint appointment with the Rollins School of Public Health in

Atlanta, Georgia. Dr. Malebranche is known as a dynamic speaker nationwide and has appeared in documentaries on CNN, ABC News Primetime, TV One, and Black Entertainment Television (BET) for his expertise on HIV in the black community. Dr. Malebranche also served as a member of the President's Advisory Council on HIV/AIDS (PACHA) from 2006–2008, and is the current HIV/AIDS expert on webmd.com.

Rod McCullom has written and produced for ABC News, New York City's ABC Channel 7, Chicago's NBC Channel 5, *EXTRA*, and other shows. He is a contributor to *Ebony*, was a columnist and featured contributor to *The Advocate*, and his work has appeared at the *Los Angeles Times*, *Out.com*, NPR, MTV/LOGO, *After Elton*, *Colorlines*, and many others. Rod has extensively covered HIV/AIDS issues and reported from AIDS 2010 in Vienna. He is also a contributor to the 2010 anthology *Obama and the Gays: A Political Marriage*. Rod blogs on LGBT news, pop culture and politics at the award-winning Rod 2.0 at Rod20.com.

Alphonso Morgan is an author, producer, and entertainment attorney originally from Minneapolis, Minnesota. He received his BA from Howard University and his law degree from Georgetown University Law Center. His first novel, *Sons*, was released in 2005 to critical acclaim—being nominated for two Lambda Literary Awards among others. He is currently in New York preparing for the publication of his next novel, *Americano*.

Jarrett Neal earned a BA in English from Northwestern University and an MFA in Writing from the School of the Art Institute of Chicago. A 2010 fellow at the Lambda Literary Writer's Retreat for Emerging LGBT Voices, his writing has appeared in *Q Review*, *Nolos*, and *Lucid Moon*. He is assistant director of the Center for Teaching and Learning at Aurora University and lives in Oak Park, Illinois.

Antron Reshaud Olukayode is a walking, breathing, revolutionizing poet, playwright, songwriter, actor, visual and performance artist, and HIV/AIDS activist. Born Antron Reshaud Brown on April 26, 1984, he has self-published three books, *Bohemian Rebel Naked and Exposed Vol. 1*, *The Rising Vol. 2*, and *Fearless Revolution Vol. 3*.

Curtis Pate III was born in Peru, Indiana in 1977, but his family relocated to New Jersey before his first birthday. A true Jersey boy, he lived with his family (mom, dad, older bro) until he graduated from high school in 1995, then left home to attend Hampton University for a year and half before transferring to Rutgers University in New Jersey. It was there he acquired two BAs and the love of his life.

Robert E. Penn is a writer/filmmaker. His documentary *Art from Adversity* premiered in June 2011. Penn's cinematography for Kewulay Kamara's film about Sierra Leone screened in April 2011. He created theatrical video for Ron Brown's 2011 dance "On Earth Together" and Brian Freeman's 2010 revival of satire *Fierce Love*. Penn produced and directed six Public Service Announcements promoting HIV-testing for New Jersey's 2010 "Status is Everything" campaign. His story "Learning to Speak Heterosexual" appears in *Voices Rising* (Redbone Press, 2007). New York State Council on the Arts awarded Penn a 2006 Individual Artist Grant in Film and Video/New Media Technologies.

Frank Roberts (Editor) is a co-founding member of the National Black Justice Coalition. A doctoral candidate in the humanities at NYU, he is a recipient of the Ford Foundation Doctoral Dissertation Fellowship. Along with writing and teaching at NYU, he has also held academic appointments at Emory University and Spelman College. Prior to graduate school, he worked briefly as a research assistant to the late civil rights attorney Johnnie Cochran. A proud native New Yorker, he lives in downtown Manhattan. Visit www.frankrobertsonline. com.

B. Scott is a multi-ethnic American television personality, radio show host and internet celebrity who is best known for his YouTube videos, which have been viewed more than 40 million times, and for his website lovebscott.com. He has interviewed celebrities such as Mariah Carey, Ne-Yo, Chaka Khan, and Jennifer Lopez and has made numerous television appearances, including *The Tyra Banks Show* and Oxygen's *Hair Battle Spectacular*. He also hosted *The B. Scott Show* on Jamie Foxx's channel, The Foxxhole, on Sirius XM Satellite Radio.

Will Sheridan Jr. played college basketball for the Villanova Wildcats from 2003 to 2007. After graduation, he played as an international basketball player in Italy. He is now a singer, musician, and recording artist signed with Royal Advisor Records. He is also a businessman and manager in a company in the fashion industry.

José David Sierra, better known as Jessica Wild, is a Puerto Rican drag queen, dancer, actor, choreographer, professional makeup artist, singer, and reality television personality who has been performing since 1997. Sierra was born in 1980 in Caguas, Puerto Rico and appeared on the second season of Logo's popular reality series *RuPaul's Drag Race*. In March 2011, Jessica Wild (in collaboration with DJ Ranny) released her first dance single "You Like It Wild."

Ron Simmons is a photographer, teacher, and community activist who earned his bachelor and master degrees from the State University of New York at Albany and his doctorate in Mass Communications from Howard University. He served as the still photographer and the Washington, D.C., field producer on *Tongues Untied* (1989), the award-winning black gay documentary film. In 1991, he authored the noted essay "Some Thought on the Challenges Facing Black Gay Intellectuals" in the anthology *Brother to Brother: New Writings by Black Gay Men*. Since 1992, Simmons has served as the President/CEO of Us Helping Us, People Into Living, Inc.

Rob Smith served for five years in the United States Army and deployed to Kuwait and Iraq, eventually earning the Army Commendation Medal and Combat Infantryman Badge. A freelance writer and graduate of Syracuse University, he has lectured about "Don't Ask, Don't Tell" (DADT), coming out, and homophobia at various colleges and universities across the country. His articles and opinion pieces about various gay political issues have appeared at *The Huffington Post*, *USA Today*, *Metro Weekly*, and *Salon.com* among others.

Charles Stephens was born and grew up in Atlanta, Georgia. A graduate of Georgia State University, he works in the nonprofit sector. His writing has appeared in the anthologies *Think Again* and *If We Have to Take Tomorrow*, and the online literary journal *Loose Change*. Currently he is co-editing a collection of writings on the legacy of Joseph Beam and *In the Life*.

Kevin E. Taylor is the Pastor of Unity Fellowship Church, New Brunswick, which he founded in January 2001. He is a publisher, author, and an empowerment coach. Kevin is also an award-winning TV producer, having worked with BET since 1991 and through his own video production company, where he created such programs as *Access Granted*, *Notarized*, *Testimony*, *VideoLink* and *Lyrically Speaking* and interviewed such artists as Natalie Cole, Tina Turner, Stevie Wonder, Aaliyah, Lenny Kravitz, and Mariah Carey.

André St. Clair Thompson is a professional in production and creative management and an interdisciplinary artist. He holds a M.F.A. in Acting from California Institute of the Arts (CalArts), a M.A. in Performance Studies from New York University/Tisch School of the Arts and an Honors B.A. in Sexuality and Society from Brown University. As a black, gay, cross-dressing male, immigrant of working class upbringing, and a new American citizen, he is interested in producing art that nurtures non-mainstream voices and promotes cultural and aesthetic diversity of viewpoint, experience and expression.

Craig Washington was born and lovingly raised by Anna and Leon Washington in Queens, New York and has lived in Atlanta since 1992. He has been living with HIV for more than twenty-five years. Craig has been engaged in community organizing and writing for social change and HIV advocacy for many years. He has written various articles and editorials for the *Atlanta Voice*, *Southern Voice*, *Atlanta Journal Constitution*, the *Washington Blade* and the anthology *Not In My Family: AIDS in the African American Community*.

Tim'm T. West is a critically acclaimed author, poet, activist, and rapper who is Cincinnati-born and raised in Arkansas. He has degrees from Duke, The New School, and Stanford Universities and has spent much of his adult professional life between secondary and post-secondary teaching and youth advocacy and HIV education and prevention. Tim'm taught Philosophy and English at Houston Community College before relocating in the summer of 2011 to Chicago, IL. More information about his vast body of creative work can be found at: www.reddirt.biz.

Nathan Hale Williams is an award-winning TV/film producer, writer, entertainment attorney, and TV personality. He is the star of Sundance Channel's hit docu-series, *Girls Who*

Like Boys Who Like Boys and has also appeared on Showtime's *American Candidate*. Following his first film, *The Ski Trip*, Nathan produced the NAACP and GLAAD-nominated film *Dirty Laundry*. For television, Nathan has executive produced several shows, including *My Model Looks Better Than Your Model*, *Leading Women/Men*, and *Inside Black Culture* (Director). His popular weekly column, "Girl's Best Friend," appears on Essence.com.

Emanuel Xavier is an American poet, spoken word artist, author, editor, literary events curator, and actor born and raised in the Bushwick area of Brooklyn. He is one of the most significant voices to emerge from the neo-Nuyorican poetry movement using political, sexual and religious themes throughout his work. His background is Puerto Rican and Ecuadorian.

Victor Yates is a freelance writer. His new book, *The Taste of Scars*, is set to be released by Addison Craft Publishing. Yates is the winner of the Elma Stuckey Writing Award (first place in poetry). His writing has appeared in *The Voice*, *The Catalyst*, *Prism*, *Windy City Times* and on the website Best Gay Blogs.